John Robinson, George Washington, John Carey, George Robinson

Official Letters to the Honorable American Congress

Vol. I

John Robinson, George Washington, John Carey, George Robinson

Official Letters to the Honorable American Congress
Vol. I

ISBN/EAN: 9783744687836

Printed in Europe, USA, Canada, Australia, Japan

Cover: Foto ©ninafisch / pixelio.de

More available books at **www.hansebooks.com**

AMERICAN STATE PAPERS,

BEING

A COLLECTION

Of Original and Authentic Documents

RELATIVE TO THE WAR

BETWEEN THE

UNITED STATES

AND

GREAT BRITAIN.

Publiſhed by Special Permiſſion.

VOLUME THE FIRST.

1795.

OFFICIAL LETTERS

TO THE HONORABLE

AMERICAN CONGRESS,

Written, during the War between the

UNITED COLONIES AND GREAT BRITAIN,

BY HIS EXCELLENCY,

GEORGE WASHINGTON,

COMMANDER IN CHIEF OF THE
CONTINENTAL FORCES,

NOW

PRESIDENT of the UNITED STATES.

Copied, by Special Permiffion, from the Original Papers preferved in the Office of the Secretary of State, Philadelphia.

VOL. I.

LONDON:

PRINTED FOR CADELL JUNIOR AND DAVIES, G. G. AND J. RO-
BINSON, B. AND J. WHITE, W. OTRIDGE AND SON, J. DE-
BRETT, R. FAULDER, AND T. EGERTON.

1795.

RESPECTING the fource from which the following letters have been drawn, and the grounds on which the reader is expected to reft his belief of their authenticity, it may be fufficient to inform him (and, for the truth of the affertion, to appeal to His Excellency, Thomas Pinckney, the American Minifter Plenipotentiary), that permiffion was obtained from the proper authority, to tranfcribe, from the original papers preferved in the Secretary of State's office in Philadelphia, thefe and fundry other authentic documents relating to the conteft between the colonies and the mother country, viz. Letters from the Commanders of the continental forces, and other perfons employed in the public fervice,—intercepted Letters from British Officers and other adherents to the royal caufe,—Communications from the Governors, Conventions, and Committees of the feveral American States,—Difpatches from Agents and Commiffioners,—Inftructions,—Reports of Committees of Congrefs,—parts of the Secret Journals hitherto unpublifhed,—and various

various other pieces elucidative of the events which led to and finally established American Independence.

That permission was granted early in the year 1792, and immediate advantage was taken of the indulgence; though, from various circumstances, of little consequence to the reader to know, the publication has been so long delayed. Even at this late period, the editor contents himself with laying before the public but a part of the collection,—intending, if these volumes meet with a favorable reception, to continue the publication, and present his readers with a variety of interesting pieces penned by the leaders and principal agents in the American Revolution, and tending to throw light on many important transactions that have hitherto been either enveloped in total darkness, or, at best, but obscurely perceived, and imperfectly understood.

Some parts of these letters may perhaps appear too full of minutiæ to interest that class of readers, who, unaccustomed to enter into the investigation of causes or consequences, delight only in recitals of battles, sieges, and other striking occurrences which constitute the more prominent features of history. But, to the reasoning philosophic reader, who wishes to explore the secret springs of action, —to trace events to their remote and latent causes, —to discover and examine the subordinate and collateral circumstances (oft trifling in appearance, and generally overlooked by the vulgar eye), which, in the struggles of contending nations, give

a prea preponderancy to the one or the other scale,—those minute details will, it is presumed, be far from unacceptable, as furnishing him with that species of information, upon which alone he can venture to ground a decisive opinion, and which he might elsewhere seek in vain.

The inclosures, frequently referred to in these volumes, would still further contribute to set every circumstance in a clearer and stronger light; and it was the editor's original intention that they should have accompanied the letters to which they respectively belong. Obstacles however, *at present* insurmountable, stand in the way of their immediate publication: but, when these are removed, the papers alluded to shall make their appearance in form of an Appendix,—such parts of them at least, as are of a curious and interesting nature.

Meanwhile the reader will observe that it was deemed as yet premature to publish certain passages of these letters: some omissions have of course taken place, which are every where pointed out by asterisks, and which will be supplied at a proper season, probably not far distant.—On the other hand, in perhaps half a dozen instances, a single word has been hazarded on conjecture, to fill up a chasm, where either the original or the copy happened to be torn or defaced; in which cases, the supplemental words are inclosed within crotchets and printed in Italic.—A few entire letters, moreover, as appears by reference made to them in subsequent ones, are here wanted to complete the chain of correspondence. These the editor

tor can give no account of, as the originals appear to have been loft from the files of office.

About a dozen letters, written by the general's fecretary*, are here inferted;—a few from the general himfelf to the board of war, or committee of Congrefs,—one to the prefident of the New-York Convention, and one to R. Morris, efquire, in the department of finance. Thefe it was thought improper to omit: nor did it feem worth while, on account of a few exceptions, to make any alteration in the general title of the book.

* Mr. R. H. Harrifon, refpecting whom, the reader is requefted to correct an error in Vol. I. page 240, line 6, where, inftead of '*aides*,' he fhould read '*fecretaries*'.—Another miftake occurs in page 26 of the fame volume, line 32, where '*fourth*' fhould be read inftead of '*fourteenth*.'

FROM
GENERAL WASHINGTON
TO CONGRESS.

To the Honorable Members of the Continental Congress, at Philadelphia.

GENTLEMEN,   *New-York, June* 24, 1775.

THE rain on friday afternoon and saturday,—the advice of several gentlemen of the Jerseys and this city, by no means to cross Hudson's river at the lower ferry—and some other circumstances, too trivial to mention, prevented my arrival at this place, until the afternoon of this day.

In the morning, after giving general Schuyler such orders, as, from the result of my inquiry into matters here, appear necessary, I shall set out on my journey to the camp at Boston, and shall proceed with all the dispatch in my power. Powder is so essential an article, that I cannot help again repeating the necessity of a supply. The camp at Boston, from the best account I can get from thence, is but very poorly supplied. At this place, they have scarce any. How they are provided at general Wooster's camp, I have not been able yet to learn.

Governor Tryon is arrived, and general Schuyler directed to advise you of the line of conduct he moves in. I fear it will not be very favorable to the American cause.

I have only to add, that I am, with great respect and regard, gentlemen, your most obedient and obliged humble servant, G° WASHINGTON.

———

To JOHN HANCOCK, *Esquire, President of Congress.*

New York, sunday, 24th June, 1775, 5 *o'clock,* P. M.
SIR,
   UPON my arrival here this afternoon, I was informed that an express was in town, from the provincial camp in Massachusetts-Bay; and having seen, among the papers in his possession, a letter directed to you as president of the Congress, I have taken the liberty to open it. I was induced to take that liberty, by several gentlemen of New-York who were anxious to know the particulars of the affair of the seventeenth instant, and agreeable to the orders of many members of the Congress, who judged it necessary that I should avail myself of the best information in the course of my journey.

You will find, sir, by that letter, a great want of powder in the provincial army, which I sincerely hope the Congress will supply as speedily and as effectually as in their power. One thousand pounds in weight were sent to the camp at Cambridge, three days ago, from this city; which has left this place almost destitute of that necessary article; there being at this time, from the best information, not more than four barrels of powder in the city of New-York.

I propose to set off for the provincial camp to-morrow, and will use all possible dispatch to join the forces there.

Please to make my compliments to the gentlemen of the
                Congress;

Congress; and believe me to be, sir, your obliged friend, and humble servant, G. W.

[N. B. *All the subsequent letters, not otherwise expressly directed, are addressed to the President of Congress for the time being.*]

Sir, Camp at Cambridge, *July* 10, 1775.

I Arrived safe at this place on the third instant, after a journey attended with a good deal of fatigue, and retarded by necessary attentions to the successive civilities which accompanied me in my whole route.

Upon my arrival, I immediately visited the several posts occupied by our troops; and, as soon as the weather permitted, reconnoitred those of the enemy. I found the latter strongly intrenched on Bunker's-hill, about a mile from Charlestown, and advanced about half a mile from the place of the late action, with their centries extended about one hundred and fifty yards on this side of the narrowest part of the neck leading from this place to Charlestown. Three floating batteries lie in Mystick river near their camp, and one twenty-gun ship below the ferry place between Boston and Charlestown. They have also a battery on Copse-hill, on the Boston side, which much annoyed our troops in the late attack. Upon the neck, they have also deeply intrenched and fortified. Their advanced guards, till last saturday morning, occupied Brown's houses, about a mile from Roxbury meeting-house, and twenty roods from their lines: but, at that time, a party from general Thomas's camp surprised the guard, drove them in, and burned the houses. The bulk of their army, commanded by general Howe, lies on Bunker's-hill, and the remainder on Roxbury-neck, except the light horse, and a few men in the town of Boston.

On our side, we have thrown up intrenchments on Winter and Prospect hills,—the enemy's camp in full view, at the distance of little more than a mile. Such intermediate points as would admit a landing, I have since my arrival taken care to strengthen, down to Sewal's farm, where a strong intrenchment has been thrown up. At Roxbury, general Thomas has thrown up a strong work on the hill, about two hundred yards above the meeting-house; which, with the brokenness of the ground, and a great number of rocks, has made that pass very secure. The troops raised in New-Hampshire, with a regiment from Rhode-Island, occupy Winter-hill: a part of those from Connecticut, under general Putnam, are on Prospect-hill. The troops in this town are entirely of the Massachusetts: the remainder of the Rhode-Island-men are at Sewal's Farm. Two regiments of Connecticut, and nine of the Massachusetts, are at Roxbury. The residue of the army, to the number of about seven hundred, are posted in several small towns along the coast, to prevent the depredations of the enemy.

Upon the whole, I think myself authorised, to say, that, considering the great extent of line and the nature of the ground, we are as well secured, as could be expected in so short a time, and under the disadvantages we labor. These consist in a want of engineers to construct proper works and direct the men, a want of tools, and a sufficient number of men to man the works in case of an attack. You will observe, by the proceedings of the council of war which I have the honor to inclose, that it is our unanimous opinion, to hold and defend these works as long as possible. The discouragement it would give the men, and its contrary effects on the ministerial troops, thus to abandon our encampment in their face, formed with so much labor,—added to the certain destruction of a considerable and valuable extent of country, and our uncertainty of finding a place in all respects so capable of making a stand,—are leading reasons for this determination. At the same time we are very sensible of the difficulties which attend the defence of lines of so

great

great extent, and the dangers which may ensue from such a division of the army.

My earnest wish to comply with the instructions of the Congress, in making an early and complete return of the state of the army, has led into an involuntary delay of addressing you; which has given me much concern. Having given orders for this purpose immediately on my arrival,— and unapprised of the imperfect obedience which had been paid to those of the like nature from general Ward, I was led from day to day to expect they would come in, and therefore detained the messenger. They are not now so complete as I could wish: but much allowance is to be made for inexperience in forms, and a liberty which had been taken (not given) on this subject. These reasons, I flatter myself, will no longer exist; and, of consequence, more regularity and exactness will in future prevail. This, with a necessary attention to the lines, the movements of the ministerial troops, and our immediate security, must be my apology, which I beg you to lay before Congress with the utmost duty and respect.

We labor under great disadvantages for want of tents: for, though they have been helped out by a collection of now useless sails from the sea-port towns, the number is far short of our necessities. The colleges and houses of this town are necessarily occupied by the troops; which affords another reason for keeping our present situation. But I most sincerely wish the whole army was properly provided to take the field, as I am well assured, that (besides greater expedition and activity in case of alarm) it would highly conduce to health and discipline. As materials are not to be had here, I would beg leave to recommend the procuring a farther supply from Philadelphia, as soon as possible.

I should be extremely deficient in gratitude as well as justice, if I did not take the first opportunity to acknowledge the readiness and attention, which the provincial Congress and different committees have shewn; to make every thing as convenient

convenient and agreeable as poffible. But there is a vital and inherent principle of delay, incompatible with military fervice, in tranfacting bufinefs through fuch numerous and different channels. I efteem it therefore my duty to reprefent the inconvenience which muft unavoidably enfue from a dependence on a number of perfons for fupplies; and fubmit it to the confideration of Congrefs, whether the public fervice will not be beft promoted by appointing a commiffary-general for thefe purpofes. We have a ftriking inftance of the preference of fuch a mode, in the eftablifhment of Connecticut, as their troops are extremely well provided under the direction of Mr. Trumbull, and he has at different times affifted others with various articles. Should my fentiments happily coincide with thofe of your honors on this fubject, I beg leave to recommend Mr. Trumbull as a very proper perfon for this department. In the arrangement of troops collected under fuch circumftances, and upon the fpur of immediate neceffity, feveral appointments are omitted, which appear to be indifpenfably neceffary for the good government of the army—particularly a quarter-mafter-general, a commiffary of mufters, and a commiffary of artillery. Thefe I muft earneftly recommend to the notice and provifion of the Congrefs.

I find myfelf already much embarraffed, for want of a military cheft. Thefe embarraffments will increafe every day: I muft therefore requeft that money may be forwarded as foon as poffible. The want of this moft neceffary article will (I fear) produce great inconveniences, if not prevented by an early attention. I find the army in general, and the troops raifed in Maffachufetts in particular, very deficient in neceffary cloathing. Upon inquiry, there appears no probability of obtaining any fupplies in this quarter: and, on the beft confideration of this matter I am able to form, I am of opinion that a number of hunting fhirts (not lefs than ten thoufand) would in a great degree remove this difficulty, in the cheapeft and quickeft manner. I know nothing, in a

fpeculative

speculative view, more trivial, yet, if put in practice, would have a happier tendency to unite the men, and abolish those provincial distinctions which lead to jealousy and dissatisfaction.

In a former part of this letter, I mentioned the want of engineers. I can hardly express the disappointment I have experienced on this subject,—the skill of those we have being very imperfect, and confined to the mere manual exercise of cannon; whereas the war in which we are engaged requires a knowledge, comprehending the duties of the field, and fortification. If any persons thus qualified are to be found in the southern colonies, it would be of great public service to forward them with all expedition.

Upon the article of ammunition, I must re-echo the former complaints on this subject. We are so exceedingly destitute, that our artillery will be of little use, without a supply both large and seasonable. What we have must be reserved for the small arms, and that managed with the utmost frugality. * * *

The state of the army you will find ascertained with tolerable precision in the returns which accompany this letter. Upon finding the number of men to fall so far short of the establishment, and below all expectation, I immediately called a council of the general officers, whose opinion (as to the mode of filling up the regiments, and providing for the present exigency) I have the honor of inclosing, together with the best judgment we are able to form of the ministerial troops. From the number of boys, deserters, and negroes, that have been enlisted in the troops of this province, I entertain some doubts whether the number required can be raised here: and all the general officers agree that no dependence can be put on the militia, for a continuance in camp, or regularity and discipline during the short time they may stay. This unhappy and devoted province has been so long in a state of anarchy, and the yoke * * * * * been laid so heavily on it, that great allowances are to be made for troops raifed under fuch circumftances.. The deficiency of numbers, difcipline, and ftores, can only lead to this conclufion—that their fpirit has exceeded their ftrength. But at the fame time I would humbly fubmit to the confideration of Congrefs the propriety of making fome further provifion of men from the other colonies. If thefe regiments fhould be completed to their eftablifhment, the difmiffion of thofe unfit for duty on account of their age and character would occafion a confiderable reduction; and, at all events, they have been enlifted upon fuch terms, that they may be difbanded when other troops arrive. But fhould my apprehenfions be realifed, and the regiments here not filled up, the public caufe would fuffer by an abfolute dependence upon fo doubtful an event, unlefs fome provifion is made againft fuch a difappointment.

It requires no military fkill, to judge of the difficulty of introducing proper difcipline and fubordination into an army, while we have the enemy in view, and are in daily expectation of an attack: but it is of fo much importance, that every effort will be made, which time and circumftances will admit. In the mean time I have a fincere pleafure in obferving that there are materials for a good army—a great number of able-bodied men, active, zealous in the caufe, and of unqueftionable courage.

I am now, fir, to acknowledge the receipt of your favor of the twenty-eighth, inclofing the refolutions of Congrefs, of the twenty-feventh ultimo, and a copy of a letter from the committee of Albany; to all which I fhall pay due attention.

Generals Gates and Sullivan have both arrived in good health.

My beft abilities are at all times devoted to the fervice of my country: but I feel the weight, importance, and variety of my prefent duties too fenfibly, not to wifh a more immediate and frequent communication with the Congrefs. I fear it may often happen in the courfe of our prefent operations,

that

that I shall need that assistance and direction from them, which time and distance will not allow me to receive.

Since writing the above, I have also to acknowledge your favor of the fourth instant by Fessenden, and the receipt of the commissions, and articles of war. The former are yet eight hundred short of the number required. This deficiency you will please to supply as soon as you conveniently can. Among the other returns, I have also sent one of our killed, wounded, and missing, in the late action; but have been able to procure no certain account of the loss of the ministerial troops. My best intelligence fixes it at about five hundred killed, and six or seven hundred wounded: but it is no more than conjecture,—the utmost pains being taken on their side to conceal it. I have the honor to be, &c.   G. W.

P. S. Having ordered the commanding officer to give me the earliest intelligence of every motion of the enemy by land or water, discernible from the heights of his camp, I this instant, as I was closing my letter, received the inclosed from the brigade major. The design of this manœuvre I know not:—perhaps it may be to make a descent somewhere along the coast:—it may be for New-York; or it may be practised as a deception on us. I thought it not improper however to mention the matter to you: I have done the same to the commanding officer at New-York; and I shall let it be known to the committee of safety here, so that intelligence may be communicated, as they shall think best, along the sea-coast of this government.

Sir,   *Camp at Cambridge, July* 14, 1775.

SINCE I did myself the honor of addressing you on the tenth instant, nothing material has happened in the camp. From some authentic and later advices of the state of the ministerial troops, and the great inconvenience of calling in the militia in the midst of harvest, I have been induced for the present

present to wave it:—but in the mean time recruiting parties have been sent throughout this province, to fill up the regiments to the establishment of the provincial Congress At the same time that I received these advices, I also obtained a list of the officers of the enemy killed and wounded in the late battle at Charlestown, which I take this opportunity to inclose.

The great scarcity of fresh provisions in their army has led me to take every precaution to prevent a supply: for this purpose, I have ordered all the cattle and sheep to be drawn from the low grounds and farms within their reach. A detachment from general Thomas's camp, on wednesday night, went over to Long-Island, and brought from thence twenty cattle and a number of sheep, with about fifteen laborers who had been put on by a Mr. Ray Thomas, to cut the hay, &c. By some accident they omitted burning the hay, and returned the next day at noon to complete it; which they effected, amidst the firing of the shipping, with the loss of one man killed and another wounded.

Last evening also a party of the Connecticut-men strolled down on the marsh at Roxbury, and fired upon a centry; which drew on a heavy fire from the enemy's lines and floating batteries, but attended with no other effect than the loss of one killed by a shot from the enemy's lines. In the mean time, we are, on both sides, continuing our works: but there has been no other movement than what I have noticed above. I shall endeavor to give a regular and particular account of all transactions, as they occur, which you will please to lay before the honorable Congress. I have the honor to be, &c. G. W.

SIR, Camp at Cambridge, *July* 21, 1775.

SINCE I did myself the honor of addressing you the fourteenth instant, I have received advice from governor Trumbull,

Trumbull, that the assembly of Connecticut had voted, and that they are now raising, two regiments of seven hundred men each, in consequence of an application from the provincial Congress of Massachusetts-Bay. The Rhode-Island assembly has also made an augmentation for this purpose. These reinforcements, with the riflemen who are daily expected, and such recruits as may come in to fill up the regiments here, will, I apprehend, compose an army sufficiently strong to oppose any force which may be brought against us at present. I am very sensible that the heavy expense, necessarily attendant upon this campaign, will call for the utmost frugality and care, and would therefore, if possible, avoid enlisting one unnecessary man. As this is the first certain account of the destination of these new-raised troops, I thought proper to communicate my sentiments as early as possible, lest the Congress should act upon my letter of the tenth, and raise troops in the southern colonies, which, in my present judgment, may be dispensed with.

For these eight days past, there have been no movements in either camp, of any consequence. On our side, we have continued the works without any intermission; and they are now so far advanced as to leave us little to apprehend on that score. On the side of the enemy, they have also been very industrious in finishing their lines, both on Bunker's-hill and Roxbury-neck. In this interval also, their transports have arrived from New-York; and they have been employed in landing and stationing their men. I have been able to collect no certain account of the numbers arrived: but the inclosed letter, wrote (though not signed) by Mr. Sheriff Lee, and delivered me by captain Darby (who went express with an account of the Lexington battle) will enable us to form a pretty accurate judgment. The increase of tents and men in the town of Boston is very obvious: but all my accounts from thence agree that there is a great mortality, occasioned by the want of vegetables and fresh meat; and that their loss in the late battle at Charlestown (from the few recoveries

of

of their wounded) is greater than at firſt ſuppoſed. The condition of the inhabitants detained in Boſton is very diſtreſſing: they are equally deſtitute of the comfort of freſh proviſions; and many of them are ſo reduced in their circumſtances, as to be unable to ſupply themſelves with ſalt. Such fiſh as the ſoldiery leave is their principal ſupport. Added to all this, ſuch ſuſpicion and jealouſy prevails, that they can ſcarcely ſpeak, or even look, without expoſing themſelves to ſome ſpecies of military execution.

I have not been able, from any intelligence I have received, to form any certain judgment of the future operations of the enemy. Sometimes I have ſuſpected an intention of detaching a part of their army to ſome part of the coaſt, as they have been building a number of flat-bottomed boats, capable of holding two hundred men each. But, from their works, and the language held at Boſton, there is reaſon to think they expect the attack from us, and are principally engaged in preparing themſelves againſt it. I have ordered all the whale-boats along the coaſt to be collected: and ſome of them are employed every night to watch the motions of the enemy by water, ſo as to guard as much as poſſible againſt any ſurpriſe. * * *

Next to the more immediate and preſſing duties of putting our lines in as ſecure a ſtate as poſſible, attending to the movements of the enemy, and gaining intelligence,—my great concern is to eſtabliſh order, regularity, and diſcipline, without which, our numbers would embarraſs us, and, in caſe of action, general confuſion muſt infallibly enſue. In order to this, I propoſe to divide the army into three diviſions:—at the head of each, will be a general officer:—theſe diviſions to be again ſubdivided into brigades, under their reſpective brigadiers. But the difficulty ariſing from the arrangement of the general officers, and waiting the farther proceedings of the Congreſs on this ſubject, has much retarded my progreſs in this moſt neceſſary work. I ſhould

be

be very happy to receive their final commands, as any determination would enable me to proceed in my plan. * * *

In addition to the officers mentioned in mine of the tenth instant, I would humbly propose that some provision should be made for a judge-advocate, and provost-marshal. The necessity of the first appointment was so great, that I was obliged to nominate a Mr. Tudor, who was well recommended to me, and now executes the office under an expectation of receiving captain's pay—an allowance (in my opinion) scarcely adequate to the service, in new-raised troops, where there are court-martials every day. However, as that is the proportion in the regular army, and he is contented, there will be no necessity of an addition.

I must also renew my request as to money, and the appointment of a paymaster. I have forbore urging matters of this nature, from my knowledge of the many important concerns which engage the attention of the Congress: but as I find my difficulties thicken every day, I make no doubt, suitable regard will be paid to a necessity of this kind. The inconvenience of borrowing such sums as are constantly requisite must be too plain for me to enlarge upon, and is a situation from which I should be very happy to be relieved.

Upon the experience I have had, and the best consideration of the appointment of the several offices of commissary-general, muster-master general, quarter-master-general, paymaster-general, and commissary of artillery, I am clearly of opinion that they not only conduce to order, dispatch, and discipline, but that it is a measure of economy. The delay, the waste, and unpunishable neglect of duty, arising from these offices being in commission in several hands, evidently shew that the public expense must be finally enhanced. I have experienced the want of these officers, in completing the returns of men, ammunition, and stores. The latter are yet imperfect, from the number of hands in which they are dispersed. I have inclosed the last weekly return, which is more accurate than the former; and hope in a little time we shall be perfectly regular in this as well as several other necessary branches of duty.

I have made inquiry into the establishment of the hospital, and find it in a very unsettled condition. There is no principal director, nor any subordination among the surgeons: of consequence, disputes and contention have arisen, and must continue until it is reduced to some system. I could wish it was immediately taken into consideration, as the lives and health of both officers and men so much depend upon a due regulation of this department. I have been particularly attentive to the least symptoms of the small pox; and hitherto we have been so fortunate as to have every person removed so soon, as not only to prevent any communication, but any alarm or apprehension it might give in the camp. We shall continue the utmost vigilance against this most dangerous enemy.

In an army properly organised, there are sundry offices of an inferior kind, such as waggon-master, master-carpenter, &c: but I doubt whether my powers are sufficiently extensive for such appointments. If it is thought proper to repose such a trust in me, I shall be governed, in the discharge of it, by a strict regard to economy and the public interest.

My instructions from the honorable Congress direct that no troops are to be disbanded without their express direction, nor to be recruited to more than double the number of the enemy. Upon this subject I beg leave to represent, that, unless the regiments in this province are more successful in recruiting than I have reason to expect, a reduction of some of them will be highly necessary, as the public is put to the whole expense of an establishment of officers, while the real strength of the regiment (which consists in the rank and file) is defective. In case of such a reduction, doubtless some of the privates and all the officers would return home: but many of the former would go into the remaining regiments; and, having had some experience, would fill them up with
useful

useful men. I so plainly perceive the expense of this campaign will exceed any calculation hitherto made, that I am particularly anxious to strike off every unnecessary charge. You will therefore, sir, be pleased to favor me with explicit directions from the Congress, on the mode of this reduction (if it shall appear necessary) that no time may be lost when such necessity appears.

Yesterday we had an account that the light-house was on fire:—by whom, and under what orders, I have not yet learned: but we have reason to believe it has been done by our irregulars.

You will please to present me to the Congress, with the utmost duty and respect; and believe me to be, &c. G. W.

P. S. Captain Darby's stay in England was so short, that he brings no other information than what the inclosed letter, and the news-papers which will accompany this, contain. General Gage's dispatches had not arrived; and the ministry affected to disbelieve the whole account, treating it as a fiction, or, at most, an affair of little consequence.—The fall of stocks was very inconsiderable.

Camp at Cambridge, July 21, 1775, 5 o'clock, P. M.
SIR,

SINCE closing the letters which accompany this, I have received an account of the destruction of the light-house; a copy of which I have the honor to inclose,—and of again assuring you that I am, with great respect, &c.

G. W.

P. S. I have also received a more authentic account of the loss of the enemy in the late battle, than any yet received. Dr. Winship, who lodged in the same house with an officer of the marines, assures me they had exactly one thousand and forty-three killed and wounded,—of whom three hundred fell on the field, or died within a few hours. Many of the wounded are since dead.

SIR,

SIR, Camp at Cambridge, July 27, 1775.

NOTHING material has occurred in either camp, since I had the honor of addressing you on the twenty-first instant by express: but on tuesday, three men-of-war and nine transports sailed out of Boston harbor, and stood a course about E. S. E.

One Groves, who came out of Boston the same evening, informed the officer at one of the out-posts, that the transports had on board six hundred men, and were bound to Block-Island, Fisher's-Island, and Long-Island, to plunder them, and bring off what cattle they may find. The fellow returned again into Boston under such suspicious circumstances, that it has led me to doubt the truth of his intelligence.

A deserter, who came in afterwards, informs me that it was given out in their camp, that they were either gone for Indians or fresh provisions; and that each transport had but twenty men on board. Upon this intelligence, I immediately wrote to governor Cooke of Rhode-Island, and to general Wooster, that they might take proper precautions for removing the cattle off those islands and the coasts, and to prevent any surprise. As we are confirmed, by every account, in the scarcity of fresh provisions in the enemy's camp, and particularly by this deserter, it is very probable this voyage may be only intended for a supply: but as it may possibly be otherwise, I thought it best to transmit the intelligence to the honorable Congress, that they may forward it to the southward, or take such other steps as they may judge proper.

Since writing the above, three more deserters have come out,—which makes four in twenty-four hours. Their accounts correspond with those of the first who came out, and which I have related above. I have the honor to be, &c.

G. W.

SIR,

Sir, Camp at Cambridge, Aug. 4, 1775.

I AM to acknowledge the receipt of your favor of the twenty-fourth July, accompanied by two hundred and eighty-four commiffions, which are yet much fhort of the neceffary number. I am much honored by the confidence repofed in me, of appointing the feveral officers recommended in mine of the tenth ultimo; and fhall endeavor to felect fuch perfons as are beft qualified to fill thefe important pofts. * * * *

In the renewal of thefe commiffions, fome difficulties occur, in which I fhould be glad to know the pleafure of the honorable Congrefs. The general officers of the Maffachufetts have regiments; thofe of Connecticut have both regiments and companies; and the other field officers have companies each. From Rhode-Ifland, the general officer has no regiment, but the field officers have companies: but I do not find that they have or expect pay under more than one commiffion. Should the commiffions, now to be delivered, purfue thefe different eftablifhments, there will be a diftinction between general and field officers of the fame rank. In order to put New-Hampfhire, Maffachufetts, and Rhode-Ifland, upon a line with Connecticut, it would be neceffary to difmifs a number of officers in poffeffion of commiffions, without any fault of theirs. On the other hand, to bring the Connecticut generals and field officers to the fame fcale with the others, will add to the number of officers, and may be deemed inconfiftent with the terms on which they entered into the fervice, although you add nothing to the expenfe, except in the article of provifions. Upon the whole, it is a cafe which I would wifh the honorable Congrefs to confider and determine.

Colonel Gridley of this province, who is at the head of the artillery, has the rank of major-general from the provincial Congrefs. Will it be proper to renew his commiffion here in the fame manner?—It is proper here to remark, that, in this cafe, he will take rank of all the brigadiers-general, and even the majors-general, whofe commiffions are fubfequent in date ۱. and this can anfwer no good purpofe, but may be productive of many bad confequences.

Thefe are matters of fome importance: but I am embarraffed with a difficulty of a fuperior kind. The eftimate, made in Congrefs, fuppofed all the regiments to be formed upon one eftablifhment: but they are different in different provinces, and even vary in the fame province, in fome particulars. In Maffachufetts, fome regiments have ten companies, others eleven: the eftablifhment of the former is five hundred and ninety men, officers included;—of the latter, fix hundred and forty-nine. The eftablifhment of Rhode-Ifland and New-Hampfhire is five hundred and ninety to a regiment, officers included:—Connecticut has a thoufand men to a regiment. Should the Maffachufetts regiments be completed, with the new levies from Rhode-Ifland and Connecticut, and the riflemen, the number will exceed twenty-two thoufand. If they fhould not be completed,—as each regiment is fully officered, there will be a heavy expenfe to the public, without an adequate fervice. The reduction of fome of them feems to be neceffary, and yet is a matter of much delicacy, as we are fituated. I moft earneftly requeft it may be taken into immediate confideration, and the time and mode of doing it pointed out by the honorable Congrefs. By an eftimate I have made from the general return,—when the new levies arrive, and the regiments are completed, there will be twenty-four thoufand four hundred and fifty men on the pay and provifion of the United Colonies. Some of the recruiting officers, who have been out on that fervice, have returned with very little fuccefs; fo that we may fafely conclude, the number of two thoufand and fixty-four, now wanting to complete, will rather increafe than diminifh. There are the regiment of artillery, confifting of four hundred and ninety-three men, and one under colonel Sergeant (who has not received any commiffion, although he had orders to raife a regiment,

giment, from the provincial Congress here) which are not included in the above estimate. This last regiment consists of two hundred and thirty-four men by the last return; but a company has since joined.

By adverting to the general return, which I have the honor of inclosing (N° 1), it will be seen, what regiments are most deficient.

If the Congress does not chuse to point out the particular regiments, but the provinces in which the reduction is to be made, the several Congresses and Assemblies may be the proper channel to conduct this business, which I would also conceive the most advisable, from their better acquaintance with the merits, terms, and time of service, of the respective officers. Reducing some regiments, and, with the privates thereof, filling up others, would certainly be the best method of accomplishing this work if it were practicable : but the experiment is dangerous, as the Massachusetts-men, under the privilege of chusing their own officers, do not conceive themselves bound, if those officers are disbanded.

As general Gage is making preparations for winter by contracting for quantities of coal, it will suggest to us the propriety of extending our views to that season. I have directed that such huts as have been lately made of boards should be done in such a manner, that, if necessary, they may serve for covering during the winter. But I need not enlarge upon the variety of necessities, such as clothing, fuel, &c, (both exceedingly scarce, and difficult to be procured) which that season must bring with it, if the army or any considerable part of it is to remain embodied.

From the inactivity of the enemy since the arrival of their whole reinforcement,—their continual addition to their lines, —and many other circumstances,—I am inclined to think, that, finding us so well prepared to receive them, the plan of operations is varied, and they mean, by regular approaches, to bombard us out of our present line of defence, or are waiting in expectation that the colonies must sink under the

weight

weight of the expense, or the prospect of a winter campaign so discourage our troops, as to break up our army. If they have not some such expectations, the issue of which they are determined to wait, I cannot account for the delay, when their strength is lessened every day by sickness, desertions, and little skirmishes.

Of these last we have had only two worthy of notice. Having some reason to suspect they were extending their lines at Charlestown, I, last saturday evening, ordered some of the riflemen down, to make a discovery, or bring off a prisoner. They were accidentally discovered sooner than they expected, by the guard coming to relieve, and obliged to fire upon them. We have reason to believe they killed several. They brought in two prisoners, whose account (confirmed by some other circumstances) removed my suspicions in part. Since that time, we have, on each side, drawn in our centries, and there have been scattering fires along the line. This evening we have heard of three captains who have been taken off by the riflemen, and one killed by a cannon-shot from Roxbury, besides several privates: but as the intelligence is not direct, I only mention it as a report which deserves credit.—The other happened at the light-house. A number of workmen having been sent down to repair it, with a guard of twenty-two marines and a subaltern,—major Tupper, last monday morning about two o'clock, landed there with about three hundred men, attacked them, killed the officer and four privates; but being detained by the tide, in his return he was attacked by several boats; but he happily got through, with the loss of one man killed, and another wounded. The remainder of the ministerial troops (three of whom are badly wounded) he brought off prisoners, with ten tories, all of whom are on their way to Springfield-jail. The riflemen, in these skirmishes, lost one man, who (we hear) is a prisoner in Boston-jail. The enemy, in return, endeavored to surprise our guard at Roxbury: but they, being apprised of it by a deserter, had time to prepare for it: but by some negligence or misconduct in the officer of the guard, they burned the George tavern on the neck; and have every day since been cannonading us from their lines, both at Roxbury and Charlestown, but with no other effect than the loss of two men. On our part, except straggling fires from the small arms about the lines, which we endeavor to restrain, we have made little or no return.

Our situation, in the article of powder, is much more alarming than I had the most distant idea of. Having desired a return to be made out (on my arrival) of the ammunition, I found three hundred and three barrels and a half of powder mentioned as in the store; but on ordering a new supply of cartridges yesterday, I was informed, to my very great astonishment, that there was no more than thirty-six barrels of the Massachusetts store, which, with the stock of Rhode-Island, New-Hampshire, and Connecticut, makes nine thousand nine hundred and thirty-seven pounds,—not more than nine rounds a man. As there had been no consumption of powder since, that could in any degree account for such a deficiency, I was very particular in my inquiries, and found that the committee of supplies, not being sufficiently acquainted with the nature of a return, or misapprehending my request, sent in an account of all the ammunition which had been collected by the province; so that the report included not only what was in hand, but what had been spent.

Upon discovering this mistake, I immediately went up to confer with the speaker of the house of representatives, upon some measures to obtain a supply from the neighboring townships, in such a manner as might prevent our poverty being known; as it is a secret of too great consequence to be divulged in the general court, some individual of which might perhaps indiscreetly suffer it to escape him, so as to find its way to the enemy,—the consequences of which are terrible even in idea. I shall also write to the governors of Rhode-Island and Connecticut, and the committee of safety in New-Hampshire, on this subject, urging, in the most

forcible

forcible terms, the neceffity of an immediate fupply, if in their power. I need not enlarge on our melancholy fituation: it is fufficient that the exiftence of the army and the falvation of the country depends upon fomething being done for our relief, both fpeedy and effectual, and that our fituation be kept a profound fecret.

In the inclofures, N° 2 and 3, I fend the allowance of provifions, &c, made by the provinces of Connecticut and Maffachufetts. The mode and quantity are different from what has fallen within my experience, and, I am confident, muft prove very wafteful and expenfive. If any alteration can be fafely made (which I much doubt), there might be a great faving to the public.

A gentleman of my family, affifted by a deferter who has fome fkill in fortification, has, by my direction, fketched out two draughts of our refpective lines at Charleftown and Roxbury, which, with the explanations, will convey fome idea of our fituation, and, I hope, prove acceptable to the members of the honorable Congrefs. They are the inclofures, N° 4 and 5.

Since I had the honor of addreffing you laft, I have been applied to, by a committee of the general court, for a detachment of the army, to protect the inhabitants of the eaftern parts of this province from fome apprehended depredations on their coafts. I could have wifhed to have complied with their requeft: but, after due confideration, and confulting the general officers, together with thofe members of Congrefs who are here, I thought it my duty to excufe myfelf. The application and my anfwer are the inclofures, N° 6 and 7, which I hope will be approved by the honorable Congrefs.

Since I began this letter, the original (of which the inclofure N° 8 is a copy) fell into my hands. As the writer is a perfon of fome note in Bofton, and it contains fome advices of importance not mentioned by others, I thought proper to forward it as I received it. By comparing the hand-writing with another letter, it appears the writer is one Belcher Noyes,

Noyes, a person probably known to some of the gentlemen, delegates from this province, who can determine from his principles and character, what credit is due to him.

The army is now formed into three grand divisions, under the command of the generals Ward, Lee, and Putnam;— each division into two brigades, consisting of about six regiments each, commanded by generals Thomas and Spencer at Roxbury,—Heath at Cambridge,—Sullivan and Greene at Winter-hill. By this, you will please to observe, there is a deficiency of one brigadier-general (occasioned by Mr. Pomroy's not acting under his commission) which I beg may be filled up as soon as possible. I observe the honorable Congress have also favored me with the appointment of three brigade-majors. I presume they have or intend to appoint the rest soon, as they cannot be unacquainted that one is necessary to each brigade; and, in a new-raised army, it will be an office of great duty and service.

General Gage has at length liberated the people of Boston, who land in numbers at Chelsea every day. The terms on which the passes are granted, as to money, effects, and provisions, correspond with Mr. Noyes's letter.

We have several reports that general Gage is dismantling Castle-William, and bringing all the cannon up to town: but, upon a very particular inquiry, accounts are so various, that I cannot ascertain the truth of it. * * *

On the first instant, a chief of the Caghnewaga tribe, who lives about six miles from Montréal, came in here, accompanied by a colonel Bayley of Cohofs. His accounts of the temper and disposition of the Indians are very favorable. He says they have been strongly solicited by governor Carleton to engage against us; but his nation is totally averse;—that threats, as well as entreaties, have been used without effect;— that the Canadians are well-disposed to the English colonies; and, if any expedition is meditated against Canada, the Indians in that quarter will give all their assistance. I have endeavored to cherish these favorable dispositions, and have recommended to him to cultivate them on his return. What I have said, I enforced with a prefent, which I underftood would be agreeable to him: and as he is reprefented to be a man of weight and confequence in his own tribe, I flatter myfelf his vifit will have a good effect. His accounts of general Carleton's force and fituation at St. John's correfpond with what we have already had from that quarter.

The acceffion of Georgia to the meafures of the Congrefs is a happy event, and muft give a fincere pleafure to every friend of America.

Auguft 5.——We have accounts this morning of two exploftons at the caftle; fo that its deftruction may now be fuppofed certain.

I have this morning been alarmed with an information that two gentlemen from Philadelphia (Mr. Hitchbourn and captain White), with letters for general Lee and myfelf, have been taken by captain Ayfcough at Rhode-Ifland, the letters intercepted and fent forward to Bofton,—with the bearers, as prifoners; that the captain exulted much in the difcoveries he had made: and my informer (who was alfo in the boat, but releafed) underftood them to be letters of confequence. I have therefore difpatched the exprefs immediately back, though I had before refolved to detain him till Feffenden's return. I fhall be anxious till I am relieved from the fufpenfe I am in, as to the contents of thofe letters.

It is exceedingly unfortunate that gentlemen fhould chufe to travel the only road on which there is danger. Let the event of this be what it will, I hope it will ferve as a general caution againft trufting any letters that way in future.

Nothing of confequence has occurred in camp thefe two days.—The inhabitants of Bofton continue coming out at Chelfea, but under a new reftriction, that no *men* fhall come out without fpecial licence, which is refufed to all mechanics, fince the tory laborers were taken at the light-houfe. I have the honor to be, &c. G. W.

[*The*

[*The following letter bears no date, but appears to have been written on or about the twenty-sixth of August, 1775.*]

SIR,

THE inclosed letter came under such a direction and circumstances, as led me to suppose it contained some interesting advices, either respecting a supply of powder, or the clothing lately taken at Philadelphia. I therefore took the liberty of breaking the seal, for which I hope the service and my motives will apologise.

As the filling up the place of vacant brigadier-general will probably be of the first business of the honorable Congress, I flatter myself it will not be deemed assuming, to mention the names of two gentlemen, whose former services, rank and age, may be thought worthy of attention on this occasion. The former is colonel John Armstrong, of Pennsylvania; he served during the last war, in most of the campaigns to the southward; was honored with the command of the Pennsylvania forces, and his general military conduct and spirit much approved by all who served with him: besides which, his character was distinguished by an enterprise against the Indians, which he planned with great judgment, and executed with equal courage and success. It was not till lately that I had reason to believe he would enter again on public service; and it is now wholly unsolicited and unknown on his part. The other gentleman is colonel Fry, of Massachusetts-Bay. He entered into the service as early as 1745, and rose through the different military ranks, in the succeeding wars, to that of colonel, until last June, when he was appointed a major-general by the Congress of this province. From these circumstances, together with the favorable report made to me of him, I presume he sustained the character of a good officer, though I do not find it distinguished by any peculiar service.

Either

Either of thefe gentlemen, or any other whom the honorable Congrefs fhall pleafe to favor with this appointment, will be received by me with the utmoft deference and refpect.

The late adjournment having made it impracticable to know the pleafure of the Congrefs as to the appointment of brigade-majors, beyond the number of three which they were pleafed to leave to me,—and the fervice not admitting of farther delay,—I have continued the other three; which I hope their honors will not difapprove. Thefe latter were recommended by the refpective corps to which they belong, as the propereft perfons for thefe offices until farther direction, and have difcharged the duty ever fince. They are the majors Box, Scammel, and Samuel Brewer.

Laft faturday night we took poffeffion of a hill confiderably advanced beyond our former lines; which brought on a very heavy cannonade from Bunker's hill, and afterwards a bombardment, which has been fince kept up with little fpirit on their part, or damage on ours. The work having been continued ever fince, is now fo advanced, and the men fo well covered, as to leave us under no apprehenfions of much farther lofs. In this affair, we had killed—one adjutant, one volunteer, and two privates. The fcarcity of ammunition does not admit of our availing ourfelves of the fituation, as we otherwife might do: but this evil, I hope, will foon be remedied, as I have been informed of the arrival of a large quantity at New-York, fome at New-London, and more hourly expected at different places. I need not add to what I have already faid on this fubject.—Our late fupply was very feafonable, but far fhort of our neceffities.

The late adjournment of the honorable Congrefs having been made before my letter of the fourteenth inftant was received, I muft now beg leave to recall their attention to thofe parts of it which refpect the provifion for the winter, the reduction of the troops, the double commiffions under different eftablifhments, and colonel Gridley's appointment of major-general;

general; in all which, I hope to be honored with their commands as foon as poffible.

The advocate-general has fent me a memorial refpecting his fervice, which I have the honor to inclofe (N° 1): and from the variety and multiplicity of duty in a new army, as well as his regular fervice and attendance, I am induced to recommend him to the farther notice of the honorable Congrefs.

The treatment of our officers, prifoners at Bofton, induced me to write to general Gage on that fubject. His anfwer and my reply I have the honor to lay before the Congrefs, in the inclofures N° 2, 3, 4; fince which I have heard nothing from him.

I remain, with the greateft refpect and regard, &c. G. W.

To the Honorable PETER VANBRUGH LIVINGSTON, *Efq. Prefident of the Provincial Convention, New-York.*

SIR, *Camp at Cambridge, Auguft,* 30, 1775.

* * * MR. Livingfton and fome other gentlemen from your city brought us the acceptable news of the fafe arrival of a large quantity of powder, and five hundred ftand of arms. Our fituation is fuch as requires your immediate affiftance and fupply in that article. We have lately taken poffeffion of a hill confiderably advanced towards the enemy; but our poverty prevents our availing ourfelves of any advantage of fituation. I muft therefore moft earneftly entreat that meafures may be taken to forward to this camp, in the moft fafe and expeditious manner, whatever ammunition can be fpared from the immediate and neceffary defence of the province. The value of whatever may be fent in confequence of this requeft will be paid by order from hence when delivered, or negotiated with the honorable continental Congrefs at Philadelphia, as may be agreed with the proprietors. I only requeft that no time may be loft through any

fuch

such difficulties, as our situation is so critical, and the exigence so great. The mode of conveyance I must leave with the provincial Congress, or the committee of the city. I doubt not they will take every precaution to make it safe and expeditious.—I have the honor to be, &c. G. W.

SIR, *Camp at Cambridge, Sept.* 7, 1775.

I DO myself the honor of addressing you in consequence of an application from the commissary-general, who is, by my direction, taking all proper precautions on the approach of winter. I desired him to commit to writing such proposals as his experience and knowledge of the country might entitle him to make; which he has done in the paper which I have the honor to inclose. The difficulty of procuring a sufficient quantity of salt, which I objected to him, he has fully obviated, by assuring me that there is so much now actually in store, in this and the neighboring towns, as will remove all possibility of a disappointment.

I propose to do myself the honor of writing, in a few days, fully and particularly on several heads, to which I must now refer. In the mean time, I have only to inform the honorable Congress, that I have received a small supply of seven thousand pounds of powder this week from Rhode-Island, and in a few days expect seven tons of lead, and five hundred stand of arms, a part of the same importation; and to request that more money may be forwarded with all expedition, the military chest being nearly exhausted.

I am, with the greatest respect, &c. G. W.

SIR, *Camp at Cambridge, Sept.* 21, 1775.

I HAVE been in daily expectation of being favored with the commands of the honorable Congress, on the subject of my two last letters. The season now advances so fast,

fast, that I cannot any longer defer laying before them such farther measures as require their immediate attention, and in which I wait their direction.

The mode in which the present army has been collected has occasioned some difficulty in procuring the subscription of both officers and soldiers to the continental articles of war. Their principal objection has been, that it might subject them to a longer service than that for which they engaged under their several provincial establishments. It is in vain to attempt to reason away the prejudices of a whole army: * * * I have therefore forbore pressing them, as I did not experience any such inconvenience from their adherence to their former rules, as would warrant the risk of entering into a contest upon it; more especially as the restraints, necessary for the establishment of essential discipline and subordination, indisposed their minds to every change, and made it both duty and policy to introduce as little novelty as possible. With the present army, I fear such a subscription is impracticable: but the difficulty will cease with this army.

The Connecticut and Rhode-Island troops stand engaged to the first of December only; and none longer than the first of January. A dissolution of the present army therefore will take place, unless some early provision is made against such an event. Most of the general officers are of opinion the greater part of them may be re-enlisted for the winter, or another campaign, with the indulgence of a furlough to visit their friends, which may be regulated so as not to endanger the service. How far it may be proper to form the new army entirely out of the old, for another campaign, rather than from the contingents of the several provinces, is a question which involves in it too many considerations of policy and prudence, for me to undertake to decide. It appears to be impossible to draw it from any other source than the old army, for this winter; and, as the pay is ample, I hope a sufficient number will engage in the service for that time at least. But there are various opinions of the temper of the

men

men on the subject; and there may be great hazard in deferring the trial so long.

In the continental establishment, no provision has been made for the pay of artificers, distinct from that of the common soldiers; whereas, under the provincial, such as found their own tools, were allowed one shilling per diem advance, and particular artisans, more. The pay of the artillery also now differs from that of the province; the men have less, the officers more; and, for some ranks, no provision is made, as the Congress will please to observe by the list which I have the honor to inclose (N° 1). These particulars, though seemingly inconsiderable, are the source of much complaint and dissatisfaction, which I endeavor to compose in the best manner I am able.

By the returns of the rifle companies, and that batallion, they appear to exceed their establishment very considerably. I doubt my authority to pay these extra men without the direction of the Congress: but it would be deemed a great hardship, wholly to refuse them, as they have been encouraged to come.

The necessities of the troops having required pay, I directed that those of the Massachusetts should receive for one month, upon their being mustered, and returning a proper roll: but a claim was immediately made for pay by lunar months; and several regiments have declined taking up their warrants on this account. As this practice was entirely new to me, though said to be warranted by former usage, here the matter now waits the determination of the honorable Congress. I find, in Connecticut and Rhode-Island, this point was settled by calendar months: in Massachusetts, though mentioned in the Congress, it was left undetermined; which is also the case of New-Hampshire.

The inclosure, N° 2, is a petition from the subalterns, respecting their pay. Where there are only two of these in a company, I have considered one as an ensign, and ordered him pay as such, as in the Connecticut forces. I must beg leave

leave to recommend this petition to the favor of the Congress; as I am of opinion the allowance is inadequate to their rank and service, and is one great source of that familiarity between the officers and men, which is so incompatible with subordination and discipline. Many valuable officers of those ranks, finding themselves unable to support the character and appearance of officers, (I am informed) will retire as soon as the term of service is expired, if there is no alteration.

For the better regulation of duty, I found it necessary to settle the rank of the officers, and to number the regiments; and, as I had not received the commands of the Congress on the subject, and the exigence of the service forbade any farther delay, the general officers were considered as having no regiments,—an alteration, which, I understand, is not pleasing to some of them, but appeared to me and others to be proper, when it was considered, that, by this means, the whole army is put upon one footing, and all particular attachments dissolved.

Among many other considerations which the approach of winter will demand, that of clothing appears to be one of the most important. So far as regards the preservation of the army from cold, they may be deemed in a state of nakedness. Many of the men have been without blankets the whole campaign: and those, which have been in use during the summer, are so much worn as to be of little service. In order to make a suitable provision in these articles, and at the same time to guard the public against imposition and expense, it seems necessary to determine the mode of continuing the army: for, should these troops be clothed under their present engagement, and, at the expiration of the term of service, decline renewing it, a set of unprovided men may be sent to supply their places.

I cannot suppose it to be unknown to the honorable Congress, that, in all armies, it is an established practice to make an allowance to officers, of provisions and forage, proportionate to their rank. As such an allowance formed no

part

part of the continental establishment, I have hitherto forbore to issue the orders for that purpose: but, as it is a received opinion of such members of the Congress as I have had an opportunity of consulting, as well as throughout the army, that it must be deemed a matter of course and implied in the establishment of the army, I have directed the following proportion of rations, being the same allowed in the American armies last war :———major-general, fifteen; brigadier-general, twelve; colonel, six; lieutenant-colonel, five; major, four; captain, three; subaltern, two; staff, two.

If these should not be approved by the honorable Congress, they will please to signify their pleasure, as to the alterations they would have made in the whole or in part.

I am now to inform the honorable Congress, that, encouraged by the repeated declarations of the Canadians and Indians, and urged by their requests, I have detached colonel Arnold with a thousand men, to penetrate into Canada by way of Kennebeck river, and, if possible, to make himself master of Quebec. By this manœuvre, I proposed either to divert Carleton from St. John's, which would leave a free passage to general Schuyler;—or, if this did not take effect, Quebec, in its present defenceless state, must fall into his hands an easy prey. I made all possible inquiry, as to the distance, the safety of the route, and the danger of the season being too far advanced; but found nothing in either, to deter me from proceeding, more especially as it met with very general approbation from all whom I consulted upon it. But, that nothing might be omitted, to enable me to judge of its propriety and probable consequences, I communicated it by express to general Schuyler, who approved of it in such terms, that I resolved to put it in immediate execution. They have now left this place seven days; and, if favored with a good wind, I hope soon to hear of their being safe in Kennebeck river. For the satisfaction of the Congress, I here inclose a copy of the proposed route (N° 3). I also do myself the honor of inclosing a manifesto, which I caused to be printed here, and

of

†

of which colonel Arnold has taken a suitable number with him. This is the inclosure, N° 4. I have also forwarded a copy of his instructions (N° 5):—from all which, I hope the Congress will have a clear view of the motives, plan, and intended execution of this enterprise, and that I shall be so happy as to meet with their approbation in it.

I was the more induced to make this detachment, as it is my clear opinion, from a careful observation of the movements of the enemy, corroborated by all the intelligence we receive by deserters and others, (of the former of whom we have some every day) that the enemy have no intention to come out, until they are reinforced. They have been wholly employed for some time past in procuring materials for barracks, fuel, and making other preparations for winter. These circumstances, with the constant additions to their works which are apparently defensive, have led to the above conclusion, and enabled me to spare this body of men where I hope they will be usefully and successfully employed.

The state of inactivity, in which this army has lain for some time, by no means corresponds with my wishes, by some decisive stroke to relieve my country from the heavy expense its subsistence must create. After frequently reconnoitring the situation of the enemy in the town of Boston, collecting all possible intelligence, and digesting the whole, a surprise did not appear to me wholly impracticable, though hazardous. I communicated it to the general officers some days before I called them to a council, that they might be prepared with their opinions. The result I have the honor of inclosing (N° 6). I cannot say that I have wholly laid it aside: but new events may occasion new measures. Of this I hope the honorable Congress can need no assurance, that there is not a man in America who more earnestly wishes such a termination of the campaign, as to make the army no longer necessary.

The season advances so fast, that I have given orders to prepare barracks and other accommodations for the winter.

The great scarcity of tow-cloth in this country, I fear, will totally disappoint us in our expectations of procuring hunting-shirts. Governor Cooke informs me, few or none are to be had in Rhode-Island; and governor Trumbull gives me little encouragement to expect many from Connecticut.

I have filled up the office of quarter-master-general which the Congress was pleased to leave to me, by the appointment of major Mifflin, which I hope and believe will be universally acceptable.

It gives me great pain to be obliged to solicit the attention of the honorable Congress to the state of this army, in terms which imply the slightest apprehension of being neglected. But my situation is inexpressibly distressing, to see the winter fast approaching upon a naked army; the time of their service within a few weeks of expiring; and no provision yet made for such important events. Added to these, the military chest is totally exhausted: the paymaster has not a single dollar in hand: the commissary-general assures me he has strained his credit, for the subsistence of the army, to the utmost. The quarter-master-general is precisely in the same situation; and the greater part of the troops are in a state not far from mutiny, upon the deduction from their stated allowance. I know not to whom I am to impute this failure: but I am of opinion, if the evil is not immediately remedied, and more punctuality observed in future, the army must absolutely break up. I hoped I had so fully expressed myself on this subject (both by letter, and to those members of the Congress who honored the camp with a visit), that no disappointment could possibly happen: I therefore hourly expected advice from the paymaster that he had received a fresh supply, in addition to the hundred and seventy-two thousand dollars delivered him in August; and thought myself warranted to assure the public creditors that in a few days they should be satisfied. But the delay has brought matters to such a crisis, as admits of no farther uncertain expectation. I have therefore sent off this express, with orders to make all possible dispatch. It is my most earnest request that he may be returned with all possible expedition, unless the honorable Congress have already forwarded what is so indispensably necessary.

I have the honor to be, &c. G. W.

Sir,   *Camp at Cambridge, Sept. 30, 1775.*

THE reverend Mr. Kirkland, the bearer of this, having been introduced to the honorable Congress, can need no particular recommendation from me. But as he now wishes to have the affairs of his mission and public employ put upon some suitable footing, I cannot but intimate my sense of the importance of his station, and the great advantages which have and may result to the United Colonies, from his situation being made respectable.

All accounts agree that much of the favorable disposition, shewn by the Indians, may be ascribed to his labor and influence. He has accompanied a chief of the Oneidas to this camp, which I have endeavored to make agreeable to him, both by civility and some small presents. Mr. Kirkland being also in some necessity for money to bear his travelling charges and other expenses, I have supplied him with thirty-two pounds lawful money.

I cannot but congratulate the honorable Congress on the happy temper of the Canadians and Indians, our accounts of which are now fully confirmed by some intercepted letters from officers in Canada, to general Gage and others in Boston, which were found on board the vessel lately taken, going into Boston with a donation of cattle and other fresh provisions for the ministerial army.

I have the honor to be, &c. G. W.

Sir, Camp at Cambridge, Oct. 5, 1775.

I WAS honored with your favor of the twenty-sixth ultimo, late the night before last; and a meeting of the general officers having been called upon a business which will make a considerable part of this letter, I took the opportunity of laying before them those parts of yours which respect the continuance and new-modelling of the army, the fuel, clothing, and other preparations for the ensuing winter. They have taken two or three days to consider; and, as soon as I am possessed of their opinions, I shall lose no time in transmitting the result, not only on the above subjects, but the number of troops necessary to be kept up.

I have also directed the commissary-general and the quarter-master-general to prepare estimates of the expense of their departments for a certain given number of men, from which a judgment may be made, when the number of men to be kept in pay is determined:—all which I shall do myself the honor to lay before the Congress, as soon as they are ready.

I have now a painful though a necessary duty to perform, respecting Dr. Church, director-general of the hospital. About a week ago, Mr. secretary Ward of Providence sent up to me one Wainwood, an inhabitant of Newport, with a letter directed to major Cane in Boston, in [*occult*] characters, which he said had been left with Wainwood some time ago, by a woman who was kept by Dr. Church. She had before pressed Wainwood to take her to captain Wallace, Mr. Dudley the collector, or George Rome; which he declined. She then gave him the letter, with a strict charge to deliver it to either of those gentlemen. He, suspecting some improper correspondence, kept the letter, and after some time opened it; but, not being able to read it, laid it up, where it remained until he received an obscure letter from the woman, expressing an anxiety after the original letter. He then communicated the whole matter to Mr. Ward, who

sent

sent him up with the papers to me. I immediately secured the woman: but for a long time she was proof against every threat and persuasion to discover the author. However, at length she was brought to a confession, and named Dr. Church. I then immediately secured him and all his papers. Upon his first examination, he readily acknowledged the letter, said it was designed for his brother Fleming, and, when deciphered, would be found to contain nothing criminal. He acknowledged his never having communicated the correspondence to any person here but the girl, and made many protestations of the purity of his intentions. Having found a person capable of deciphering the letter, I in the mean time had all his papers searched, but found nothing criminal among them; but it appeared on inquiry, that a confidant had been among the papers before my messenger arrived. I then called the general officers together for their advice, the result of which you will find in the inclosure, N° 1. The deciphered letter is the inclosure, N° 2. The army and country are exceedingly irritated: and upon a free discussion of the nature, circumstances, and consequence of this matter, it has been unanimously agreed to lay it before the honorable Congress for their special advice and direction; at the same time suggesting to their consideration, whether an alteration of the twenty-eighth article of war may not be necessary.

As I shall reserve all farther remarks upon the state of the army till my next, I shall now beg leave to request the determination of Congress, as to the property and disposal of such vessels and cargoes as are designed for the supply of the enemy, and may fall into our hands. There has been an event of this kind at Portsmouth (as by the inclosure, N° 3), in which I have directed the cargo to be brought hither for the use of the army, reserving the settlement of any claims of capture to the decision of Congress.

As there are many unfortunate individuals whose property has been confiscated by the enemy, I would humbly suggest to the consideration of Congress the humanity of applying, in part or in the whole, such captures to the relief of those sufferers, after compensating any expense of the captors, and for their activity and spirit. I am the more induced to request this determination may be speedy, as I have directed three vessels to be equipped in order to cut off the supplies; and, from the number of vessels hourly arriving, it may become an object of some importance. In the disposal of these captures, for the encouragement of the officers and men, I have allowed them one-third of the cargoes, except military stores, which, with the vessels, are to be reserved for the public use. I hope my plan, as well as the execution, will be favored with the approbation of Congress.

One Mr. Fisk, an intelligent person, came out of Boston on the third instant, and gives us the following advices:—that a fleet, consisting of a sixty-four, and twenty-gun ship, two sloops of eighteen guns, and two transports with six hundred men, were to sail from Boston as yesterday; that they took on board two mortars, four howitzers, and other artillery calculated for the bombardment of a town;—their destination was kept a profound secret:—that an express sloop of war, which left England the eighth August, arrived four days ago;—that general Gage is recalled, and last sunday resigned his command to general Howe;—that lord Percy, colonel Smith, and other officers who were at Lexington, are ordered home with Gage;—that six ships of the line and two cutters were coming out under sir Peter Dennis;—that five regiments and a thousand marines are ordered out, and may be expected in three or four weeks:—no prospect of accommodation; but the ministry determined to push the war to the utmost.

I have an express from colonel Arnold, and herewith send a copy of his letter and an inclosure, N° 4 and 5.—I am happy in finding he meets with no discouragement.—The claim of the rifle officers, to be independent of all the superior officers except colonel Arnold, is without any countenance or authority from me, as I have signified in my last dispatch both to
colonel

colonel Arnold and captain Morgan.—The captain of the brig from Quebec for Boston informs me that there is no suspicion of any such expedition; and that, if Carleton is not drove from St. John's, so as to be obliged to throw himself into Quebec, it must fall into our hands, as it is left without a regular soldier, and many of the inhabitants are most favorably disposed to the American cause;—and that there is the largest stock of ammunition ever collected in America.

In the above vessel some letters were also found, from an officer at Quebec, to general Gage and major Sheriff at Boston, containing such an account of the temper of the Canadians, as cannot but afford the highest satisfaction. I have thought it best to forward them: they are the inclosures, N° 6 and 7.

I am, with the greatest respect, &c.   G. W.

Sir,   *Camp at Cambridge, Oct.* 12, 1775.

I AM honored with your several favors of the twenty-sixth and thirtieth September, and fifth October, the contents of which I shall beg leave to notice in their respective order.

Previous to the direction of Congress to consult the general officers on the best mode of continuing and providing for the army during the winter, I had desired them to turn their thoughts upon these subjects, and to favor me with the result, by a particular day, in writing. In this interval, the appointment of Dr. Franklin, Mr. Lynch, and colonel Harrison, was communicated,—an event, which has given me the highest satisfaction, as the subject was too weighty and complex for a discussion by letter. This appointment made any conclusion here unnecessary, as it is not probable any such arrangement would be agreed on, as would not be altered in some respects, upon a full and free conference. This good effect will arise from the step already taken, that every officer will

will be prepared to give his sentiments upon these important subjects.

The estimates of the commissary and quarter-master-general I have now the honor of inclosing. The first is N° 1,—the other, N° 2.

With respect to the reduction of the pay of the men, which may enter into the consideration of their support, it is the unanimous opinion of the general officers, that it cannot be touched with safety at present. * * *

Upon the presumption of there being a vacancy in the direction of the hospital, lieutenant-colonel Hand, formerly a surgeon in the eighteenth regiment, or royal Irish, and Dr. Foster, late of Charlestown, and one of the surgeons of the hospital under Dr. Church, are candidates for that office. I do not pretend to be acquainted with their respective merits, and therefore have given them no farther expectation, than that they should be mentioned as candidates for the department. I therefore need only to add upon this subject, that the affairs of the hospital require that the appointment should be made as soon as possible.

Before I was honored with your favor of the fifth instant, I had given orders for the equipment of some armed vessels, to intercept the enemy's supplies of provisions and ammunition. One of them was on a cruise between Cape Anne and Cape Cod, when the express arrived. The others will be fit for the sea in a few days, under the command of officers of the continental army, who are well recommended, as persons acquainted with the sea, and capable of such a service. Two of these will be immediately dispatched on this duty; and every particular, mentioned in your favor of the fifth instant, literally complied with.

That the honorable Congress may have a more complete idea of the plan on which these vessels are equipped, I inclose a copy of the instructions given to the captains now out (N° 4). These, with the additional instruction directed, will be given to the captains who go into the mouth of St. Laurence's river. As both officers and men most cheerfully engage in the service on the terms mentioned in these instructions, I fear that the proposed increase will create some difficulty, by making a difference between men engaged on similar service. I have therefore not yet communicated this part of the plan, but reserved an extra bounty as a reward for extraordinary activity. There are no armed vessels in this province; and governor Cooke informs me the enterprise can receive no assistance from him, as one of the armed vessels of Rhode-Island is on a long cruise, and the other unfit for the service. Nothing shall be omitted, to secure success. A fortunate capture of an ordnance ship would give new life to the camp, and an immediate turn to the issue of this campaign.

Our last accounts from colonel Arnold are very favorable: he was proceeding with all expedition; and I flatter myself (making all allowances) he will be at Quebec the twentieth instant, where a gentleman from Canada (Mr. * * *) assures me he will meet with no resistance.

In the quarter-master's estimate, there are some articles omitted, of which he informs me he cannot pretend to furnish a computation,—such as cartage, tools, &c, for which some general allowance must be made.

From the various accounts received from Europe, there may be reason to expect troops will be landed at New-York, or some other middle colony. I should be glad to know the pleasure of the Congress, whether, upon such an event, it would be expected that a part of this army should be detached, or the internal force of such colony and its neighborhood be deemed sufficient; or whether, in such case, I am to wait the particular direction of Congress.

The fleet, mentioned in my last, has been seen standing N. N. E; so that we apprehend it is intended for some part of this province, or New-Hampshire, or possibly Quebec.

The

The latest and best accounts we have from the enemy, are, that they are engaged in their new work across the south end of Boston, preparing their barracks, &c, for winter:—that it is proposed to keep from five hundred to a thousand men on Bunker's hill all winter, who are to be relieved once a week;—the rest to be drawn into Boston.

A person who has lately been a servant to major Conolly (a tool of lord Dunmore's) has given an account of a scheme to distress the southern provinces, which appeared to me of sufficient consequence to be immediately transmitted. I have therefore got it attested, and do myself the honor of inclosing it, N° 5.

The new levies from Connecticut have lately marched into camp, and are a body of as good troops as any we have; so that we have now the same strength, as before the detachment made under colonel Arnold.

I am, with the most respectful sentiments to the honorable Congress, and yourself, sir, your most obedient, &c. G. W.

Sir, *Camp at Cambridge, Octob.* 24, 1775.

MY conjecture of the destination of the late squadron from Boston, in my last, has been unhappily verified by an outrage, exceeding, in barbarity and cruelty, every hostile act practised among civilised nations. I have inclosed the account given me by Mr. Jones, a gentleman of the town of Falmouth, of the destruction of that increasing and flourishing village. He is a very great sufferer, and informs me that the time allowed for the removal of effects was so small, that valuable property of all kinds, and to a great amount, has been destroyed. The orders shewn by the captain for this horrid procedure (by which it appears the same desolation is meditated upon all the towns on the coast) made it my duty to communicate it as quickly and extensively as possible. As Portsmouth was the next place to which he proposed to go, general Sullivan was permitted to

go

go up, and give them his assistance and advice to ward off the blow. I flatter myself the like event will not happen there, as they have a fortification of some strength, and a vessel has arrived at a place called Sheepscot, with fifteen hundred pounds of powder.

The gentlemen of the Congress have nearly finished their business: but as they write by this opportunity, I must beg leave to refer you to their letter, for what concerns their commission.

We have had no occurrence of any consequence in the camp since I had the honor of addressing you last; but expect every hour to hear that Newport has shared the fate of unhappy Falmouth.

I have the honor to be, &c. G. W.

Sir, *Camp at Cambridge, Octob.* 30, 1775.

THE information, which the gentlemen who have lately gone from hence can give the Congress, of the state and situation of the army, would have made a letter unnecessary, if I did not suppose there would be some anxiety to know the intentions of the army on the subject of the re-enlistment.

Agreeable to the advice of those gentlemen, and my own opinion, I immediately began by directing all such officers as proposed to continue, to signify their intentions as soon as possible. A great number of the returns are come in, from which I find that a very great proportion of the officers of the rank of captains, and under, will retire;—from present appearances, I may say, half,—but at least, one-third. It is with some concern also that I observe, that many of the officers who retire, discourage the continuance of the men, and, I fear, will communicate the infection to them. Some have advised that those officers who decline the service should be immediately dismissed: but this would be very dangerous and inconvenient. I confess I have great anxieties

upon

upon the subject, though I still hope the pay and terms are so advantageous, that interest, and, I hope also, a regard to their country, will retain a greater proportion of the privates than their officers. In so important a matter, I shall esteem it my indispensable duty, not only to act with all possible prudence, but to give the most early and constant advice of my progress.

A supply of clothing, equal to our necessities, would greatly contribute to the encouragement and satisfaction of the men. In every point of view, it is so important, that I beg leave to call the attention of the Congress to it in a particular manner.

A sergeant has just come in from Bunker's hill, but brings no important news.

I have the honor to be, &c. G. W.

Sir, Cambridge, Nov. 2, 1775.

I COULD not suffer Mr. Randolph to quit this camp without bearing some testimony of my duty to the Congress; although his sudden departure (occasioned by the death of his worthy relative, whose loss, as a good citizen and valuable member of society, is much to be regretted) does not allow me time to be particular.

The inclosed return shews, at one view, what reliance we have upon the officers of this army, and how deficient we are like to be in subaltern officers. A few days more will enable me to inform the Congress what they have to expect from the soldiery, as I shall issue recruiting orders for this purpose, so soon as the officers are appointed,—which will be done this day,—having sent for the general officers, to consult them in the choice.

I must beg leave to recall the attention of the Congress to the appointment of a brigadier-general,—an officer as necessary to a brigade, as a colonel is to a regiment, and will be exceedingly wanted in the new arrangement.

The

'The proclamations and association, herewith inclosed, came to my hands on monday last. I thought it my duty to send them to you.——Nothing of moment has happened since my last.

With respectful compliments to the members of Congress, I have the honor to be, &c.   G. W.

SIR,   *Cambridge, Nov. 8, 1775.*

THE immediate occasion of my giving the Congress the trouble of a letter at this time is to inform them, that, in consequence of their order signified in your letter of the twentieth ultimo, I laid myself under a solemn tie of secrecy to captain M'Pherson, and proceeded to examine his plan for the destruction of the fleet in the harbor of Boston, with all that care and attention which the importance of it deserved, and my judgment could lead to. But not being happy enough to coincide in opinion with that gentleman, and finding that his scheme would involve greater expense, than (under my doubts of its success) I thought myself justified in giving into, I prevailed upon him to communicate his plan to three gentlemen of the artillery in this army, well acquainted in the knowledge and practice of gunnery. By them he has been convinced, that, inasmuch as he set out upon wrong principles, the scheme would prove abortive. Unwilling however to relinquish his favorite project of reducing the naval force of Great Britain, he is very desirous of building a number of row gallies for this purpose. But as the Congress alone are competent to the adoption of this measure, I have advised him (although he offered to go on with the building of them at his own expense, till the Congress should decide) to repair immediately to Philadelphia with his proposals; where, if they should be agreed to, or vessels of superior force, agreeable to the wishes of most others, should be resolved on, he may set instantly about them, with all the materials upon the spot:—here, they are to collect.—To him therefore I refer for further information on this head.

A vessel, said to be from Philadelphia and bound to Boston, with a hundred and twenty pipes of wine (a hundred and eighteen of which are secured) stranded at a place called Eastham, in a gale of wind on the second instant:—another, from Boston to Halifax, with dry goods, &c, (amounting, per invoice, to about two hundred and forty pounds lawful) got disabled in the same gale, near Beverly. These cargoes, with the papers, I have ordered to this place,—the vessels to be taken care of till further orders. I have also an account of the taking of a wood-sloop bound to Boston, and carried into Portsmouth by one of our armed vessels,—particulars not yet come to hand;—and this instant, of two others, from Nova Scotia to Boston, with hay, wood, live stock, &c, by another of our armed schooners.—These are in Plymouth.

These accidents and captures point out the necessity of establishing proper courts without loss of time, for the decision of property, and the legality of seizures; otherwise I may be involved in inextricable difficulties.

Our prisoners, by the reduction of Fort Chamblee (on which happy event I most sincerely congratulate the Congress), being considerably augmented, and likely to be increased, I submit it to the wisdom of Congress, whether some convenient inland towns, remote from the post-roads, ought not to be assigned them; the manner of their treatment, subsistence, &c, defined; and a commissary or agent appointed, to see that justice is done both to them and the public, proper accounts rendered, &c. Without a mode of this sort is adopted, I fear there will be sad confusion hereafter, as there are great complaints at present.

I reckoned without my host, when I informed the Congress in my last, that I should in a day or two be able to acquaint them of the disposition of the soldiery towards a new enlistment.

ment. I have been in consultation with the generals of this army ever since thursday last, endeavoring to establish new corps of officers; but find so many doubts and difficulties to reconcile, that I cannot say when they are to end, or what may be the consequences; as there appears to be such an unwillingness in the officers of one government mixing in the same regiment with those of another; and, without it, many must be dismissed who are willing to serve, notwithstanding we are deficient on the whole.

The council of officers are unanimously of opinion that the command of the artillery should no longer continue in colonel * * *; and knowing of no person better qualified to supply his place, or whose appointment will give more general satisfaction, have taken the liberty of recommending Henry Knox, esquire, to the consideration of Congress, thinking it indispensably necessary at the same time that this regiment should consist of two lieutenant-colonels, two majors, and twelve companies, agreeable to the plan and estimate handed in; which differing from the last establishment, I should be glad to be instructed on.

The commissary-general not being returned, will apologise, I hope, for my silence respecting a requisition of the expense of his clerks, &c, which I was to have obtained together with others, and forwarded.

I have heard nothing of colonel Arnold since the thirteenth ultimo. His letter of, and journal to, that date, will convey all the information I am able to give of him. I think he must be in Quebec. If any mischance had happened to him, he would, as directed, have forwarded an express.—No account yet of the armed vessels sent to St. Laurence.—I think they will meet the stores inward or outward bound.

Captain Symons, in the Cerberus lately sent from Boston to Falmouth, hath published the inclosed declaration at that place; and it is suspected he intends to make some kind of a lodgement there. I wrote immediately to colonel Finnie of this army, who went up there upon the last alarm, to

spirit

spirit up the people and oppose it at all events.—Falmouth is about a hundred and thirty miles from this camp.

I have the honor to be, &c. G. W.

P. S. I send a general return of the troops, and manifests of the cargoes and vessels taken at Plymouth.

SIR, Cambridge, Nov. 11, 1775.

* * * Inclosed, you have a copy of an act, passed this session, by the honorable council and house of representatives of this province. It respects such captures as may be made by vessels fitted out by the province, or by individuals thereof. As the armed vessels, fitted out at the continental expense, do not come under this law, I would have it submitted to the consideration of Congress, to point out a more summary way of proceeding, to determine the property and mode of condemnation of such prizes as have been or hereafter may be made, than is specified in this act.

Should not a court be established by authority of Congress, to take cognisance of prizes made by the continental vessels? Whatever the mode is which they are pleased to adopt, there is an absolute necessity of its being speedily determined on: for I cannot spare time from military affairs, to give proper attention to these matters.

The inhabitants of Plymouth have taken a sloop, laden with provisions, &c, from Halifax, bound to Boston; and the inhabitants of Beverly have, under cover of one of the armed schooners, taken a vessel from Ireland, laden with beef, pork, butter, &c, for the same place. The latter brings papers and letters of a very interesting nature, which are in the hands of the honorable council, who informed me they will transmit them to you by this conveyance. To the contents of these papers and letters I must beg leave to refer you and the honorable Congress, who will now see the absolute necessity there is, of exerting all their wisdom, to withstand the mighty efforts of our enemies.

The

The trouble I have in the arrangement of the army is really inconceivable. Many of the officers sent in their names to serve, in expectation of promotion: others stood aloof * * *; whilst a number who had declined have again sent in their names, to serve. So great has the confusion, arising from these and many other perplexing circumstances, been, that I found it absolutely impossible to fix this very interesting business exactly on the plan resolved on in the conference, though I have kept up to the spirit, as near as the nature and necessity of the case would admit of: the difficulty with the soldiers is as great,—indeed more so, if possible, than with the officers. They will not enlist, until they know their colonel, lieutenant-colonel, major, captain, &c; so that it was necessary to fix the officers the first thing; which is, at last, in some manner done; and I have given out enlisting orders.

You, sir, can much easier judge, than I can express, the anxiety of mind I must labor under on the occasion, especially at this time, when we may expect the enemy will begin to act on the arrival of their reinforcement, part of which is already come, and the remainder daily dropping in.

I have other distresses of a very alarming nature. The arms of our soldiery are so exceeding bad, that I assure you, sir, I cannot place a proper confidence in them. Our powder is wasting fast, notwithstanding the strictest care, economy, and attention, is paid to it. The long series of wet weather we have had, renders the greater part of what has been served out to the men, of no use. Yesterday I had a proof of it, as a party of the enemy, about four or five hundred, taking the advantage of a high tide, landed at Leechmore's point: we were alarmed, and of course ordered every man to examine his cartouch-box; when the melancholy truth appeared; and we were obliged to furnish the greater part of them with fresh ammunition.

The damage done at the point was the taking of a man who watched a few horses and cows: ten of the latter they carried

carried off. Colonel Thompson marched down with his regiment of riflemen, and was joined by colonel Woodbridge, with a part of his and a part of Patterson's regiment, who gallantly waded through the water, and soon obliged the enemy to embark under cover of a man-of-war, a floating battery, and the fire of a battery on Charlestown neck. We have two of our men dangerously wounded by grape-shot from the man-of-war; and, by a flag sent out this day, we are informed the enemy lost two of their men.

I have the honor to be, &c. G. W.

Sir, *Cambridge, Nov.* 19, 1775.

I Received your favors of the seventh and tenth instant, with the resolves of the honorable Congress, to which I will pay all due attention.—As soon as two capable persons can be found, I will dispatch them to Nova-Scotia, on the service resolved on in Congress.

The resolve to raise two batallions of marines will (if practicable in this army) entirely derange what has been done. It is therein mentioned, " one colonel for the two batallions:"—of course, a colonel must be dismissed. One of the many difficulties, which attended the new arrangement, was in reconciling the different interests, and judging of the merits of the different colonels.—In the dismission of this one, the same difficulties will occur.—The officers and men must be acquainted with maritime affairs; to comply with which, they must be picked out of the whole army,—one from this corps, one from another,—so as to break through the whole system, which has cost us so much time, anxiety and pains, to bring into any tolerable form. Notwithstanding any difficulties which will arise, you may be assured, sir, that I will use every endeavor to comply with their resolve.

I beg leave to submit it to the consideration of Congress (if these two batallions can be formed out of this army) whether

ther this is a time to weaken our lines, by employing any of the forces appointed to defend them, on any other service. The gentlemen who were here from the Congress know their vast extent: they must know that we shall have occasion for our whole force for that purpose; more so now than at any past time, as we may expect the enemy will take the advantage of the first hard weather, and attempt to make an impression somewhere. That this is their intention, we have many reasons to suspect.

We have had, in the last week, six deserters, and took two straggling prisoners. They all agree that two companies, with a train of artillery and one of the regiments from Ireland, were arrived at Boston;—that fresh ammunition and flints have been served out;—that the grenadiers and light infantry had orders to hold themselves in readiness at a moment's warning.

As there is every appearance that this contest will not be soon decided, and of course that there must be an augmentation of the continental army, would it not be eligible to raise two batallions of marines in New-York and Philadelphia, where there must be numbers of sailors now un-employed?—This however is matter of opinion, which I mention with all due deference to the superior judgment of the Congress.

Inclosed, you have copies of two letters,—one from colonel Arnold,—the other from colonel * * *. I can form no judgment on the latter's conduct, until I see him. Notwithstanding the great defection, I do not despair of colonel Arnold's success. He will have, in all probability, many more difficulties to encounter, than if he had been a fortnight sooner; as it is likely that governor Carleton will, with what forces he can collect after the surrender of the rest of Canada, throw himself into Quebec, and there make his last effort. There is no late account from captains Broughton and Sillman, sent to the river St. Laurence. The other cruisers have been chiefly confined to harbor, by the badness of the weather. The same reason has caused great delay in building of our barracks; which, with a most mortifying scarcity of fire-wood, discourages the men from enlisting. The last, I am afraid, is an insuperable obstacle. I have applied to the honorable house of representatives of this province, who were pleased to appoint a committee to negotiate this business: and notwithstanding all the pains they have and are taking, they find it impossible to supply our necessities. The want of a sufficient number of teams I understand to be the chief impediment.

I got returns this day from eleven colonels, of the numbers enlisted in their regiments. The whole amount is nine hundred and sixty-six men. There must be some other stimulus besides love for their country, to make men fond of the service. It would be a great encouragement, and no additional expense to the continent, were they to receive pay for the months of October and November; also a month's pay advance. The present state of the military chest will not admit of this. The sooner it is enabled to do so, the better.

The commissary-general is daily expected in camp. I cannot send you the estimate of the clerks in his department, until he arrives.

I sincerely congratulate you upon the success of your arms, in the surrender of St. John's, which I hope is a happy presage of the reduction of the rest of Canada.

I have the honor to be, &c. G. W.

Sir, *Cambridge, Novem. 28, 1775.*

I HAD the honor of writing to you on the nineteenth instant. I have now to inform you that Henry Knox, esquire, is gone to New-York, with orders to forward to this place what cannon and ordnance stores can be there procured. From thence he will proceed to general Schuyler on the same business, as you will see by the inclosed copy of instructions which I have given him. It would give me much

much satisfaction, that this gentleman, or any other whom you may think qualified, was appointed to the command of the artillery regiment. In my letter to you, of the eighth instant, I have expressed myself fully on this subject, which I beg leave to recommend to your immediate attention; as the formation of that corps will be at a stand, until I am honored with your instructions thereon. * * * *

There are two persons engaged to go to Nova-Scotia, on the business recommended in your last. By the best information we have from thence, the stores, &c. have been withdrawn some time. Should this not be the case, it is next to an impossibility to attempt any thing there, in the present unsettled and precarious state of the army. * * *

From what I can collect by my inquiries amongst the officers, it will be impossible to get the men to enlist for the continuance of the war; which will be an insuperable obstruction to the formation of the two batallions of marines on the plan resolved on in Congress. As it can make no difference, I propose to proceed on the new arrangement of the army, and, when completed, inquire out such officers and men as are best qualified for that service, and endeavor to form these two batallions out of the whole. This appears to me the best method, and will, I hope, meet the approbation of Congress.

As it will be very difficult for the men to work when the hard frost sets in, I have thought it necessary (though of little use at present) to take possession of Coble-hill, for the benefit of any future operations. It was effected, without the least opposition from the enemy, the twenty-third instant. Their inactivity on this occasion is what I cannot account for:—it is probable they are meditating a blow somewhere.

About three hundred men, women, and children, of the poor inhabitants of Boston, came out to Point-Shirley last friday. They have brought their household furniture, but are unprovided of every other necessary of life. I have recommended

mended them to the attention of the committee of the honorable council of this province, now sitting at Watertown.

The number enlisted since my last are two thousand four hundred and fifty men. * * * * Our situation is truly alarming: and of this general Howe is well apprised, it being the common topic of conversation when the people left Boston last friday.—No doubt, when he is reinforced, he will avail himself of the information.

I am making the best disposition I can for our defence, having thrown up, besides the work on Coble-hill, several redoubts, half-moons, &c, along the bay: and I fear I shall be under the necessity of calling in the militia and minutemen of the country to my assistance: I say, I fear it,—because, by what I can learn from the officers in the army, belonging to this colony, it will be next to an impossibility to keep them under any degree of discipline, and that it will be very difficult to prevail on them to remain a moment longer than they chuse themselves. It is a mortifying reflexion, to be reduced to this dilemma. There has been nothing wanting on my part, to infuse a proper spirit amongst the officers, that they may exert their influence with the soldiery. You see, by a fortnight's recruiting amongst men with arms in their hands, how little has been the success.

As the small-pox is now in Boston, I have used the precaution of prohibiting such as lately came out, from coming near our camp.—General Burgoyne, I am informed, will soon embark for England.—I think the risk too great to write you by post, whilst it continues to pass through New-York. It is certain that a post has been intercepted the beginning of last month, as they sent out several letters from Boston, with the post-mark of Baltimore on them. This goes by captain Joseph Blewer, who promises to deliver it carefully unto you.

You, doubtless, will have heard, before this reaches, of general Montgomery's having got possession of Montreal. I congratulate

congratulate you thereon. He has troubles with his troops, as well as I have.—All I can learn of colonel Arnold, is, that he is near Quebec. I hope Montgomery will be able to proceed to his assistance. I shall be very uneasy until I hear they are joined.

My best respects attend the gentlemen in Congress: and believe me, sir, your most obedient, &c.   G. W.

Sir,   *Cambridge, Novem. 30, 1775.*

I HAD the honor to write to you, the twenty-eighth instant, by captain Joseph Blewer. Last evening I received the agreeable account of the schooner Lee, commanded by captain Manly, having taken and carried into Cape-Anne a large brigantine, bound from London to Boston, laden with military stores, the inventory of which I have the pleasure to inclose you. Cape-Anne is a very open harbor, and accessible to large ships; which made me immediately send off colonel Glover and Mr. Palfrey, with orders to raise the minute-men and militia of that part of the country, to have the cargo landed without loss of time, and guarded up to this camp. This, I hope, they will be able to effect, before it is known to the enemy, what port she is carried into. I sincerely congratulate you on this very great acquisition; and am, sir, your most humble, &c.   G. W.

Manly has also taken a sloop in the ministerial service; and captain Adams, in the schooner Warren, has taken a schooner laden with potatoes and turnips, bound to Boston, and carried her into Portsmouth.

Sir,   *Cambridge, Dec. 4, 1775.*

I HAD the honor of writing to you the thirtieth ultimo, inclosing an inventory of the military stores taken on board the brig Nancy by captain Manly of the armed schooner Lee. I have now to inform you that he has since sent

sent into Beverly a ship named the Concord, James Lowrie master, from Greenock in Scotland, bound to Boston. She has on board dry goods and coals, to the value of three thousand six hundred and six pounds, nine shillings and sevenpence sterling, shipped by Crawford, Anderson, and Co. and consigned to James Anderson, merchant in Boston. It is mentioned in the letters found on board, that this cargo was for the use of the army: but, on a strict examination, I find it is really the property of the shippers and the person to whom consigned.—Pray what is to be done with this ship and cargo? and what with the brigantine which brought the military stores?—It was agreed, in the conference last October, " that all vessels employed merely as transports, and unarmed, with their crews, be set at liberty, upon giving security to return to Europe; but that this indulgence be not extended longer than till the first of April next." In the shippers' letter, they mention: " you must procure a certificate from the general and admiral, of the Concord's being in the government service, such as the Glasgow packet brought with her, which was of great service, procured a liberty to arm her, which was refused us; also gave her a preference for some recruits that went out in her." In another part of the letter, they say: " Captain Lowrie will deliver you the contract for the coals: we gave it to him, as it perhaps might be of use, as a certificate of his ship being employed in the government service." Every letter on board breathes nothing but enmity to this country: and a vast number of them there are.

It is some time since I recommended to the Congress that they would institute a court for the trial of prizes made by the continental armed vessels; which I hope they have ere now taken into their consideration: otherwise I should again take the liberty of urging it in the most pressing manner.

The conduct of a great number of the Connecticut troops has laid me under the necessity of calling in a body of the militia much sooner than I apprehended there would be an occasion for such a step. I was afraid some time ago that

they

they would incline to go home when the time of their enlistment expired. I called upon the officers of the several regiments, to know whether they could prevail on the men to remain until the first of January, or till a sufficient number of other forces could be raised to supply their place. I suppose they were deceived themselves: I know they deceived me by assurances that I need be under no apprehension on that score, for the men would not leave the lines. Last friday shewed how much they were mistaken, as the major part of the troops of that colony were going away with their arms and ammunition. We have however, by threats, persuasion, and the activity of the people of the country who sent back many of them that had set out, prevailed upon the most part to stay. There are about eighty of them missing.

I have called in three thousand men from this province; and general Sullivan, who lately returned from the province of New-Hampshire, having informed me that a number of men were there ready at the shortest notice, I have demanded two thousand from that province. These two bodies, I expect, will be in by the tenth instant, to make up the deficiency of the Connecticut-men whom I have promised to dismiss on that day, as well as the numbers to whom I was obliged to grant furloughs before any would enlist.—As the same defection is much to be apprehended when the time of the Massachusetts-Bay, New-Hampshire, and Rhode-Island forces is expired, I beg the attention of Congress to this important affair.

I am informed that it has been the custom of these provinces in the last war, for the legislative power to order every town to provide a certain quota of men for the campaign. This or some other mode should be at present adopted, as I am satisfied the men cannot be had without. This the Congress will please to take into their immediate consideration. My suspicions on this head I shall also communicate to the governors
Trumbull

Trumbull and Cooke, also to the New-Hampshire convention.

The number enlisted in the last week are about thirteen hundred men. By this you see how slow this important work goes on. * * *

An express is just come in from general Schuyler, with letters from colonel Arnold and general Montgomery, copies of which I have the honor to inclose you. Upon the whole, I think affairs carry a pleasing aspect in that quarter. The reduction of Quebec is an object of such great importance, that I doubt not the Congress will give every assistance in their power for the accomplishing it this winter.

By the last accounts from the armed schooners sent to the river St. Laurence, I fear we have but little to expect from them: they were falling short of provision, and mention that they would be obliged to return; which at this time is particularly unfortunate, as, if they chose a proper station, all the vessels coming down that river must fall into their hands. The plague, trouble, and vexation I have had with the crews of all the armed vessels, is inexpressible. I do believe there is not on earth a more disorderly set:—every time they come into port, we hear of nothing but mutinous complaints. Manly's success has lately, and but lately, quieted his people. The crews of the Washington and Harrison have actually deserted them; so that I have been under the necessity of ordering the agent to lay the latter up, and get hands for the other on the best terms he could.

The house of representatives and the honorable board have sent me a vote of theirs relative to the harbor of Cape-Cod, which you have herewith. I shall send an officer thither to examine what can be done for its defence, though I do not think I shall be able to give them such assistance as may be requisite; for I have at present neither men, powder, nor cannon to spare. The great want of powder is what the attention of Congress should be particularly applied to. I

dare

dare not attempt any thing offensive, let the temptation or advantage be ever so great, as I have not more of that most essential article, than will be absolutely necessary to defend our lines, should the enemy attempt to attack them.

By recent information from Boston, general Howe is going to send out a number of the inhabitants, in order, it is thought, to make more room for his expected reinforcements. There is one part of the information I can hardly give credit to:—a sailor says that a number of those coming out have been inoculated, with design of spreading the small-pox though this country and camp. I have communicated this to the general court; and recommended their attention thereto.

They are arming one of the transports in Boston, with which they mean to decoy some of our armed vessels. As we are apprised of their design, I hope they will be disappointed.

My best respects wait on the gentlemen in Congress, and I am, sir, your most humble, &c.   G. W.

P. S. I was misinformed when I mentioned that one regiment had arrived at Boston: a few companies of the seventeenth and artillery are all that are yet come.—Near three hundred persons are landed on Point-Shirley from Boston.

Sir,   *Cambridge, Decemb.* 7, 1775.

I WROTE you, the fourth instant, by express, to which I beg you will be referred. My fears, that Broughton and Sillman would not effect any good purpose, were too well founded. They are returned, and brought with them three of the principal inhabitants from the island of St. John's. * * * They brought the governor's commission, the province seal, &c, &c. As the captains acted without any warrant for such conduct, I have thought it but justice to discharge these gentlemen, whose families were left in the utmost distress.

I am

I am credibly informed that James Anderson, the consignee and part owner of the ship Concord and cargo, is not only unfriendly to American liberty, but actually in arms against us,—being captain of the Scotch company at Boston. Whether your being acquainted with this circumstance, or not, will operate against the vessel and cargo, I will not take upon me to say: but there are many articles on board, so absolutely necessary for the army, that, whether she is made a prize or not, we must have them.

I have the honor to be, &c.   G. W.

Sir,   *Cambridge, Decemb.* 11, 1775.

* * * The numbers enlisted last week are   men. If they go on at this slow rate, it will be a long time before this army is complete. I have wrote to the governors of Connecticut and Rhode-Island, also to the convention of New-Hampshire, on this subject. A copy of my letter to them I have the honor to inclose herewith. A letter to same purport I sent to the legislature of this province.

The militia are coming in fast. I am much pleased with the alacrity which the good people of this province, as well as those of New-Hampshire, have shewn upon this occasion. I expect the whole will be in this day and to-morrow, when what remains of the Connecticut [*troops*], who have not enlisted, will have liberty to go to their fire-sides.

The commissary-general is still by his indisposition detained from camp. He committed an error, when making out the ration-list: for he was then serving out (and has continued so to do) six ounces per man per week of butter, though it is not included in the list approved of by Congress. I do not think it would be expedient to put a stop thereto; as every thing, that would have a tendency to give the soldiery room for complaint, must be avoided.

The information I received that the enemy intended spreading

†

ing the small-pox amongst us, I could not suppose them capable of.—I now must give some credit to it, as it has made its appearance on several of those who last came out of Boston.—Every necessary precaution has been taken to prevent its being communicated to this army; and the general court will take care that it does not spread through the country.

I have not heard that any more troops are arrived at Boston; which is a lucky circumstance, as the Connecticut troops, I now find, are for the most part gone off.—The houses in Boston are lessening every day: they are pulled down, either for fire-wood, or to prevent the effects of fire, should we attempt a bombardment or an attack upon the town.—Coble-hill is strongly fortified, without any interruption from the enemy. * * * This is what at present occurs, from, sir, your most obedient, &c.   G. W.

P. S. The weekly returns of enlistments not being yet received for more than ten regiments, amounting to seven hundred and twenty-five men, I cannot fill up the blank in this letter: but this, added to the former, makes in the whole five thousand two hundred and fifty-three.

Sir, *Cambridge, Decemb.* 14, 1775.

I Received your favor of the second instant, with the several resolves of Congress therein inclosed.—The resolves relative to captures made by continental armed vessels only want a court established for trial, to make them complete. This, I hope, will be soon done, as I have taken the liberty to urge it often to the Congress.

I am somewhat at a loss to know whether I am to raise the two batallions of marines here, or not. As the delay can be attended with but little inconvenience, I will wait a farther explanation from Congress, before I take any steps therein.

I am much pleased that the money will be forwarded with all possible expedition, as it is much wanting; also that Conolly and his associates are taken. It has been a very fortunate

tunate discovery. I make no doubt but that the Congress will take every necessary measure to dispossess lord Dunmore of his hold in Virginia: the sooner steps are taken for that purpose, the more probability there will be of their being effectual. * * * *

I will make application to general Howe, and propose an exchange for Mr. Ethan Allen. I am much afraid I shall have a like proposal to make for captain Martindale of the armed brigantine Washington, and his men, who, it is reported, was taken a few days past by a man-of-war, and carried into Boston.—We cannot expect to be always successful.

You will doubtless hear of the barbarity of captain Wallace on Conanicut island, ere this reaches your hands.

About a hundred and fifty more of the poor inhabitants are come out of Boston. The small-pox rages all over the town: such of the military as had it not before are now under inoculation. This, I apprehend, is a weapon of defence they are using against us. What confirms me in this opinion, is, that I have information that they are tearing up the pavement, to be provided against a bombardment.

I wrote you this day by Messrs. Pennel and De Pliarné, who will lay before the Congress, or a committee thereof, proposals for furnishing the continent with arms and ammunition. I refer you to themselves for further particulars.

I have the honor to be, &c.   G. W.

Chelsea, Decemb. 16, 1775.

OBSERVATIONS OF THE DAY.

LAST evening, eight men came in a boat from Boston, to our guard at the ferry,—six of them captains of vessels.—They brought the following account:

Yesterday, one large mortar was carried over to Bunker's hill:—the troops filling water, carrying it on board the transports:—provisions scarce,—not more than sufficient for

six

six weeks. One regiment of foot, and three companies of the light horse, sail for Halifax this day.

Dorchester, December 16, 1775.

Sailed out of Boston harbor this morning, eight large and two small vessels, taken to be tenders;—by their firing, appeared to be going a voyage out to sea.

Mr. Joshua Pico came last-night from Boston. He confirms the information that the regiment of foot, and some companies of light horse, were preparing to embark for Halifax.

SIR, *Cambridge, Decemb.* 16, 1775.

THE information, contained in the above, coming so many different ways, corroborated by several vessels having sailed this day from Boston,—I thought it my duty to transmit it to you. Though Halifax is the place given out for their destination, it is possible they may be bound elsewhere. I shall communicate this intelligence to governors Cooke and Trumbull, and to the convention of New-York, for their government.

I remain, sir, your most obedient, &c. G. W.

SIR, *Cambridge, Decemb.* 19, 1775.

CAPTAIN Manly, of the Lee armed schooner, took and sent into Beverly the sloop Betsey, A. Atkinson master. She is an armed vessel, dispatched by lord Dunmore, with Indian corn, potatoes, and oats, for the army in Boston. The packets of letters found on board, I have the honor to send you with this by captain James Chambers, they being of so much importance, that I do not think it would be prudent to trust them by a common express.

As lord Dunmore's schemes are fully laid open in these letters, I need not point out to the Congress the necessity there is of a vigorous exertion being adopted by them, to disposfefs his lordſhip of the ſtrong hold he has got in Virginia.— I do not mean to dictate: but I am ſure they will pardon me for giving them freely my opinion, which is, that the fate of America a good deal depends on his being obliged to evacuate Norfolk this winter, or not.

I have Kirkland well ſecured, and think I will ſend him to you for examination. By moſt of the letters relative to him, he is a dangerous fellow. John Stewart's letters and papers are of a very intereſting nature. Governor Tonyn's and many other letters from Auguſtine ſhew the weakneſs of the place; at the ſame time, of what vaſt conſequence it would be for us to poſſeſs ourſelves of it, and the great quantity of ammunition contained in the forts.—Indeed theſe papers are of ſo great conſequence, that I think this but little inferior to any prize our famous Manly has taken.

We now work at our eaſe on Leechmore's hill. On diſcovering our party there yeſterday morning, the ſhip which lay oppoſite began a cannonade, to which Mount Horam added ſome ſhells.—One of our men was wounded.—We fired a few ſhot from two eighteen-pounders which are placed on Coble-hill, and ſoon obliged the ſhip to ſhift her ſtation. She now lies in the ferry-way: and, except a few ſhells from the mount in Boſton (which do no execution), we have no interruption in proſecuting our works, which will in a very ſhort time be completed. When that is done,—when we have powder to ſport with,—I think, if the Congreſs reſolve on the execution of the propoſal made relative to the town of Boſton, it can be done.

I have ſent a letter in this day to general Howe, of which a copy goes herewith. My reaſon for pointing out brigadier-general Preſcot as the object who is to ſuffer Mr. Allen's fate, is, that, by letters from general Schuyler, and copies of letters from general Montgomery to Schuyler, I am given to underſtand that Preſcot is the cauſe of Allen's ſufferings.—I thought it beſt to be deciſive on the occaſion, as did the generals whom I conſulted thereon.

The

The returns of men enlisted since my last amount to about eighteen hundred, making in the whole seven thousand one hundred and forty. The militia that are come in, both from this province and New-Hampshire, are very fine-looking men, and go through their duty with great alacrity. The dispatch made, both by the people in marching and by the legislative powers in complying with my requisition, has given me infinite satisfaction.

Your letter of the eighth instant, with the explanatory resolve respecting my calling forth the militia and minute-men, is come to hand; to which I shall pay all due attention. You have removed all the difficulties which I labored under, about the two batallions of marines. I shall obey the orders of Congress in looking out for proper officers to command that corps.—I make no doubt but, when the money arrives to pay off the arrears and the month's advance, that it will be a great encouragement for the men to enlist.

Inclosed is a letter I lately received from Mr. James Lovell. His case is truly pitiable. I wish some mode could be fallen upon to relieve him from the cruel situation he is now in.—I am sensible of the impropriety of exchanging a soldier for a citizen: but there is something so cruelly distressing in regard to this gentleman, that I dare say you will take it under your consideration.

I am, with great respect, &c.   G. W.

SIR,   *Cambridge, Dec.* 25, 1775:

I HAD the honor to address myself to you on the nineteenth instant, since which I have received undoubted information that the genuine instructions given to Conolly have not reached your hands; that they are very artfully concealed in the tree of his saddle, and covered with canvas so nicely that they are scarcely discernible; that those which were found upon him were intended to deceive, if he was caught.

caught.—You will moft certainly have his faddle taken to pieces, in order to difcover this deep-laid plot.

Inclofed is a copy of general Howe's letter in anfwer to the one I wrote him the eighteenth inftant. The conduct I am to obferve towards brigadier Prefcot in confequence of thefe letters, the Congrefs will oblige me by determining for me.

The gentlemen by whom you fent the money are arrived. The fum they brought, though large, is not fufficient to anfwer the demands of the army, which at this time are remarkably heavy: there is three months' pay due, one month's advance, two dollars for each blanket,—the arms, that are left by thofe who are difmiffed, to be paid for,—befides the demands which are on the commiffary and quarter-mafter generals. You will therefore fee the neceffity of another remittance, which I beg may be as foon as you conveniently can.

I will take the opportunity of the return of thefe gentlemen, to fend colonel Kirkland to you for examination, and that you may difpofe of him as to you may feem proper.

A committee from the general court of this province called on me the other day, informing me that they were in great want of ordnance for the defence of the colony; that, if what belonged to them, now in ufe here, was kept for the continent, they would be under the neceffity of providing themfelves with others: of courfe what is kept muft be paid for. There are many of the cannon of very little ufe: fuch of them as are good, I cannot at prefent part with: perhaps when I receive the fupply from New-York and Canada, it may be in my power to fpare them.

Mr. Wadfworth has fent in his report refpecting Cape-Cod harbor, a copy of which you will receive herewith; alfo a letter from a Mr. Jacob Bailey, put into my hands by colonel Little. It contains fome things that may not be unworthy the confideration of Congrefs.

We have made good progrefs in the works on Leechmore's point. They would have been finifhed ere this, but

for

for the severity of the weather, which prevents our people from working.

I received a letter from governor Cooke, which expresses the fears of the people of Rhode-Island, lest the ships, which we had information were sailed with some troops on board, were destined for Newport. I sent major-general Lee there, to point out to them such defence as he may think the place capable of. I sincerely wish he may be able to do it with effect, as that place, in its present state, is an asylum for such as are disaffected to American liberty.

Our returns of enlistments, to this day, amount to eight thousand five hundred men.

I have the honor to be, &c. G. W.

P. S. Inclosed is an estimate of the demands of the army.

SIR, *Cambridge, Dec.* 31, 1775.

I WROTE to you the twenty-fifth instant; since which I am not honored with any of your favors. The estimate I then inclosed you was calculated to pay the troops, &c, up to the first of January. That cannot be done for want of funds in the paymaster-general's hands; which causes a great murmuring amongst those who are going off. —The monthly expenses of this army amount to near two hundred and seventy-five thousand dollars, which I take the liberty of recommending to the observation of Congress, that their future remittances may be governed thereby.

It sometimes happens that persons would wish to deposit money in the hands of the paymaster-general, for his bills on the treasury at Philadelphia. He has hitherto declined such offers, not having authority from Congress to draw.—Would it not be proper to give this power?—If it should be approved of, you will please to point out the mode that the Congress would chuse to have it done in.

The clothing sent to the quarter-master-general is not sufficient to put half our army into regimentals; nor is there a possibility of getting any quantity here. I have wrote to
general

general Schuyler, that I wish what was lodged at Albany could be spared for these troops, as general Montgomery would clothe the men under his command at Montréal. If this can be done, it will be of infinite service; and no time should be lost in forwarding them to this camp.

In forming the regiments for the new establishment, I thought it but justice to appoint the officers, detached under colonel Arnold, to commissions in them. Their absence at present is of very great detriment to the service, especially in recruiting: I would therefore wish, if the Congress intend raising troops in or for Canada, that they could be taken in there. The sooner I have their opinion of this matter, the better; that, if they can be commissioned in Canada, I may appoint officers here to replace them.

Inclosed you have a copy of a representation sent me to by the legislative body of this province, respecting four companies stationed at Braintree, Weymouth, and Hingham. As they were never regimented, and were doing duty at a distance from the rest of the army, I did not know whether to consider them as a part of it; nor do I think myself authorised to direct payment for them without the approbation of Congress.

It has been represented to me that the free negroes who have served in this army are very much dissatisfied at being discarded. As it is to be apprehended that they may seek employ in the ministerial army, I have presumed to depart from the resolution respecting them, and have given licence for their being enlisted. If this is disapproved of by Congress, I will put a stop to it.

* * * I must remark that the pay of the assistant engineers is so very small, that we cannot expect men of science will engage in it. Those gentlemen, who are in that station, remained under the expectation that an additional allowance would be made them by the respective provinces in which they were appointed, to that allowed by the Congress.

Captain Freeman arrived this day at camp from Canada.

He

He left Quebec the twenty-fourth ultimo, in confequence of general Carleton's proclamation which I have the honor to fend you herewith. He fawe olonel Arnold, the twenty-fixth, and fays that he was joined at Point-à-tremble by general Montgomery, the firft inftant;—that they were about two thoufand ftrong, and were making every preparation for attacking Quebec;—that general Carleton had with him about twelve hundred men, the majority of whom are failors;—that it was his opinion the French would give up the place if they get the fame conditions granted to the inhabitants of Montréal. * * *

Captains Semple and Harbefon take under their care Mr. Kirkland. * * * Captain Mathews and Mr. Robinfon will accompany them. The two latter were taken prifoners by lord Dunmore, who was fending them to Bofton, from whence there is little doubt but they would be forwarded to England, to which place I am credibly informed captain Martindale and the crew of the Wafhington are fent; alfo colonel Allen, and the prifoners taken with him in Canada. This may account for general Howe's filence on the fubject of an exchange of prifoners mentioned in my letter to him.

General Lee is juft returned from his excurfion to Rhode-Ifland:—he has pointed out the beft method the ifland would admit of for its defence:—he has endeavored all in his power to make friends of thofe that were our enemies. You have, inclofed, a fpecimen of his abilities in that way, for your perufal. I am of opinion that, if the fame plan was purfued through every province, it would have a very good effect.

I have long had it on my mind to mention to Congrefs that frequent applications had been made to me refpecting the chaplains' pay, which is too fmall to encourage men of abilities. Some of them, who have left their flocks, are obliged to pay the parfon acting for them more than they receive. I need not point out the great utility of gentlemen whofe lives and converfation are unexceptionable, being employed for that fervice in this army. There are two ways of making it worth the attention of fuch: one is an advancement

vancement of their pay; the other, that one chaplain be appointed to two regiments. This laſt, I think, may be done without inconvenience.—I beg leave to recommend this matter to Congreſs, whoſe ſentiments hereon I ſhall impatiently expect.

Upon a farther converſation with captain Freeman, he is of opinion that general Montgomery has with him near three thouſand men, including colonel Arnold's. He ſays that lord Pitt had received repeated orders from his father to return home; in conſequence of which, he had embarked, ſome time in October, with a captain Green who was maſter of a veſſel belonging to Philadelphia.

By a number of ſalutes in Boſton harbor yeſterday, I fancy admiral Shuldham is arrived.—Two large ſhips were ſeen coming in.

Our enliſtments now amount to nine thouſand ſix hundred and fifty.

Thoſe gentlemen, who were made priſoners by lord Dunmore, being left deſtitute of money and neceſſaries, I have advanced them a hundred pounds lawful money belonging to the public, for which I have taken captain Mathews's draught on the treaſury of Virginia, which goes incloſed.

I have the honor to be, &c.   G. W.

P. S. You have, incloſed, the returns of the army.

Sir,   *Cambridge, January* 4, 1776.

SINCE my laſt of the thirty-firſt ultimo, I have been honored with your favor of the twenty-ſecond, incloſing ſundry reſolves, which ſhall, in matters they reſpect, be made the rule of my conduct.

The reſolution relative to the troops in Boſton, I beg the favor of you, ſir, to aſſure Congreſs, ſhall be attempted to be put in execution the firſt moment I ſee a probability of ſucceſs, and in ſuch a way as a council of officers ſhall think moſt likely to produce it: but, if this ſhould not happen as ſoon as you may expect or my wiſhes prompt to, I requeſt that

that Congress will be pleased to advert to my situation, and do me the justice to believe, that circumstances, and not want of inclination, are the cause of delay.

It is not in the pages of history perhaps to furnish a case like ours:—to maintain a post within musket-shot of the enemy, for six months together, without *   , and at the same time to disband one army, and recruit another, within that distance of twenty-odd British regiments,—is more, probably, than ever was attempted. But if we succeed as well in the last, as we have heretofore in the first, I shall think it the most fortunate event of my whole life.

By a very intelligent gentleman, a Mr. Hutchinson from Boston, I learn, that it was admiral Shuldham that came into the harbor on saturday last;—that two of the five regiments from Cork are arrived at Halifax;—two others have sailed for Quebec; but what was become of them, could not be told:—and the other (the fifty-fifth) has just got into Boston. Certain it is also, that the greatest part of the seventeenth regiment is arrived there. Whether we are to conclude from hence that more than five regiments have been sent out, or that the companies of the seventeenth, arrived at Boston, are part of the regiments destined for Halifax and Quebec, I know not.

We also learn from this gentleman and others, that the troops, embarked for Halifax (as mentioned in my letter of the sixteenth) were really designed for that place, but recalled from Nantasket road, upon advice being received of the above regiments there. I am also informed of a fleet now getting ready under the convoy of the Scarborough and Fowey men-of-war,—consisting of five transports and two bomb vessels, with about three hundred marines, and several flat-bottomed boats. It is whispered that they are designed for Newport, but generally thought in Boston that it is meant for Long-Island: and it is probable it will be followed by

* *Left blank in the original to guard against the danger of miscarriage.—Read,* "without powder."

more troops, as the other transports are taking in water,—to lie, as others say, in Nantasket road, to be out of the ice. A large quantity of biscuit is also baking.

As the real design cannot with certainty be known, I submit it, with all due deference, to the superior judgment of Congress, whether it would not be consistent with prudence to have some of the Jersey troops thrown into New-York, to prevent an evil, which would be almost irremediable, should it happen,—I mean, the landing of troops at that place, or upon Long-Island near it.

As it is possible you may not yet have received his majesty's " *most gracious*" speech, I do myself the honor to inclose one of many, which were sent out of Boston yesterday. It is full of * * *, and explicitly holds forth his royal will to be, that vigorous measures must be pursued, to deprive us of our * * *. These measures, whatever they be, I hope will be opposed by more vigorous ones, and rendered unavailing and fruitless, though sanctioned and authorised by the name of majesty,—a name, which ought to promote the blessings of his people, and not their oppression.

I am, Sir, &c.   G. W.

Sir,   Cambridge, *Jan.* 11, 1776.

EVERY account I have out of Boston confirms the embarkation of troops mentioned in my last, which, from the season of the year and other circumstances, must be destined for some expedition to the southward of this. I have therefore thought it prudent to send major-general Lee to New-York. I have given him letters recommendatory to governor Trumbull, and to the committee of safety at New-York. I have good hopes that in Connecticut he will get many volunteers, who (I have some reason to think) will accompany him on this expedition, without more expense to the continent than their maintenance. But should it be otherwise, and that they should expect pay, I think it is a

trifling

trifling confideration, when put in competition with the importance of the object, which is to put the city of New-York, with fuch parts of the North river and Long-Ifland as to him fhall feem proper, in that ftate of defence, which the feafon of the year and circumftances will admit of,—fo as, if poffible, to prevent the enemy from forming a lodgement in that government, which, I am afraid, contains too many perfons difaffected to the caufe of liberty and America. I have alfo wrote to lord Stirling to give him all the affiftance that he can with the troops under his command in the continental fervice, provided it does not interfere with any orders he may receive from Congrefs relative to them.

I hope the Congrefs will approve of my conduct in fending general Lee upon this expedition :—I am fure I mean it well; as experience teaches us that it is much eafier to prevent an enemy from pofting themfelves, than it is to diflodge them after they have got poffeffion.

The evening of the eighth inftant, a party of our men, under the command of major Knoulton, were ordered to go and burn fome houfes which lay at the foot of Bunker's hill, and at the head of Charleftown. They were alfo ordered to bring off the guard, which, we expected, confifted of an officer and thirty men. They croffed the mill-dam about half after eight o'clock, and gallantly executed their bufinefs,— having burned eight houfes, and brought with them a fergeant and four privates of the tenth regiment. There was but one man more there, who making fome refiftance, they were obliged to difpatch. The gun that killed him was the only one difcharged by our men, though feveral hundred were fired by the enemy from within their works, but in fo confufed a manner, that not one of our people was hurt.

Our enliftments go on very heavily.

I am, with great refpect, &c.   G. W.

SIR,

Sir,   *Cambridge, Jan.* 14, 1776.

I AM exceedingly sorry that I am under the neceffity of applying to you, and calling the attention of Congrefs to the ftate of our arms, which is truly alarming. Upon the diffolution of the old army, I was apprehenfive that the new would be deficient in this inftance: and, that the want might be as inconfiderable as poffible, I gave it out in orders, that the arms of fuch men as did not re-enlift (or fuch of them as were good) fhould be retained at the prices which fhould be affixed by perfons appointed to infpect and value them: and, that we might be fure of them, I added that there would be a ftoppage of pay for the months of November and December, from thofe who fhould carry their firelocks away without their being firft examined. I hoped, by thefe precautions, to have procured a confiderable number: but, fir, I find with much concern, that, from the badnefs of the arms, and the difobedience of too many in bearing them off without a previous infpection,—very few were collected. Neither are we to expect that many will be brought in by the new recruits,—the officers, who are out enlifting, having reported that few men who have arms will engage in the fervice; and that they are under the difagreeable alternative of taking men without arms, or of getting none. Unhappy fituation, and much to be deplored!—efpecially when we have every reafon to convince us, that we have to contend with a formidable army, well provided of every neceffary; and that there will be a moft vigorous exertion of minifterial vengeance againft us, as foon as they think themfelves in a condition for it. I hope it is in the power of Congrefs to afford us relief:—if it is not, what muft, what can be done?

Our treafury is almoft exhaufted, and the demands againft it very confiderable. A conftant fupply of money, to anfwer every claim and exigency, would much promote the good of the fervice. In the common affairs of life, it is ufeful:

in war, it is abfolutely neceffary and effential. I would beg leave, too, to remind you of the tents, and of their importance,—hoping that if an opportunity has offered, you have procured them. I fear that our army will not be raifed to the new eftablifhment in any reafonable time, if ever: the enlifting goes on fo very flow, that it almoft feems at an end.

In my letter of the fourth inftant, I wrote you that I had received certain intelligence from a Mr. Hutchinfon and others, that two of the five regiments from Cork were arrived at Halifax, one at Bofton, and the two others had failed for Quebec, and had not been heard of. I am now affured (as a matter to be relied on) by four captains of fhips, who left England about the fecond of November, and who appear to be men of veracity, that the whole of thefe regiments (except the two companies that arrived at Bofton fome time ago), when they failed, were at Milford Haven, where they had been obliged to put in, by a violent ftorm, the nineteenth of October; that they would not be able to leave it for a confiderable time, as they were under the neceffity of repairing their veffels, and getting fome new ones taken up.—Such is the uncertainty and contradiction in what I now hear, that it is not poffible to know what to believe or difbelieve.

I wrote to the general court yefterday, and to the convention of New-Hampfhire, immediately upon feeing the great deficiency in our arms,—praying that they would intereft themfelves in the matter, and furnifh me with all in their power. Whether I fhall get any, or what quantity, I can not determine, not having received their anfwers.—The fame application will be made to the governments of Connecticut and Rhode-Ifland.

I do myfelf the honor to fend you fundry newfpapers I received from the above-mentioned captains, as they may be later than any you have feen, and contain fome interefting intelligence.—I have the honor to be, &c. G. W.

SIR,

SIR, *Cambridge, Jan.* 19, 1776.

TAKING it for granted that general Schuyler has not only informed you of the fall of the brave and much-to-be-lamented general Montgomery, but of the situation of our affairs in Canada (as related by general Wooster, colonel Arnold, colonel Campbell, and others), I shall not take up much more of your time on this subject, than is necessary to inclose you a copy of his letter to me, with the result thereon, as appears by the council of war, which I immediately summoned on the occasion, and at which Mr. Adams, by my particular desire, was good enough to attend.

It may appear strange, sir, as I had not men to spare from these lines, that I should presume (without first sending to Congress, and obtaining an express direction) to recommend to the governments of Massachusetts, Connecticut, and New-Hampshire, to raise each a regiment, on the continental account, for this service. I wish most ardently that the urgency of the case would have admitted of the delay. I wish also that the purport of general Schuyler's letter had not, unavoidably as it were, laid me under an indispensable obligation to do it:—for having informed you in his letter (a copy of which he inclosed me) of his dependence on this quarter, for men, I thought you might also have some reliance on my exertions. This consideration, added to my fears of the fatal consequences of delay,—to an information of your having designed three thousand men for Canada,—to a belief, founded chiefly on general Schuyler's letters, that few or none of them were raised,—and to my apprehensions for New-York, which led me to think that no troops could be spared from that quarter,—induced me to lose not a moment's time in throwing in a force there; being well assured that general Carleton will improve to the utmost the advantages gained, leaving no artifices untried, to fix the Canadians and Indians (who, we find, are too well disposed to take part with the strongest) in his interest.

If these reasons are not sufficient to justify my conduct in the opinion of Congress,—if the measure contravenes any resolution of theirs,—they will please to countermand the levying and marching of the regiments as soon as possible, and do me the justice to believe that my intentions were good, if my judgment has erred.

The Congress will please also to observe, that the measure of supporting our posts in Canada appeared of such exceeding great importance, that the general officers (agreeing with me in sentiment, and unwilling to lay any burden which can possibly be avoided,—although it may turn out an ill-timed piece of parsimony) have resolved that the three regiments for Canada shall be part of the thirteen militia regiments which were requested to reinforce this army,—as appears by the minutes of another council of war, held on the sixteenth instant. I shall (being much hurried and fatigued) add no more in this letter, than my duty to Congress, and that I have the honor to be, &c. G. W.

P. S. I inclose you a copy of my letter to the governments of Massachusetts, Connecticut, and New-Hampshire; also a copy of a resolution of this colony, in answer to an application of mine for arms.

Since writing the above, I have been informed by a message from the general court of Massachusetts, that they have resolved upon the raising of a regiment for Canada, and appointed the field officers for it, in the western parts of this government. I am also informed by express from governor Trumbull, that he and his council of safety had agreed upon the raising of a regiment for the same purpose; which was anticipating my application to that government.

If commissions (and they are applied for) are to be given by Congress to the three regiments going to Canada, you will please to have them forwarded, as I have none by me for that purpose.

SIR,

Sir,   *Cambridge, Jan.* 24, 1776.

    THE commiffary-general being at length [*recovered*] from a long and painful illnefs, I have it in my power to comply with the requifition of Congrefs, in forwarding an eftimate of the expenfe attending his office, as alfo that of the quarter-mafter-general.

    You will pleafe to obferve that the commiffary, by his account of the matter, has entered into no fpecial agreement with any of the perfons he has found occafion to employ (as thofe, to whofe names fums are annexed, are of their own fixing), but left it to Congrefs to afcertain their wages. I fhall fay nothing therefore on this head, farther than relates to the propofition of Mr. * * *, to be allowed one eighth for his trouble and the delivery of the other feven eighths of provifions, which to me appears exorbitant in the extreme, however conformable it may be to cuftom and ufage: I therefore think that reafonable ftipends had better be fixed upon. Both the quarter-mafter and commiffary generals affure me that they do not employ a fingle perfon ufelefsly: and as I have too good an opinion of them to think they would deceive me, I believe them.

    I fhall take the liberty, in this place, of recommending the expediency, indeed the abfolute neceffity, of appointing fit and proper perfons to fettle the accounts of this army. To do it with precifion, requires time, care, and attention: the longer it is left undone, the more intricate they will be, the more liable to error, and difficult to explain and rectify;—as alfo the perfons in whofe hands they are (if difpofed to take undue advantage) will be lefs fubject to detection. I have been as attentive as the nature of my office would admit of, in granting warrants for money on the paymafter: but it would be abfolutely impoffible for me to go into an examination of all the accounts incident to this army, and the vouchers appertaining to them, without devoting fo large a portion of my time to the bufinefs, as might not only prove injurious, but fatal to it in other respects. This ought, in my humble opinion, to be the particular business of a select committee of Congress, or one appointed by them, who, once in three months at furthest, should make a settlement with the officers in the different departments.

Having met with no encouragement from the governments of Massachusetts and New-Hampshire, from my application for arms, and expecting no better from Connecticut and Rhode-Island, I have, as the last expedient, sent one or two officers from each regiment into the country, with money, to try if they can buy. In what manner they succeed, Congress shall be informed as soon as they return.

Congress, in my last, would discover my motives for strengthening these lines with the militia: but whether,—as the weather turns out exceedingly mild, insomuch as to promise nothing favorable from ice,—and no appearance of powder,—I shall be able to attempt any thing decisive, time only can determine. No man upon earth wishes more ardently to destroy the nest in Boston, than I do:—no person would be willing to go greater lengths than I shall, to accomplish it, if it shall be thought advisable. But if we have neither powder to bombard with, nor ice to pass on, we shall be in no better situation than we have been in all the year:—we shall be worse, because their works are stronger.

I have accounts from Boston, which I think may be relied on, that general Clinton, with about four or five hundred men, hath left that place within these four days. Whether this is part of the detachment which was making up (as mentioned in my letter of the fourth instant, and then at Nantasket) or not, is not in my power to say. If it is designed for New-York or Long-Island as some think, throwing a body of troops there may prove a fortunate circumstance. If they go farther south agreeable to the conjectures of others, I hope there will be men to receive them.

Notwithstanding the positive assertions of the four cap-

tains

tains from Portſmouth, noticed in my letter of the fourteenth, I am now convinced from ſeveral corroborating circumſtances,—the accounts of deſerters, and of a lieutenant Hill, of lord Percy's regiment, who left Ireland the fifth of November, and was taken by a privateer from Newburyport,—that the ſeventeenth and fifty-fifth regiments are arrived at Boſton, and other troops at Halifax, agreeable to the information of Hutchinſon and others. Lieutenant Hill ſays that the tranſports of two regiments only were forced into Milford Haven.

Congreſs will think me a little remiſs, I fear, when I inform them that I have done nothing yet towards raiſing the batallion of marines: but I hope to ſtand exculpated from blame, when they hear the reaſon, which was, that already having twenty-ſix incomplete regiments, I thought it would be adding to an expenſe, already great, in officers, to ſet two entire corps of officers on foot, when perhaps we ſhould not add ten men a week by it to our preſent numbers. In this opinion the general officers have concurred, which induced me to ſuſpend the matter a little longer.—Our enliſtments, for the two laſt weeks, have not amounted to a thouſand men, and are diminiſhing. The regiment for Canada (it is thought) will ſoon be filled, as the men are to chuſe all but their field officers, who are appointed by the court.

On ſunday evening, thirteen of the Caghnewaga Indians arrived here on a viſit. I ſhall take care that they be ſo entertained during their ſtay, that they may return impreſſed with ſentiments of friendſhip for us, and alſo of our great ſtrength. One of them is colonel Louis, who honored me with a viſit once before.

I have the honor to be, &c.   G. W.

Sir,   *Cambridge, Jan.* 30, 1776.

YOUR favors of the sixth and twentieth inftant I received yefterday, with the feveral refolves of Congrefs alluded to; for which I return you my thanks.

Knowing the great importance Canada will be of to us in the prefent interefting conteft, and the relief our friends there ftand in need of, I fhould be happy, were it in my power to detach a batallion from this camp: but it cannot be done. On the nineteenth inftant, I had the honor to write to you, which will fully convey the refolutions of a council of war, and the fentiments of the general officers here, as to the propriety and expediency of fending troops from thefe lines, for the defence of which we have been and now are obliged to call in the militia;—to which I beg leave to refer you. You may reft affured that my endeavors and exertions fhall not be wanting, to ftimulate the governments of Connecticut and New-Hampfhire to raife and forward reinforcements as faft as poffible; nor in any other inftance that will promote the expedition.

I fhall, in obedience to the order of Congrefs, though interdicted by general Howe, propofe an exchange of governor Skene for Mr. Lovell and family, and fhall be happy to have an opportunity of putting this deferving man (who has diftinguifhed his fidelity and regard to his country to be too great for perfecution and cruelty to overcome) in any poft agreeable to his wifhes and inclination.

I do not know that there is any particular rank annexed to the office of aide-de-camp. Generally they are captains, and rank as fuch: but higher rank is often given on account of particular merit and particular circumftances.— Aides to the king have the rank of colonels.—Whether any diftinction fhould be made between thofe of your commander-in-chief and the other generals, I really know not:—I think there ought.

You may rely that Conolly had inftructions concealed in his

his faddle. Mr. * * * who was one of lord Dunmore's family, and another gentleman who wifhes his name not to be mentioned, faw them cafed in tin, put in the tree, and covered over. He probably has exchanged his faddle, or withdrew the papers when it was mended, as you conjecture. Thofe that have been difcovered are fufficiently bad; but I doubt not of the others being worfe, and containing more diabolical and extenfive plans. I hope he will be taken proper care of, and meet with rewards equal to his merits.

I fhall appoint officers in the places of thofe who are in Canada, as I am fully perfuaded they will wifh to continue there, for making our conqueft complete in that quarter.— I wifh their bravery and valor may be attended with the fmiles of fortune.

It gives me great pleafure to hear of the meafures Congrefs are taking for manufacturing powder. I hope their endeavors will be crowned with fuccefs. I too well know and regret the want of it. It is fcarcely poffible to defcribe the difadvantages an army muft labor under, when not provided with a fufficient fupply of this neceffary. It may feem ftrange, that, after having received about eleven tons, added to about five tons which I found here, and no general action has happened, we fhould be fo deficient in this article, and require more. But you will pleafe to confider, that, befides its being in its nature fubject to wafte, and (whilft the men lay in bad tents) unavoidably damaged by fevere and heavy rains (which could not have been prevented, unlefs it had been entirely withdrawn from the men, and an attack hazarded againft us without ammunition in their hands),—the armed veffels, our own occafional firings, and fome fmall fupplies I have been obliged to afford the feaport towns threatened with deftruction,—to which may be added the fupply to the militia, and going off of the old troops,—have occafioned, and ever will, a large confumption of it, and wafte, in fpite of all the care in the world. The king's troops never have lefs than fixty rounds a man

in

in their poffeffion, independent of their ftores.—To fupply an army of twenty thoufand men in this manner, would take near four hundred barrels, allowing nothing for ftores, artillery, &c. I have been always afraid to place more than twelve or fifteen rounds at a time in the hands of our men, left, any accident happening to it, we fhould be left deftitute, and be undone.—I have been thus particular, not only to fhew our poverty, but to exculpate myfelf from even a fufpicion of unneceffary wafte.

I fhall inform the paymafter-general of the refolution of Congrefs refpecting his draughts, and the mode and account of them.

The companies at Chelfea and Malden are and have always been regimented.—It was not my intention to replace with continental troops the independent companies at Hingham, Weymouth, and Braintree. Thefe places are expofed, but not more than Cape Ann, Beverly, Salem, Marblehead, &c, &c, &c.

Is it the intention of Congrefs that the officers of the army fhould pay poftage?—They are not exempted by the refolve of the ninth inftant.

The Congrefs will be pleafed, I have no doubt, to recollect that the five hundred thoufand dollars, now coming, are but little more than enough to bring us up to the firft day of this month; that to-morrow will be the laft of it; and, by their refolves, the troops are to be paid monthly.

I wifh it was in my power to furnifh Congrefs with fuch a general as they defire, to fend to Canada. Since the unhappy reverfe of our affairs in that quarter, general Schuyler has informed me, that, though he had thoughts of declining the fervice before, he would now act. My letter of the eleventh will inform them of general Lee's being at New-York. He will be ready to obey their orders; fhould they incline to fend him: but, if I am not greatly deceived, he or fome other fpirited able officer will be wanted there in the fpring, if not fooner; as we have undoubted intelligence that general Clinton has failed with some troops.—The reports of their number are various, from between four and five hundred to nineteen companies of grenadiers and light infantry. It is also imagined that the regiments, which were to sail the first of December, are intended for that place or Virginia.—General Putnam is a most valuable man, and a fine executive officer : but I do not know how he would conduct in a separate department. He is a younger major-general than Mr. Schuyler, who, as I have observed, having determined to continue in the service, will, I expect, repair into Canada.—A copy of my letter to him, on this and other subjects, I inclose you, as it will explain my motives for not stopping the regiments from these governments.

When captain Cockran arrives, I will give him every assistance in my power, in obedience to the orders of Congress : but I fear it will be the means of laying up our own vessels, as these people will not bear the distinction. Should this be the consequence, it will be highly prejudicial to us, as we sometimes pick up their provision-vessels, and may continue to distress them in this way.

Last week captain Manly took a ship and a brig bound to Boston from Whitehaven, with coals chiefly, and some potatoes, for the army.—I have, for his great vigilance and industry, appointed him commodore of our little squadron; and he now hoists his flag on board the schooner Hancock.

I congratulate you upon the recovery of Smith, and am exceedingly glad to hear of the measures Congress are taking for the general defence of the continent. The clouds thicken fast :—where they will burst, I know not : but we should be armed at all points.

I have not succeeded in my applications to these governments for arms. They have returned for answer, that they cannot furnish any.—Whether I shall be more lucky in the last resource left me in this quarter, I cannot determine, having not received returns from the officers sent out to purchase of the people. I greatly fear that but very few will

will be procured in this way, as they are exceedingly scarce, and but a small part of what there are, fit for service.—When they make their report, you shall be informed.

The quarter-master-general has just received from general Schuyler clothing for the soldiery, amounting to about seventeen hundred pounds York currency. It has come very seasonably, as they are in great want, and will contribute a little to their relief.

Since writing the above, I saw Mr. * * *, and mentioning that nothing had been found in the tree of Conolly's saddle, he told me there had been a mistake in the matter; that the instructions were artfully concealed on the two pieces of wood which are on the mail-pillion of his portmanteau-saddle; that, by order of lord Dunmore, he saw them contrived for the purpose, the papers put in, and first covered with tin, and over that with a waxed canvas cloth.—He is so exceedingly pointed and clear in his information, that I have no doubt of its being true.—I could wish them to be discovered, as I think they contain some curious and extraordinary plans.

In my letter of the twenty-fourth instant, I mentioned the arrival of thirteen of our Caghnewaga friends. They honored me with a talk to-day, as did three of the tribes of the St. John's and Pasmiquoddi Indians;—copies of which I beg leave to inclose you.—I shall write to general Schuyler respecting the tender of service made by the former, and not to call for their assistance, unless he shall at any time want it, or be under the necessity of doing it to prevent their taking the side of our enemies.

I had the honor of writing you on the nineteenth of November, and then I informed you of having engaged two persons to go to Nova-Scotia on the business recommended in your letter of the tenth; and also that the state of the army would not then admit of a sufficient force being sent, for carrying into execution the views of Congress respecting the dock-yards, &c.——I would now beg leave to mention,

mention, that, if the persons, sent for information, should report favorably of the expediency and practicability of the measure, it will not be in my power to detach any men from these lines: the situation of our affairs will not allow it.—I think it would be advisable to raise them in the eastern parts of this government. If it is attempted, it must be by people from the country.—A colonel * * * and a captain * * * have been with me:—they think the men necessary may be easily engaged there, and the measure practicable:—provided there are not more than two hundred British troops at Halifax, they are willing and ready to embark in the matter, upon the terms mentioned in their plan, which I inclose you. I would wish you to advert to the considerations inducing them to the expedition, as I am not without apprehension, should it be undertaken upon their plan, that the innocent and guilty will be involved in one common ruin.—I presume they do not expect to receive more than the five or ten thousand pounds mentioned in their scheme, and to be at every expense.—If we had men to spare, it might be undertaken for less than either, I conceive.—Perhaps, if Congress do not adopt their proposition, they will undertake to raise men for that particular purpose, who may be disbanded as soon as it is effected, and upon the same terms that are allowed the continental troops in general.—Whatever may be the determination of Congress upon the subject, you will please to communicate it to me immediately: for the season most favorable for the enterprise is advancing fast; and we may expect in the spring, that there will be more troops there, and the measure be more difficult to execute.—I have the honor to be, &c. G. W.

Sir, Cambridge, Feb. 9, 1776.

THE purport of this letter will be directed to a single object:—through you, I mean to lay it before Congress; and—at the same time that I beg their serious attention to the

the subject,—to ask pardon for intruding an opinion, not only unasked, but, in some measure, repugnant to their resolves.

The disadvantages attending the limited enlistment of troops are too apparent to those who are eye-witnesses of them, to render any animadversions necessary: but to gentlemen at a distance, whose attention is engrossed by a thousand important objects, the case may be otherwise.

That this cause precipitated the fate of the brave and much-to-be-lamented general Montgomery, and brought on the defeat which followed thereupon, I have not the most distant doubt:—for, had he not been apprehensive of the troops leaving him at so important a crisis, but continued the blockade of Quebec, a capitulation (from the best accounts I have been able to collect) must inevitably have followed. And that we were not at one time obliged to dispute these lines under disadvantageous circumstances (proceeding from the same cause, to wit, the troops disbanding of themselves before the militia could be got in), is to me a matter of wonder and astonishment; and proves that general Howe was either unacquainted with our situation, or restrained by his instructions from putting any thing to a hazard till his reinforcements should arrive.

The instance of general Montgomery—(I mention it, because it is a striking one;—for a number of others might be adduced)—proves, that, instead of having men to take advantage of circumstances, you are in a manner compelled, right or wrong, to make circumstances yield to a secondary consideration. Since the first of December, I have been devising every means in my power to secure these encampments; and, though I am sensible that we never have, since that period, been able to act upon the offensive, and at times not in a condition to defend, yet the cost of marching home one set of men,—bringing in another,—the havoc and waste occasioned by the first,—the repairs necessary for the second,—with a thousand incidental charges and inconveniences which have arifen, and which it is fcarce poffible either to recollect or defcribe,—amount to near as much, as the keeping up a refpectable body of troops the whole time, ready for any emergency, would have done.—To this may be added, that you never can have a well-difciplined army.

To bring men well acquainted with the duties of a foldier, requires time. To bring them under proper difcipline and fubordination, not only requires time, but is a work of great difficulty, and, in this army where there is fo little diftinction between the officers and foldiers, requires an uncommon degree of attention. To expect then the fame fervice from raw and undifciplined recruits as from veteran foldiers, is to expect what never did and perhaps never will happen. Men who are familiarifed to danger meet it without fhrinking; whereas thofe who have never feen fervice often apprehend danger where no danger is. Three things prompt men to a regular difcharge of their duty in time of action,—natural bravery,—hope of reward,—and fear of punifhment. The two firft are common to the untutored and the difciplined foldier; but the latter moft obvioufly diftinguifhes the one from the other. A coward, when taught to believe, that, if he breaks his ranks and abandons his colors, he will be punifhed with death by his own party,—will take his chance againft the enemy: but a man who thinks little of the one, and is fearful of the other, acts from prefent feelings, regardlefs of confequences.

Again, men of a day's ftanding will not look forward: and from experience we find, that, as the time approaches for their difcharge, they grow carelefs of their arms, ammunition, camp utenfils, &c. Nay even the barracks themfelves have felt uncommon marks of wanton depredation, and lay us under frefh trouble and additional expenfe in providing for every frefh fet, when we find it next to impoffible to procure fuch articles as are abfolutely neceffary in the firft inftance. To this may be added the feafoning which new recruits muft have to a camp, and the lofs confequent

fequent thereupon. But this is not all.—Men, engaged for a fhort limited time only, have the officers too much in their power: for, to obtain a degree of popularity in order to induce a fecond enliftment, a kind of familiarity takes place, which brings on a relaxation of difcipline, unlicenfed furloughs, and other indulgences incompatible with order and good government; by which means, the latter part of the time for which the foldier was engaged is fpent in undoing what you were aiming to inculcate in the firft.

To go into an enumeration of all the evils we have experienced in this late great change of the army, and the expenfes incidental to it,—to fay nothing of the hazard we have run, and muft run, between the difcharging of one army and enliftment of another, unlefs an enormous expenfe of militia is incurred,—would greatly exceed the bounds of a letter. What I have already taken the liberty of faying will ferve to convey a general idea of the matter; and therefore I fhall, with all due deference, take the freedom to give it as my opinion, that, if the Congrefs have any reafon to believe that there will be occafion for troops another year, and confequently of another enliftment, they would fave money, and have infinitely better troops, if they were, even at a bounty of twenty, thirty, or more dollars, to engage the men already enlifted (till January next), and fuch others as may be wanted to complete the eftablifhment, for and during the war. I will not undertake to fay that the men can be had upon thefe terms: but I am fatisfied that it will never do, to let the matter alone, as it was laft year, till the time of fervice was near expiring. The hazard is too great in the firft place:—in the next, the trouble and perplexity of difbanding one army and raifing another at the fame inftant, and in fuch a critical fituation as the laft was, is fcarcely in the power of words to defcribe, and fuch as no man, who has experienced it once, will ever undergo again.

If Congrefs fhould differ from me in fentiment upon this
point,

point, I have only to beg that they will do me the justice to believe, that I have nothing more in view than what to me appears necessary to advance the public weal, although in the first instance it will be attended with a capital expense;—and that I have the honor to be, &c.   G. W.

Sir,   *Cambridge, Feb. 9, 1776.*

IN compliance with the resolves of Congress, I have applied to general Howe for the exchange of Mr. Lovell. A copy of my letter, and his answer thereto, you have inclosed.

Captain Watters and captain Tucker, who command two of the armed schooners, have taken and sent into Glocester a large brigantine, laden with wood, a hundred and fifty butts for water, and forty suits of bedding, bound from La Have in Nova-Scotia, for Boston. She is one of the transports in the ministerial service. The captain says that he was at Halifax, the seventeenth of January, and that general Massey was arrived there with two regiments from Ireland.

The different prizes were all libelled immediately on the receipt of the resolves of Congress pointing out the mode; but none of them yet brought to trial, owing to a difference between the law passed in this province, and the resolutions of Congress. The general court are making an amendment to their law, by which the difficulties that now occur will be removed, as I understand it is to be made conformable to your resolves. The unavoidable delay attending the bringing the captures to trial is grievously complained of by the masters of these vessels, as well as the captors. Many of the former have applied for liberty to go away without waiting the decision,—which I have granted them.

I beg leave to recall the attention of Congress to their appointing a commissary in these parts, to attend the providing of necessaries for the prisoners who are dispersed in these provinces. Complaints are made by some of them, that they
                                                               are

are in want of bedding and many other things. As I understand that Mr. Franks has undertaken that businefs, I wish he was ordered to send a deputy immediately to see that the prisoners get what is allowed them by Congrefs; also to supply the officers with money as they may have occasion. It would save me much time and much trouble.

There are yet but few companies of the militia come in. This delay will, I am much afraid, fruftrate the intention of their being called upon, as the feafon is flipping faft away when they may be of fervice.

The demands of the army were fo very prefling before your laft remittance came to hand, that I was under the neceflity of borrowing twenty-five thoufand pounds lawful money from this province. They very cheerfully lent it, and paffed a vote for as much more, if required. I have not repaid the fum borrowed, as I may ftand in need of it before the arrival of another fupply, which the demands of the commiffary-general, quartermafter-general, and paying off the arrearages, will very foon require.

Your efteemed favor of the twenty-ninth ultimo is juft come to hand. It makes me very happy to find my conduct hath met the approbation of Congrefs. I am entirely of your opinion, that, fhould an accommodation take place, the terms will be fevere or favorable in proportion to our ability to refift, and that we ought to be on a refpectable footing to receive their armaments in the fpring. But how far we fhall be provided with the means, is a matter I profefs not to know, under my prefent unhappy want of arms, ammunition, and, I may add, men,—as our regiments are very incomplete. The recruiting goes on very flow, and will, I apprehend, be more fo, if for other fervice the men receive a bounty, and none is given here.

I have tried every method I could think of, to procure arms for our men. They really are not to be had in thefe governments (belonging to the public); and if fome method is not fallen upon, in the fouthern governments, to fupply us, us, we shall be in a distressed situation for want of them. There are near two thousand men now in camp without firelocks.—I have wrote to the committee of New-York this day, requesting them to send me those arms which were taken from the disaffected in that government. The Congress interesting themselves in this request will doubtless have a good effect. I have sent officers into the country, with money to purchase arms in the different towns. Some have returned, and brought in a few:—many are still out:—what their success will be, I cannot determine.

I was in great hopes that the expresses, resolved to be established between this place and Philadelphia, would ere now have been fixed. It would, in my opinion, rather save than increase the expense; as many horses are destroyed by one man coming the whole way. It will certainly be more expeditious, and safer, than writing by the post or private hands, which I am often under the necessity of doing.

I am, with great respect, &c. G. W.

Sir, *Cambridge, Feb.* 9, 1776.

I BEG leave to inform you, at the request of the committee of pay-table of the colony of Connecticut, that I have not advanced, to any of the regiments from that government, any money except the sum of seven thousand one hundred and seventy-two dollars and one-ninth on the twentieth of November last to major general Putnam, for the thirty-fourth regiment under his command. I should have paid them in the same manner I did the rest of the army, had I not been prevented by the colonels, who expressed their inclination to receive the whole at once upon their return home at the expiration of service, as was customary in their colony. For this reason, I never included them in my estimates of money, and have made no provision for their payment, always imagining that whatever payments the colony made them, Congress would apply to their credit in the general account against the United Colonies, or refund upon application.

I have the honor to be, &c. G. W.

Sir, *Cambridge, Feb.* 14, 1776.

THROUGH you, I beg leave to lay before Congress the inclosed letter from lord Drummond to general Robertson, which came to my hands a few days ago in order to be sent into Boston.

As I never heard of his lordship being vested with power to treat with Congress upon the subject of our grievances, nor of his having laid any propositions before them for an accommodation, I confess it surprised me much, and led me to form various conjectures of his motives, and intended application to general Howe and admiral Shuldham for a passport for the safe-conduct of such deputies as Congress might appoint for negotiating terms of reconciliation between Great Britain and us.—Whatever his intentions are, however benevolent his designs may be, I confess that his letter has embarrassed me much; and I am not without suspicion of its meaning more than the generous purposes it professes. I should suppose, that, if the mode for negotiation, which he points out, should be adopted (which I hope will never be thought of), it ought to have been fixed and settled previous to any application of this sort; and at best, that his conduct in this instance is premature and officious, and leading to consequences of a fatal and injurious nature to the rights of this country. His zeal and desire perhaps of an amicable and constitutional adjustment's taking place may have suggested and precipitated the measure. Be that as it may, I thought it of too much importance, to suffer it to go in without having the express direction of Congress for that purpose; and that it was my indispensable duty to transmit them the original, to make such interpretations and inferences as they may think right.

Messrs.

Messrs. Willard and Child, who were sent to Nova-Scotia in pursuance of the resolve of Congress, have just returned, and made their report, which I do myself the honor to inclose you. They have not answered the purposes of their commission by any means, as they only went a little way into that country, and found their intelligence upon the information of others. You will see the reasons they assign in excuse or justification of their conduct, in the report itself.

Last night a party of regulars, said to be about five hundred, landed on Dorchester neck, and burned some of the houses there, which were of no value to us; nor would they have been, unless we take post there : they then might be of some service. A detachment went after them as soon as the fire was discovered : but, before it could arrive, they had executed their plan, and made their retreat.

Inclosed is a letter for David Franks esquire, from Mr. Chamier in Boston, upon the subject of victualling such of the king's troops as may be prisoners within the limits of his contract, which I beg the favor of you to deliver him, and that proper agents may be appointed by him, to see that it is done. I could wish, too, that Congress would fall upon some mode for supplying the officers with such money as they may really stand in need of, and depute proper persons for that purpose, and furnishing the privates with such clothing as may be absolutely necessary. I am applied to, and wearied by their repeated requests. In some instances I have desired the committees to give the prisoners within their appointments what they should judge absolutely necessary for their support,—as the only means in my power of relieving their distress. But I imagine, that, if there were persons to superintend this business, their wants would be better attended to, and many exorbitant charges prevented and saved to the continent; and the whole would then be brought into a proper account.

I am, sir, with great esteem, &c.   G. W.

P. S. I send a return of the strength of the regiments.

Sir,   *Cambridge, Feb.* 18, 1776.

THE late freezing weather having formed some pretty strong ice from Dorchester point to Boston neck, and from Roxbury to the Common, thereby affording a more expanded and consequently a less dangerous approach to the town, I could not help thinking,—notwithstanding the militia were not all come in, and we had little or no powder to begin our operation by a regular cannonade or bombardment,—that a bold and resolute assault upon the troops in Boston with such men as we had (for it could not take many men to guard our own lines at a time when the enemy were attacked in all quarters) might be crowned with success: and therefore, seeing no certain prospect of a supply of powder on the one hand, and a certain dissolution of the ice on the other, I called the general officers together, for their opinion, agreeably to the resolve of Congress, of the twenty-second of December. The result will appear in the inclosed council of war; and, being almost unanimous, I must suppose it to be right; although, from a thorough conviction of the necessity of attempting something against the ministerial troops before a reinforcement should arrive, and while we were favored with the ice, I was not only ready, but willing, and desirous of making the assault, under a firm hope (if the men would have stood by me) of a favorable issue, notwithstanding the enemy's advantage of ground, artillery, &c.

Perhaps the irksomeness of my situation may have given different ideas to me, than those which influenced the gentlemen I consulted, and might have inclined me to put more to the hazard, than was consistent with prudence:—if it had, I am not sensible of it, as I endeavored to give it all the consideration that a matter of such importance required. True it is, and I cannot help acknowledging, that I have many disagreeable sensations on account of my situation:

for,

for, to have the eyes of the whole continent fixed with anxious expectation of hearing of some great event,—and to be restrained in every military operation, for want of the necessary means of carrying it on,—is not very pleasing, especially as the means, used to conceal my weakness from the enemy, conceal it also from our friends, and add to their wonder.

I do not utter this by way of complaint. I am sensible that all that the Congress could do, they have done; and I should feel most powerfully the weight of conscious ingratitude, were I not to acknowledge this. But as we have accounts of the arrival of powder in captain Mason, I would beg to have it sent on in the most expeditious manner: otherwise we not only lose all chance of the benefits resulting from the season, but of the militia, who are brought in at a most enormous expense, upon a presumption that we should, long ere this, have been amply supplied with powder, under the contracts entered into with the committee of Congress.

The militia, contrary to an express requisition, are come and coming in without ammunition. To supply them alone with twenty-four rounds (which is less, by three fifths than the regulars are served with) will take between fifty and sixty barrels of powder; and to complete the other troops to the like quantity, will take near as much more, and leave in store not more than about sixty barrels, besides a few rounds of cannon cartridges ready filled for use. This, sir, Congress may be assured, is a true state of our powder, and will, I hope, bear some testimony of my incapacity for action in such a way as may do any essential service.

February 21.——When I began this letter, I proposed to have sent it by express. But recollecting that all my late letters have been as expressive of my want of powder and arms as I could paint them, and that Mr. Hooper was to set off in a day or two, I thought it unnecessary to run the continent to the expense of an express, merely to repeat what I had

had so often done before, when I am certain that Congress, knowing our necessities, will delay no time that can possibly be avoided in supplying them.

My duty is offered to Congress; and, with great respect and esteem, I have the honor to be, &c. G. W.

P. S. Hearing of the arrival of a small parcel of powder in Connecticut, I have been able to obtain three thousand weight of it, which is in addition to the sixty barrels before mentioned.

Sir, Cambridge, Feb. 26, 1776.

I HAD the honor of addressing you on the eighteenth and twenty-first instant, by Mr. Hooper; since which, nothing material has occurred.

We are making every necessary preparation for taking possession of Dorchester heights as soon as possible, with a view of drawing the enemy out. How far our expectations may be answered, time only can determine: but I should think, if any thing will induce them to hazard an engagement, it will be our attempting to fortify these heights; as, on that event's taking place, we shall be able to command a great part of the town and almost the whole harbor, and to make them rather disagreeable than otherwise, provided we can get a sufficient supply of what we greatly want.

Within these three or four days, I have received sundry accounts from Boston, of such movements there,—(such as taking the mortars from Bunker's hill,—the putting them, with several pieces of heavy ordnance, on board of ship, with a quantity of bedding,—the ships all taking in water,— the baking a large quantity of biscuit,—&c,)—as to indicate an embarkation of the troops from thence. A Mr. Ides, who came out yesterday, says that the inhabitants of the town generally believe that they are about to remove either to New-York or Virginia, and that every vessel in the harbor on tuesday last was taken up for government's service, and two months' pay advanced them. Whether they really intend to embark, or whether the whole is a feint, is impossible for me to tell. However I have thought it expedient to send an express to general Lee, to inform him of it—(in order that he may not be taken by surprise, if their destination should be against New-York),—and continued him on to you. If they do embark, I think the possessing themselves of that place, and of the North river, is the object they have in view, thereby securing the communication with Canada, and rendering the intercourse between the northern and southern United Colonies exceedingly precarious and difficult. To prevent them from effecting their plan, is a matter of the highest importance, and will require a large and respectable army, and the most vigilant and judicious exertions.

Since I wrote by Mr. Hooper, some small parcels of powder have arrived from Connecticut, which will give us a little assistance.

On thursday night a party of our men at Roxbury made the enemy's out-centries, consisting of a corporal and two privates, prisoners, without firing a gun or giving the least alarm.

I shall be as attentive to the enemy's motions as I can, and obtain all the intelligence in my power; and, if I find them embark, shall in the most expeditious manner detach a part of the light troops to New-York, and repair thither myself if circumstances shall require it. I shall be better able to judge what to do, when the matter happens. At present, I can only say that I will do every thing that shall appear proper and necessary.

Your letter of the twelfth instant, by colonel Bull, came to hand yesterday evening: and I shall, agreeable to your recommendation, pay proper notice to him.—The supply of cash came very seasonably, as our treasury was just exhausted, and nothing can be done here without it.

I have the honor to be, &c. G. W.

P. S. This was intended to have been sent by exprefs: but meeting with a private opportunity, the exprefs was countermanded.

Sir, *Cambridge, March* 7, 1776.

ON the twenty-fixth ultimo I had the honor of addreffing you, and then mentioned that we were making preparations for taking poffeffion of Dorchefter heights.—I now beg leave to inform you, that, a council of general officers having determined a previous bombardment and cannonade expedient and proper, in order to harrafs the enemy and divert their attention from that quarter,—on faturday, funday, and monday nights laft, we carried them on from our pofts at Coble-hill, Leechmore's-point, and Lam's-dam. Whether they did the enemy any confiderable and what injury, I have not yet heard, but have the pleafure to acquaint you that they greatly facilitated our fchemes, and would have been attended with fuccefs equal to our moft fanguine expectations, had it not been for the unlucky burfting of two thirteen, and three ten-inch mortars, among which was the brafs one taken in the ordnance brig. To what caufe to attribute this misfortune, I know not,—whether to any defect in them, or to the inexperience of the bombardiers. But to return,—on monday evening, as foon as our firing commenced, a confiderable detachment of our men, under the command of brigadier-general Thomas, croffed the neck, and took poffeffion of the two hills, without the leaft interruption or annoyance from the enemy; and by their great activity and induftry, before the morning, advanced the works fo far as to be fecure againft their fhot. They are now going on with fuch expedition, that in a little time I hope they will be complete, and enable our troops ftationed there to make a vigorous and obftinate ftand. During the whole cannonade, which was inceffant the laft two nights, we were fortunate enough to lofe but two men,—one, a lieutenant, by a cannon ball's taking off his thigh,—the other, a private, by the explosion of a shell, which also slightly wounded four or five more.

Our taking possession of Dorchester heights is only preparatory to taking post on Nuke-hill, and the points opposite the south end of Boston. It was absolutely necessary that they should be previously fortified, in order to cover and command them. As soon as the works on the former are finished and complete, measures will be immediately adopted for securing the latter, and making them as strong and defensible as we can. Their contiguity to the enemy will make them of much importance, and of great service to us.

As mortars are essential, and indispensably necessary for carrying on our operations, and for the prosecution of our plans, I have applied to two furnaces to have some thirteen-inch ones cast with all expedition imaginable, and am encouraged to hope, from the accounts I have had, that they will be able to do it. When they are done, and a proper supply of powder obtained, I flatter myself, from the posts we have just taken and are about to take, that it will be in our power to force the ministerial troops to an attack, or to dispose of them in some way that will be of advantage to us. I think from these posts they will be so galled and annoyed, that they must either give us battle or quit their present possessions. I am resolved that nothing on my part shall be wanting, to effect the one or the other.

It having been the general opinion that the enemy would attempt to dislodge our people from the hills, and force their works as soon as they were discovered, which probably might have brought on a general engagement,—it was thought advisable that the honorable council should be applied to, to order in the militia from the neighboring and adjacent towns. I wrote to them on the subject, which they most readily complied with: and, in justice to the militia, I cannot but inform you that they came in at the appointed time, and manifested the greatest alertness, and determined resolution to have acted like men engaged in the cause of freedom.

When

When the enemy firſt diſcovered our works in the morning, they ſeemed to be in great confuſion, and, from their movements, to have intended an attack. It is much to be wiſhed that it had been made: the event, I think, muſt have been fortunate, and nothing leſs than ſucceſs and victory on our ſide, as our officers and men appeared impatient for the appeal, and to have poſſeſſed the moſt animated ſentiments and determined reſolution.

On tueſday evening a conſiderable number of their troops embarked on board of their tranſports, and fell down to the caſtle, where part of them landed before dark. One or two of the veſſels got a-ground, and were fired at by our people with a field-piece, but without any damage.—What was the deſign of this embarkation and landing, I have not been able to learn. It would ſeem as if they meant an attack; for it is moſt probable, that, if they make one on our works at Dorcheſter at this time, they will firſt go to the caſtle, and come from thence. If ſuch was their deſign, a violent ſtorm that night, and which laſted till eight o'clock the next day, rendered the execution of it impracticable. It carried one or two of their veſſels a-ſhore, which have ſince got off.

In caſe the miniſterial troops had made an attempt to diſlodge our men from Dorcheſter hills, and the number detached upon the occaſion had been ſo great as to have afforded a probability of a ſucceſsful attack's being made upon Boſton,—on a ſignal given from Roxbury for that purpoſe, agreeable to a ſettled and concerted plan, four thouſand choſen men, who were held in readineſs, were to have embarked at the mouth of Cambridge river, in two diviſions, the firſt under the command of brigadier-general Sullivan, the ſecond under brigadier-general Greene,—the whole to have been commanded by major-general Putnam. The firſt diviſion was to land at the powder-houſe, and gain poſſeſſion of Beacon-hill and Mount-Horam,—the ſecond at Barton's point or a little ſouth of it, and, after ſecuring that poſt, to join the other diviſion, and force the enemy's gates and works

works at the neck, for letting in the Roxbury troops. Three floating batteries were to have preceded, and gone in front of the other boats, and kept up a heavy fire on that part of the town where our men were to land.

How far our views would have succeeded, had an opportunity offered for attempting the execution, is impossible for me to say: nothing less than experiment could determine with precision. The plan was thought to be well digested; and, as far as I could judge from the cheerfulness and alacrity which distinguished the officers and men who were to engage in the enterprise, I had reason to hope for a favorable and happy issue.

The militia who were ordered in from the adjacent towns brought with them three days' provision. They were only called upon to act under the idea of an attack's being immediately made, and were all discharged this afternoon.

I beg leave to remind Congress that three major-generals are essential and necessary for this army; and that, by general Lee's being called from hence to the command in Canada, the left division is without one. I hope they will fill up the vacancy by the appointment of another. General Thomas is the first brigadier, stands fair in point of reputation, and is esteemed a brave and good officer. If he is promoted, there will be a vacancy in the brigadier-generals, which it will be necessary to supply by the appointment of some other gentleman that shall be agreeable to Congress: but justice requires me to mention that William Thompson, esquire, of the rifle regiment, is the first colonel in this department, and, as far as I have had an opportunity of judging, is a good officer and a man of courage. What I have said of these two gentlemen, I conceived to be my duty, at the same time acknowledging, whatever promotions are made will be satisfactory to me.

March 9.——Yesterday evening, a captain Irvine, who escaped from Boston the night before with six of his crew, came to head quarters, and gave the following intelligence;

gence:—" That our bombardment and cannonade caused a great deal of surprise and alarm in town, as many of the soldiery said they never heard or thought we had mortars or shells;—that several of the officers acknowledged they were well and properly directed;—that they made much distress and confusion;—that the cannon-shot, for the greatest part, went through the houses; and he was told that one took off the legs and arms of six men lying in the barracks on the neck;—that a soldier, who came from the lines there on tuesday morning, informed him that twenty men had been wounded the night before;—(it was reported that others were also hurt, and one of the light-horse torn to pieces by the explosion of a shell: this was afterwards contradicted:) —that, early on tuesday morning, admiral Shuldham, discovering the works our people were throwing up on Dorchester heights, immediately sent an express to general Howe, to inform him that it was necessary they should be attacked and dislodged from thence, or he would be under the necessity of withdrawing the ships from the harbor, which were under his command;—that preparations were directly made for that purpose, as it was said; and, from twelve to two o'clock, about three thousand men embarked on board the transports, which fell down to the castle with a design of landing on that part of Dorchester next to it, and attacking our works on the heights at five o'clock next morning;—that lord Percy was appointed to command;—that it was generally believed the attempt would have been made, had it not been for the violent storm which happened that night, as I have mentioned before;—that he heard several of the privates, and one or two sergeants, say as they were embarking, that it would be another Bunker's-hill affair."

He further informs——" that the army is preparing to leave Boston, and that they will do it in a day or two;— that the transports necessary for their embarkation were getting ready with the utmost expedition;—that there had been great movements and confusion among the troops, the night and day preceding his coming out, in hurrying down their cannon, artillery and other stores, to the wharfs, with the utmost precipitation; and they were putting them on board the ships in such haste, that no account or memorandum was taken of them;—that most of the cannon were removed from their works, and embarked or embarking;—that he heard a woman say, whom he took to be an officer's wife, that she had seen men go under the ground at the lines on the neck, without returning;—that the ship he commanded was taken up, places fitted, and fitting, for officers to lodge, and several shot, shells, and cannon, already on board;—that the tories were to have the liberty of going where they please, if they can get seamen to man the vessels, of whom there was a great scarcity;—that, on that account, many vessels could not be carried away, and would be burned;—that many of the inhabitants apprehended the town would be destroyed; and that it was generally thought their destination is Halifax."

The account given by captain Irvine, as to the embarkation, and their being about to leave the town, I believe true. There are other circumstances corroborating; and it seems fully confirmed by a paper signed by four of the select-men of the town (a copy of which I have the honor to inclose you), which was brought out yesterday evening by a flag, and delivered to colonel Learned, by major Basset of the tenth regiment, who desired it might be delivered me as soon as possible. I advised with such of the general officers upon the occasion as I could immediately assemble; and we determined it right (as it was not addressed to me or any one else; nor authenticated by the signature of general Howe, or any other act obliging him to a performance of the promise mentioned on his part) that I should give it no answer; at the same time, that a letter should be returned, as going from colonel Learned, signifying his having laid it before me,—with the reasons assigned for not answering it.—A copy of this is sent.

To-night

To-night I shall have a battery thrown up on Nuke-hill (Dorchester point) with a design of acting as circumstances may require; it being judged advisable to prosecute our plans of fortification, as we intended before this information from the select-men came.

It being agreed on all hands that there is no possibility of stopping them in case they determine to go,—I shall order look-outs to be kept upon all the head-lands, to discover their movements and course, and moreover direct commodore Manly and his little squadron to dog them, as well for the same purpose as for picking up any of their vessels that may chance to depart their convoy. From their loading with such precipitancy, it is presumable they will not be in the best condition for sea.

If the ministerial troops evacuate the town and leave it standing, I have thoughts of taking measures for fortifying the entrance into the harbor, if it shall be thought proper, and the situation of affairs will admit of it.

Notwithstanding the report from Boston that Halifax is the place of their destination, I have no doubt but that they are going to the southward of this,—and, I apprehend, to New-York. Many reasons lead to this opinion: it is in some measure corroborated by their sending an express ship there, which, on wednesday week, got on shore and bilged at Cape-Cod. The dispatches, if written, were destroyed when she was boarded. She had a parcel of coal, and about four thousand cannon-shot, six carriage-guns, a swivel or two, and three barrels of powder.

I shall hold the riflemen and other parts of our troops in readiness to march at a moment's warning, and govern my movements by the events that happen, or such orders as I may receive from Congress, which I beg may be ample, and forwarded with all possible expedition.

On the sixth instant, a ship bound from London, with stores for the ministerial army, consisting of coal, porter, and krout, fell in with our armed vessels, four of them in company,

company, and was carried into Portsmouth. She had had a long passage, and of course brought no papers of a late date. The only letters of importance, or in the least interesting, that were found, I have inclosed.

I beg leave to mention to Congress that money is much wanted. The militia from these governments, engaged till the first of April, are then to be paid: and, if we march from hence, the expense will be very considerable, must be defrayed, and cannot be accomplished without it. The necessity of making the earliest remittance for these purposes is too obvious, for me to add more.

When I wrote that part of this letter which is antecedent to this date, I fully expected it would have gone before now by colonel Bull, not deeming it of sufficient importance to send a special messenger. But he deferred his return from time to time, and never set off till to-day. These reasons I hope will excuse the delay, and be received as a proper apology for not transmitting it sooner.

I have the honor to be, &c.   G. W.

SIR,   *Cambridge, March* 13, 1776.

IN my letter of the seventh and ninth instant which I had the honor of addressing you, I mentioned the intelligence I had received respecting the embarkation of the troops from Boston; and fully expected, before this, that the town would have been entirely evacuated. Although I have been deceived, and was rather premature in the opinion I had then formed, I have little reason to doubt but the event will take place in a very short time, as other accounts which have come to hand since, of the sailing of a great number of transports from the harbor to Nantasket road, and many circumstances corresponding therewith, seem to confirm and render it unquestionable.

Whether the town will be destroyed, is a matter of much uncertainty: but it would seem, from the destruction they are making of sundry pieces of furniture, of many of their waggons, carts, &c, which they cannot take with them as it is said, that it will not: for, if they intended it, the whole might be involved in one general ruin.

Holding it of the last importance in the present contest that we should secure New-York, and prevent the enemy from possessing it,—and conjecturing they have views of that sort, and their embarkation to be for that purpose,—I judged it necessary, under the situation of things here, to call a council of general officers to consult of such measures as might be expedient to be taken at this interesting conjuncture of affairs. A copy of the proceedings I have the honor to inclose you.

Agreeable to the opinion of the council, I shall detach the rifle regiment to-morrow, under the command of brigadier-general Sullivan, with orders to repair to New-York with all possible expedition;—which will be succeeded, the day after, by the other five in one brigade,—they being all that it was thought advisable to send from hence till the enemy shall have quitted the town. Immediately upon their departure, I shall send forward major-general Putnam, and follow myself with the remainder of the army as soon as I have it in my power,—leaving here such a number of men as circumstances may seem to require.

As the badness of the roads at this season will greatly retard the march of our men, I have, by advice of the general officers, wrote to governor Trumbull by this express, to use his utmost exertions for throwing a reinforcement of two thousand men into New-York, from the western parts of Connecticut,—and to the commanding officer there, to apply to the provincial convention or committee of safety of New-Jersey, for a thousand more for the same purpose, to oppose the enemy and prevent their getting possession in case they arrive before the troops from hence can get there; of which there is a probability, unless they are impeded by contrary winds. This measure, though it may be attended

with

with confiderable expenfe, I flatter myfelf, will meet with the approbation of Congrefs.—Paft experience, and the lines in Bofton and on Bofton neck, point out the propriety, and fuggeft the neceffity of keeping our enemies from gaining poffeffion and making a lodgement.

Should their deftination be further fouthward, or for Halifax (as reported in Bofton) for the purpofe of going into Canada,—the march of our troops to New-York will place them nearer the fcene of action, and more convenient for affording fuccours.

We have not taken poft on Nuke-hill, and fortified it, as mentioned that we fhould, in my laft. On hearing that the enemy were about to retreat and leave the town, it was thought imprudent and unadvifable to force them with too much precipitation, that we might gain a little time, and prepare for a march. To-morrow evening we fhall take poffeffion, unlefs they are gone.

As New-York is of fuch importance,—prudence and policy require that every precaution that can be devifed fhould be adopted, to fruftrate the defigns which the enemy have of poffeffing it. To this end I have ordered veffels to be provided and held ready at Norwich, for the embarkation and tranfportation of our troops thither. This I have done with a view not only of greatly expediting their arrival (as it will fave feveral days' marching), but alfo that they may be frefh and fit for intrenching and throwing up works of defence as foon as they get there, if they do not meet the enemy to contend with;—for neither of which would they be in a proper condition after a long and fatiguing march in bad roads. If Wallace, with his fhips, fhould be apprifed of the meafure, and attempt to prevent it by ftopping up the harbor of New-London, they can but purfue their march by land.

You will pleafe to obferve that it is the opinion of the general officers, if the enemy abandon the town, that it will be unneceffary to employ or keep any part of this army for its defence;

defence; and that I have mentioned, on that event's happening, I shall immediately repair to New-York with the remainder of the army not now detached, leaving only such a number of men here as circumstances may seem to require. What I partly allude to, is, that, as it will take a considerable time for the removal of such a body of men, and the divisions must precede each other in such order as to allow intermediate time sufficient for them to be covered and provided for, and many things done previous to the march of the whole, for securing and forwarding such necessaries as cannot be immediately carried, and others which it may be proper to keep here,—that directions might be received from Congress respecting the same, and as many men ordered to remain for that and other purposes, as they may judge proper. I could wish to have their commands upon the subject, and in time; as I may be under some degree of embarrassment as to their views.

Congress having been pleased to appoint colonel Thompson a brigadier-general, there is a vacancy for a colonel in the regiment he commanded, to which I would beg leave to recommend the lieutenant-colonel Hand. I shall also take the liberty of recommending captain Hugh Stephenson, of the Virginia riflemen, to succeed colonel Hand, and to be appointed in his place as lieutenant-colonel,—there being no major to the regiment since the promotion of major Magaw to be lieutenant-colonel of one of the Pennsylvania batallions, and who is gone from hence. He is, in my opinion, the fittest person in this army for it, as well as the oldest captain in the service, having distinguished himself at the head of a rifle company all the last war, and highly merited the approbation of his superior officers.

Colonel Mifflin informed me to day of his having received tent-cloths from Mr. Barrell of Philadelphia, to the amount of seven thousand five hundred pounds Pennsylvania currency, and applied for a warrant for payment of it. But, as our fund is low, and many necessary demands against it which muſt be ſatisfied,—and our calls for money are and will be exceedingly great,—I could not grant it, thinking it might be convenient for payment to be made in Philadelphia, by your order on the treaſury there.

I have the honor to be, &c.   G. W.

Sir,   *Head-Quarters, Cambridge, March* 19, 1776.

IT is with the greateſt pleaſure I inform you, that, on ſunday laſt, the ſeventeenth inſtant, about nine o'clock in the forenoon, the miniſterial army evacuated the town of Boſton, and that the forces of the United Colonies are now in actual poſſeſſion thereof. I beg leave to congratulate you, ſir, and the honorable Congreſs, on this happy event, and particularly as it was effected without endangering the lives and property of the remaining unhappy inhabitants.

I have great reaſon to imagine their flight was precipitated by the appearance of a work which I had ordered to be thrown up laſt ſaturday night on an eminence at Dorcheſter which lay neareſt to Boſton neck, called Nuke-hill.

The town, although it has ſuffered greatly, is not in ſo bad a ſtate as I expected to find it; and I have a particular pleaſure in being able to inform you, ſir, that your houſe has received no damage worth mentioning. Your furniture is in tolerable order, and the family pictures are all left entire and untouched. Captain Cazneau takes charge of the whole, until he ſhall receive further orders from you.

As ſoon as the miniſterial troops had quitted the town, I ordered a thouſand men (who had had the ſmall-pox), under command of general Putnam, to take poſſeſſion of the heights, which I ſhall endeavor to fortify in ſuch a manner as to prevent their return, ſhould they attempt it. But, as they are ſtill in the harbor, I thought it not prudent to march off with the main body of the army until I ſhould be fully ſatisfied they had quitted the coaſt. I have therefore only detached five regiments, beſides the rifle batallion, to New-York,

York, and shall keep the remainder here till all suspicion of their return ceases.

The situation in which I found their works evidently discovered that their retreat was made with the greatest precipitation. They have left their barracks and other works of wood at Bunker's hill, &c, all standing, and have destroyed but a small part of their lines. They have also left a number of fine pieces of cannon which they first spiked up, also a very large iron mortar; and, as I am informed, they have thrown another over the end of your wharf. I have employed proper persons to drill the cannon, and doubt not I shall save the most of them.—I am not yet able to procure an exact list of all the stores they have left. As soon as it can be done, I shall take care to transmit it to you.—From an estimate of what the quarter-master-general has already discovered, the amount will be twenty-five or thirty thousand pounds.

Part of the powder mentioned in yours of the sixth instant has already arrived. The remainder I have ordered to be stopped on the road, as we shall have no occasion for it here.—The letter to general Thomas, I immediately sent to him. He desired leave for three or four days, to settle some of his private affairs; after which, he will set out for his command in Canada.—I am happy that my conduct in intercepting lord Drummond's letter is approved of by Congress.—I have the honor to be, &c. G. W.

Sir, *Cambridge, March* 24, 1776.

WHEN I had the honor to address you on the nineteenth instant upon the evacuation of the town of Boston by the ministerial army, I fully expected, as their retreat and embarkation were hurried and precipitate, that, before now, they would have departed the harbor, and been far in their passage to the place of destination. But, to my surprise and disappointment, the fleet is still in Nantasket road. The purpose inducing their stay is altogether unknown; nor can I suggest any satisfactory reason for it. On wednesday night last, before the whole of the fleet fell down to Nantasket, they demolished the castle and houses belonging to it, by burning them down, and the several fortifications. They left a great number of the cannon; but have rendered all of them, except a very few, entirely useless, by breaking off the trunnions; and those they spiked up: but they may be made serviceable again:—some are already done.

There are several vessels in the docks, which were taken by the enemy (some with and others without cargoes), which different persons claim as their property and right. Are they to be restored to their former owners on making proof of their title, or to belong to the continent, as captures made from the enemy?—I wish Congress would direct a mode of proceeding against them, and establish a rule for decision: they appear to me to be highly necessary. In like manner, some of the cannon which are in Boston are said to have come from the castle. Supposing them, with those remaining at the castle, to have been purchased by and provided originally at the expense of this province,—are they now to be considered to belonging as it, or to the public? I beg leave to refer the matter to the opinion of Congress, and pray their direction how I am to conduct respecting them.

It having been suggested to me that there was considerable property, &c, belonging to persons who had, from the first of the present unhappy contest, manifested an unfriendly and inveterate disposition, in the town of Boston, I thought it prudent to write to the honorable general court upon the subject, that it might be inquired after and secured. A copy of the letter I herewith send you, and submit it to Congress through you, whether they will not determine how it is to be disposed of, and as to the appropriation of the money arising from the sale of the same.

As soon as the town was abandoned by the enemy, I judged it advisable to secure the several heights, lest they should attempt

tempt to return; and, for this purpose, have caused a large and strong work to be thrown up on Fort-hill, a post of great importance, as it commands the whole harbor, and, when fortified, if properly supported, will greatly annoy any fleet the enemy may send against the town, and render the landing of their troops exceedingly difficult, if not impracticable. This work is almost done, and in a little time will be complete: and, that the communication between the town and country may be free and open, I have ordered all the lines upon the neck to be immediately destroyed, and the other works on the sides of the town facing the country, that the inhabitants from the latter may not be impeded, and afforded an easy entrance, in case the enemy should gain possession at any future time. These matters I conceived to be within the line of my duty; of which I advised the general court, and recommended to their attention such other measures as they might think necessary for securing the town against the hostile designs of the enemy.

I have just got an inventory of stores and property belonging to the crown, which the enemy left in Boston, at the castle, and Bunker's hill,—which I have the honor to transmit you; and shall give strict orders that a careful attention be had to any more that may be found. I shall take such precautions respecting them, that they may be secure, and turn to the public advantage, as much as possible, or circumstances will admit of.

A Mr. Bulfinch from Boston, who acted as clerk to Mr. ······, having put into my hands a list of rations drawn the saturday before the troops evacuated the town, I have inclosed it for your inspection. He says, neither the staff officers nor women are included in the list; from which it appears that their number is greater than we had an idea of.

Major-general Ward and brigader-general Frye are desirous of leaving the service, and, for that purpose, have requested me to lay the matter before Congress, that they may be allowed to resign their commissions. The papers containing

ing their applications you will herewith receive. They will give you a full and more particular information upon the subject; and therefore I shall take the liberty of referring you to them.

I would mention to Congress that the commissary of artillery stores has informed me, that whatever powder has been sent to this camp has always come without any bill ascertaining the number of casks or quantity. This, it is probable, has proceeded from forgetfulness or inattention in the persons appointed to send it, or the negligence of those who brought it, though they have declared otherwise, and that they never had any. As it may in some measure prevent embezzlements (though I do not suspect any to have been made), and the commissary will know what and how much to receive, and be enabled to discover mistakes if any should happen,—I should be glad if you will direct a bill of parcels to be always sent in future.

There have been so many accounts from England, all agreeing that commissioners are coming to America, to propose terms for an accommodation, as they say,—that I am inclined to think the time of their arrival not very far off.— If they come to Boston (which probably will be the case if they come to America at all) I shall be under much embarrassment respecting the manner of receiving them, and the mode of treatment that ought to be used. I therefore pray that Congress will give me directions, and point out the line of conduct to be pursued,—whether they are to be considered as ambassadors, and to have a pass or permit for repairing through the country to Philadelphia or to any other place,— or whether they are to be restrained in any and what manner.—I shall anxiously wait their orders, and, whatever they are, comply with them literally.

I have the honor to be, &c.   G. W.

Sir,

Sir,   *Cambridge, March* 27, 1776.

I Received your favor of the eleventh inftant by faturday-night's poft; and muft beg pardon for not acknowledging it in my laft of the twenty-fourth. The hurry I was then in occafioned the neglect, and I hope will apologife for it.

I now beg leave to inform you that I have juft received intelligence, that the whole of the minifterial fleet, befides three or four fhips, got under way this evening at Nantafket road, and were ftanding out for fea; in confequence of which, I fhall detach a brigade of fix regiments immediately from hence for New-York, under the command of brigadier-general Sullivan (brigadier-general Heath having gone with the firft); which will be fucceeded by another in a day or two; and directly after, I fhall forward the remainder of the army (except four or five regiments which will be left for taking care of the barracks and public ftores, and fortifying the town, and erecting fuch works for its defence as the honorable general court may think neceffary)—and follow myfelf.

Apprehending that general Thomas will ftand in need of fome artillerifts in Canada, I have ordered two companies of the train to march immediately; and two mortars, with a quantity of fhells and fhot, to be fent him.—He fet out on the twenty-firft inftant.

Inclofed you have a copy of the return of ordnance ftores left in Bofton by the enemy. In it are not included the cannon left at the caftle, amounting to a hundred and thirty-five pieces, as reported, all of which, except a very few, they have deftroyed and rendered ufelefs, by knocking off the trunnions, and fpiking up.

I beg leave to tranfmit you the copy of a petition from the inhabitants of Nova-Scotia, brought me by * * * efquire, mentioned therein, who is now here with an Acadian. From this it appears they are in a diftreffed fituation; and, from Mr. * * *'s account, are exceedingly apprehenfive that they will be reduced to the difagreeable alternative of taking up arms and joining our enemies, or to flee their country, unlefs they can be protected againft their infults and oppreffions. He fays that their committees think many falutary and valuable confequences would be derived from five or fix hundred men being fent there, as it would not only quiet the minds of the people from the anxiety and uneafinefs they are now filled with, and enable them to take a part in behalf of the colonies, but be the means of preventing the Indians (of whom there are a good many) from taking the fide of government, and the minifterial troops from getting fuch fupplies of provifions from thence as they have done.

How far thefe good purpofes would be anfwered if fuch a force was fent as they afk for, is impoffible to determine in the prefent uncertain ftate of things. For, if the army from Bofton is going to Halifax (as reported by them before their departure), that or a much more confiderable force would be of no avail:—if not, and they poffefs the friendly difpofition to our caufe, fuggefted in the petition and declared by Mr. ***, it might be of great fervice, unlefs another body of troops fhould be fent thither by adminiftration, too powerful for them to oppofe. It being a matter of fome importance, I judged it prudent to lay it before Congrefs for their confideration; and, requefting their direction upon the fubject, fhall only add, if they determine to adopt it, that they will prefcribe the number to be fent, and whether it is to be from the regiments which will be left here.—I fhall wait their decifion, and, whatever it is, will endeavor to have it carried into execution.

I have the honor to be, &c.   G. W.

SIR,   *Head-Quarters, Cambridge, April* 1, 1776.

THIS letter will be delivered you by *** efquire, the gentleman from Nova-Scotia whom I mentioned to you in mine of the twenty-feventh ultimo. He feemed defirous of waiting on the honorable Congress, in order to lay before them the state of public affairs, and situation of the inhabitants of that province. And, as it might be in his power to communicate many things personally which could not be so well done by letter, I encouraged him in his design, and have advanced him fifty dollars to defray his expenses. The Acadian accompanies him: and, as they seem to be solid judicious men, I beg leave to recommend them both to the notice of Congress;—and am most respectfully, sir, your most obedient, &c. G. W.

Sir, *Head-Quarters, Cambridge, April* 1, 1776.

AN express arrived this morning with a letter from governor Cooke of Rhode-Island, of which the inclosed is a copy. In consequence of this important intelligence, I immediately dispatched an express after general Sullivan who is on his march to Norwich with six regiments, and ordered him to file off to Providence, if he should be so desired by governor Cooke, to whom I have wrote on the subject.

General Greene was to have marched this morning with five more regiments, by way of Providence. I have ordered him to hasten his march for that place; and hope to collect a force there, sufficient to prevent the enemy from effecting their purpose.

Whether this movement be only a feint to draw our attention from their principal object, or not, is at present impossible to determine.—I momently expect further intelligence from governor Cooke.—If the alarm should be well grounded, I shall hasten to Providence, and make the necessary dispositions for their reception. I beg you to assure the honorable Congress I shall exert myself to the utmost to frustrate the designs of the enemy.

I am sir, your most obedient, &c.

G. W.

Sir,   Cambridge, *April* 4, 1776.

 I WAS honored with your favors of the twenty-firſt and twenty-fifth ultimo, on the ſecond inſtant,—the former by Mr. Hanſon, &c,—the latter by Feſſenden. I heartily wiſh the money had arrived ſooner, that the militia might have been paid as ſoon as their time of ſervice expired. The diſappointment has given them great uneaſineſs, and they are gone home much diſſatisfied: nor have I been without ſevere complaints from the other troops on the ſame account. When I get to New-York, I hope a ſufficient ſum will be there, ready to pay every claim.

 It is not in my power to make report of the deficiency of arms in compliance with the direction of Congreſs at this time, as ſome of the regiments are at, and moſt of the others on their march to, New-York; nor do I know that it would anſwer any good purpoſe, if it were,—having made repeated applications to the ſeveral aſſemblies and conventions upon the ſubject, and conſtantly received for anſwer, that they could afford no relief.

 When I arrive at New-York, I ſhall, in purſuance of the order of Congreſs, detach four batallions to Canada, if the ſituation of affairs will admit of it; and ſhall be extremely happy if they and the troops already there can effect the important end of their going.

 In my letter of the firſt inſtant, per poſt, I incloſed you a copy of a letter from governor Cooke, adviſing me of the arrival of a ſhip of war, &c, at and near the harbor of Newport. I have now the pleaſure to inform you that the report was entirely premature, and without any foundation. You have a copy of his letter of the firſt inſtant to this effect.—I wiſh the alarm had never been given: it occaſioned general Sullivan and his brigade to make an unneceſſary and inconvenient diverſion from their route.

 Incloſed is a copy of an account, preſented by the honorable general court, of powder furniſhed the continental army

army by this colony. From the account, it appears that part of it was fupplied before the army was under my command; and therefore I know nothing of it; but have not the fmalleft doubt of the juftice of the charge. I fhall leave about two hundred barrels of this article with major-general Ward, out of which Congrefs will direct him to make a return, if they think proper,—and alfo repayment of what may have been furnifhed by the other governments.

A proclamation of general Howe's, iffued a few days before his departure from town, having fallen into my hands, I have inclofed you a copy, which will probably have been the occafion of large quantities of goods being carried away, and the removal of many perfons, which otherwife would not have happened.

Colonel Warren, paymafter-general, finding the army likely to be removed from hence, informed me the other day that the fituation of his affairs and engagements in the bufinefs of the colony are fuch, as to prevent him from perfonally attending the army; and offered, in cafe it fhould be required, to refign. This was rather embarraffing. To me it appears indifpenfably neceffary that the paymafter-general, with his books, fhould be at or near head-quarters. Indeed it is ufual for the head of every department in the army, however difperfed that army may be, to be with the commanding general, keeping deputies in the fmaller departments. On the other hand, colonel Warren's merit and attachment to the caufe are fuch, that I could do nothing lefs than defire (as fome money muft be left for the pay and contingent charges of the army which will remain here), he would wait here till Congrefs fhall be pleafed to give their fentiments upon the matter,—fending in the mean time fome perfon in whom he could confide, with the money, but little of which there will be to carry, though great the demands, as nine of the regiments which have marched to New-York have only received five hundred pounds each, towards their pay for the months of February and March,—

and fix others, not a farthing. I hope therefore this matter will be confidered by Congrefs, and the refult tranfmitted me as foon as done.

I would alfo mention to Congrefs, that the militia regiments which were laft called upon, in making up their abftracts, charged pay,—the officers, from the time they received orders to raife companies,—and the privates, from the time they refpectively engaged to come or were called upon, though they did not march for a confiderable time after,—fome not within three, four, to twenty days, during all which, they remained at home about their own private affairs, without doing any thing elfe than " preparing for the march," as they fay by way of plea. This appeared to me fo exceedingly unreafonable, and fo contrary to juftice, that the public fhould pay for a longer time than from the day of their march to that of their return, that I ordered the abftracts to be made out accordingly, and refufed to give warrants on any other terms. They fay that the enlifting orders, which went out from their governments, give them the pay they claim. The fact may be that fomething in thefe may feem to authorife it: but I muft fubmit it to Congrefs, and wifh for their decifion, whether the continent muft pay it.—I am, with great efteem, &c. G. W.

P. S. I fhall fet off to-day.

SIR, *New-York, April* 15, 1776.

I AM now to inform you that on the fourth inftant I fet out from Cambridge, and arrived here on faturday laft. I came through Providence, Norwich, and New-London, in order to fee and expedite the embarkation of the troops. The third brigade, under the command of general Greene, was at New-London when I left it, where there was a fufficient number of tranfports to embark them,—and moft probably would have arrived here before this, had it not been for a fevere ftorm which happened the night they failed,
which

which difperfed them, and, I fear, has done them fome injury.

General Spencer, with the laft brigade, marched from Roxbury the day I left Cambridge, and would be at New-London, ready to embark in the return tranfports which brought general Sullivan's divifion to this place. The whole of the troops may be reafonably expected here in the courfe of this week. The badnefs of the roads, and difficulty of procuring teams for bringing the ftores, baggage, &c, have greatly prolonged their arrival at this place.

I have not had time, fince I came, to look fully about me; but find many works of defence begun, and fome finifhed. The troops are much difperfed,—fome on Long-Ifland, others on Staten-Ifland, &c.

I have ordered four batallions from hence to Canada, and am taking meafures to have them forwarded to Albany by water with all poffible expedition. This will greatly expedite their arrival, and eafe the men of much fatigue. I have wrote general Schuyler of their coming, that he may have neceffary meafures taken to hurry their march to general Thomas.

I am informed by general Putnam that the militia, that were called in for the fupport of this town in cafe the minifterial army had arrived before our troops, are all difcharged, it being unneceffary to keep them longer.

All the fhips of war, befides the Afia, moved out of this harbor on faturday, and the Afia yefterday; fome of which are now below the Narrows, and the reft gone to fea.

Your favor of the tenth inftant, by major Sherburne, directed to general Putnam or the commanding officer here, came to hand on faturday evening, with three boxes of money, which I fhall deliver the paymafter as foon as he arrives, and tranfmit you his receipt for the fame.

Having received information from hence before my departure from Cambridge, that thirty pieces of heavy cannon were wanting, and effentially neceffary for the defence of this

this place, in addition to those already here,—I took the liberty of applying to admiral Hopkins whom I saw at New-London, for that number, with the mortars and stores he brought from Providence,—a list of which he had transmitted you. He told me, that, as many were wanting for the defence of Providence river and the harbor at New-London, it was uncertain whether I could have all I wanted; but that he would send me all that could be spared.

I have not been able to get a return of the troops since I came:—as soon as I do, I will send it you.

I am, sir, with great respect, &c.   G. W.

SIR,   *New-York, April* 18, 1776.

PERMIT me, through you, to convey to the honorable Congress the sentiments of gratitude I feel for the high honor they have done me in the public mark of approbation contained in your favor of the second instant, which came to hand last night. I beg you to assure them that it will ever be my highest ambition to approve myself a faithful servant of the public; and that, to be in any degree instrumental in procuring to my American brethren a restitution of their just rights and privileges, will constitute my chief happiness.

Agreeable to your request, I have communicated, in general orders, to the officers and soldiers under my command, the thanks of Congress for their good behavior in the service; and am happy in having such an opportunity of doing justice to their merit. They were indeed, at first, "*a band of undisciplined husbandmen:*" but it is (under God) to their bravery and attention to their duty that I am indebted for that success which has procured me the only reward I wish to receive,—the affection and esteem of my countrymen.

The medal, intended to be presented to me by your honorable body, I shall carefully preserve as a memorial of their regard. I beg leave to return you, sir, my warmest
                  thanks

thanks for the polite manner in which you have been pleased to express their sentiments of my conduct; and am, with sincere esteem and respect, sir, yours and their most obedient and most humble servant, G. W.

Sir, *New-York, April* 19, 1776.

I HAVE this moment received a letter from general Schuyler, containing inclosures of a very important nature, copies of which, I imagine, are contained in the inclosed letter to you, which I thought it my duty immediately to forward by express, that they may be laid before the honorable Congress, and proper measures pursued to prevent the fatal effects which are therein apprehended. For my own part, I have done my utmost to forward the four regiments ordered by Congress: but a variety of incidents have hitherto conspired to prevent their embarkation. The men had scarcely recovered themselves from the fatigues of their march from Boston, and are quite unprovided with necessaries. The colonels of the regiments, though repeatedly called upon for that purpose, had neglected making out the abstracts for their pay. All obstacles however are now removed; and I hope to begin the embarkation this day. Indeed it would have been best, in my opinion, to have sent the regiments, raised in this province and New-Jersey, upon that service, had not the peculiar circumstances under which they were raised prevented it. By the terms of their enlistment, they are to serve during the war, and at five dollars per month, on condition (as I am informed) that they shall not be sent out of those provinces. Besides, they are very ill provided with arms, some companies not having any. It must be a great burden upon the continent to keep such a number of useless men in pay: and yet, if they should be dismissed, and an unexpected supply of arms should arrive, it may be found very difficult to replace them.

The officers of the several corps that have arrived here have

have been so busily employed in fixing their men in quarters, that I have not yet been able to procure an exact return of their numbers. Some are yet behind. As soon as the whole are collected, I shall order the proper returns, and transmit them to Congress.

You will please to notice what colonel Hazen says of the disposition of the Indians. In my opinion, it will be impossible to keep them in a state of neutrality. They must, and, no doubt, soon will take an active part either for or against us: and I submit it to the consideration of Congress, whether it would not be best immediately to engage them on our side, and to use our utmost endeavors to prevent their minds being poisoned by ministerial emissaries, which will ever be the case while a king's garrison is suffered to remain in their country. Would it not therefore be advisable to send a sufficient force from the back counties of Pennsylvania, to take possession of the garrisons of Niagara and Detroit? This, I think, might easily be effected, and would answer the most salutary purposes. The Seneca Indians, who have hitherto appeared friendly to us, might be usefully employed in this business.

I am in hopes most of the difficulties mentioned in colonel Hazen's letter will be obviated by the appearance of the respectable committee of Congress in Canada, and the forces that have been and will be sent there. The security of that country is of the utmost importance to us. This cannot be done so effectually by conquest, as by taking strong hold of the affections and confidence of the inhabitants. It is to be lamented that any conduct of the continental troops should tend to alienate their affections from us.

The honorable Congress will be able to judge from the papers sent them by general Schuyler, and the information they may receive of the designs of the enemy, whether it is expedient to send a further reinforcement to Canada. If such should be their determination, I stand ready to execute their

their orders; and am, with respect, sir, your most obedient, humble servant,
G. W.

Inclosed is a return of the four regiments ordered to Canada; besides which, there will be two rifle companies, a company of artificers, and two artillery-men, all under the command of brigadier-general Thompson.

Sir, *New-York, April 22, 1776.*

I WAS this day honored with the receipt of your favor of the twentieth instant. I have now the pleasure to acquaint you that the four regiments designed for Canada embarked yesterday with a fair wind for Albany, under the command of colonels Greaton, Patterson, Bond, and Poor; besides which, there was a company of riflemen, a company of artificers, and two engineers,—the whole commanded by brigadier-general Thompson.

I have repeatedly mentioned to the honorable Congress the distressful situation we are in for want of arms.— With much pains and difficulty I got most of the regiments from the eastward tolerably well furnished; but find the York regiments very badly provided. Colonel Ritzema's has scarcely any: and yet these men, being enlisted during the war, and at five dollars per month, ought not (in my judgment) to be discharged; as we find it almost as difficult to get men, as arms. This is a matter of some importance, which I should be glad to receive the particular opinion of Congress upon.

Mr. Baldwin is one of the assistant engineers ordered to Canada. He is indeed a very useful man in his department, but declined the service, on account of his pay, which he says is inadequate to his support. In order to induce him to continue, I promised to represent his case to Congress; and would recommend an increase of his pay, and that he should have the rank of lieutenant-colonel, of which he is very deserving. I beg leave therefore to recommend him

him to the Congress, and that they would make provision for him accordingly.

A few days ago, application was made to me by the committee of safety for this colony, for an exchange of prisoners. For the particulars I beg leave to refer you to their letter, a copy of which you have inclosed. As there is a standing order of Congress that no sailors or soldiers shall be exchanged for citizens, I did not incline to comply with the request without the particular direction of Congress: but I have been since informed that the prisoners, mentioned in the committee's letter as citizens, are really seamen taken from private vessels, but not in arms. How far this may alter the case, or how far the reasons which induced the Congress to pass the resolve above-mentioned may still exist, must be left to their determination.

The militia, who, on my application, were ordered to this place to keep possession until I should arrive with the continental forces, were obliged to return home without their pay, as there was not then money sufficient in the treasury for that purpose, and to answer the exigencies of the army. This occasioned great uneasiness among them, and may be attended with very bad consequences in case we should have occasion for their service on any future emergency. I therefore beg the Congress would make provision for their pay, and point out particularly, whether it is to be done by the commander of the continental forces, or by the provincial assemblies or conventions from whence they are sent.

As the time for which the riflemen enlisted will expire on the first of July next, and as the loss of such a valuable and brave body of men will be of great injury to the service, I would submit it to the consideration of Congress, whether it would not be best to adopt some method to induce them to continue. They are indeed a very useful corps: but I need not mention this, as their importance is already well known to the Congress. It is necessary they should pay an
early

early attention to this matter, as we know from past experience that men are very slow in re-enlisting.

When I had the honor of seeing admiral Hopkins at New-London, he represented to me the weak state of his fleet, occasioned by sickness and the damage he received in his engagement with the enemy; and requested I would spare him two hundred men to assist him in a design he had formed of attacking Wallace. This I readily consented to; and the men are to be returned as soon as the service is performed.

I wish it was in my power at present to furnish general Lee with the companies of artillery he desires.—I have already sent two companies to Quebec; and I have not yet been able to procure a return of those that are here. I expect colonel Knox every moment, and shall then be able to determine whether any can be spared from hence. Blankets we are in great want of, ourselves; and it was with great difficulty a few could be procured for the riflemen that were ordered for Canada.

I inclose you Mr. Winthrop's receipt for two hundred thousand dollars brought some time ago from Philadelphia by major Sherburne, which you will please to deliver to the continental treasurers.

On my arrival here, I found that Mr. Livingston had been appointed by the provincial Congress a commissary, to furnish the continental troops stationed in this city with provisions. I suppose this was done because there was no continental commissary then on the spot. Mr. Livingston still claims a right of furnishing all the troops but those lately arrived from Cambridge. Mr. Trumbull is now here: and, as I consider him as the principal in that office, I should be glad to know whether any part of the continental troops is to be furnished by any other than their commissary-general. I must needs say, that to me it appears very inconsistent, and must create great confusion in the accounts as well as in the contracts.—I intended to have laid before Congress the amount

amount of the rations, as supplied by colonel Trumbull and Mr. Livingston; and called upon those gentlemen to furnish me with a separate estimate for that purpose. Colonel Trumbull has given me his, by which it appears he supplies the troops at eight pence and one third per ration. I not have yet received any from Mr. Livingston; but am informed his contract is at ten pence half-penny. The difference is immense, as it will amount to no less than two hundred pounds per day, for twenty thousand men. It is indeed to be considered that Mr. Livingston's contract is, including every other charge; and that to Mr. Trumbull's must be added store-hire, clerks, and every other contingent expense. But even then it will not amount to so much as Mr. Livingston's, by a penny per ration, which, in the gross, will be something very considerable. I thought it my duty, without prejudice or partiality, to state the matter fairly to Congress, that they might take such order upon it as to them shall seem necessary. I cannot however, in justice to Mr. Trumbull, help adding that he has been indefatigable in supplying the army; and I believe, from his connexions in New-England, is able to do it on as good terms as any person in America.

The several matters contained in the foregoing, I must beg the early attention of Congress to; and that I may be favored with an answer as soon as possible.

I have the honor to be, &c. G. W.

Sir, *New-York, April* 23, 1776.

IN a letter which I had the honor to receive from Congress some considerable time ago, they were pleased to ask what rank aides-de-camp bore in the army? from whence I concluded that they had adverted to the extraordinary trouble and confinement of those gentlemen, with a view to make them an adequate allowance. But nothing being since done or said of the matter, I take the liberty,—unsolicited by,

and

and unknown to my aides-de-camp,—to inform your honorable body that their pay is not by any means equal to their trouble and confinement.

No perſon wiſhes more to ſave money to the public, than I do: and no perſon has aimed more at it. But there are ſome caſes in which parſimony may be ill placed; and this I take to be one. Aides-de-camp are perſons in whom entire confidence muſt be placed: it requires men of abilities to execute the duties with propriety and diſpatch, where there is ſuch a multiplicity of buſineſs, as muſt attend the commander-in-chief of ſuch an army as ours: and perſuaded I am, that nothing but the zeal of thoſe gentlemen (who live with me, and act in this capacity) for the great American cauſe,—and perſonal attachment to me,—has induced them to undergo the trouble and confinement they have experienced ſince they have become members of my family.

I give into no kind of amuſements myſelf; and conſequently thoſe about me can have none, but are confined from morning till eve, hearing and anſwering the applications and letters of one and another, which will now, I expect, receive a pretty conſiderable addition, as the buſineſs of the northern and eaſtern departments (if I continue here) muſt, I ſuppoſe, paſs through my hands. If theſe gentlemen had the ſame relaxation from duty as other officers have in their common routine, there would not be ſo much in it. But, to have the mind always upon the ſtretch,—ſcarce ever unbent,—and no hours for recreation,—makes a material odds. Knowing this, and at the ſame time how inadequate the pay is, I can ſcarce find inclination to impoſe the neceſſary duties of their office upon them. To what I have here ſaid, this further remark may be made, and is a matter of no ſmall concernment to me, and, in its conſequences, to the public;—and that is, that, while the duty is hard and the pay ſmall, it is not to be wondered at, if there ſhould be found a promptneſs in them to ſeek preferment, or in me to do juſtice to them by facilitating their views; by which means I muſt loſe their aid when they have it moſt in their power to aſſiſt me.—Influenced by theſe motives, I have taken the liberty of laying the matter fully, and with all due deference, before your honorable body, not doubting its meeting with a patient hearing.

I am, ſir, with the greateſt reſpect, &c.   G. W.

Sir,   *New-York, April* 23, 1776.

THAT I might be in readineſs to take the field in the ſpring, and prepared for any ſervice Congreſs ſhould think proper to ſend me upon, this campaign,—I deſired colonel Reed, when he left Cambridge in the fall, to get me a ſet of camp equipage, tents, and a baggage-waggon, made at Philadelphia under his own inſpection, and ſent to me. This, he informs me, is now done, and ready to come on. I have therefore to beg the favor of Congreſs, through you, to order payment of them from the treaſury, as it will ſave the expenſe and hazard of a remittance from hence, where we ſtand much in need of every farthing we have.

I have the honor to be, &c.   G. W.

Sir,   *New-York, April* 25, 1776.

I Received by laſt evening's poſt a letter from Joſhua Wentworth, eſquire, of Portſmouth, whom I had appointed agent for our little fleet in that province. It is dated the fifteenth inſtant; an extract from which I have the honor of tranſcribing for your peruſal.

"The third inſtant, commodore Manly brought in the brigantine Elizabeth, one of the third diviſion which ſailed from Nantaſket, with a valuable cargo of Engliſh goods, and a few hogſheads of rum and ſugar, by a Mr. J * * *, who was paſſenger, part freighter, and a very tory. Suppoſe the cargo worth twenty thouſand pounds ſterling. Thoſe goods are, the greater part, owned by the late inhabitants of Boſton,

and

and by some that were inhabitants when the troops left it,—
the residue by this Mr. J * * *, and others of the same cast.
The complicate state of this prize required my immediate
setting off for Boston, expecting I might find some directions
for my government there ; when I waited on general Ward,
who was obliging enough to give me his opinion (but not
able to direct, having received no instructions to the point)
that the vessel and cargo must be libelled, and a dividend to
the captors would follow, of all such goods as might be legally claimed by the friends to America ; and those that were
the property of them inimical, might be decreed forfeited.
Upon further inquiry, I was informed a resolve passed in
Congress that all vessels and goods, retaken previous to a
condemnation by a British court of admiralty, were liable to
a partial decree (by every colony judge) to the captors,—
not more than one-third, nor less than one-fourth. The
present prize falls under this resolve : and any other, that
[*makes the*] property of our internal enemies liable to a full
confiscation, may be necessary for my government : therefore
shall be much obliged by your full direction of this capture,
and a copy of the continental resolves thereon. This brigantine is owned by a Mr. Richard Hart of this town, taken on
her return from the West Indies last October, and carried
into Boston, not condemned. The rum on board are seventeen hogsheads,—and four of sugar, not removed out of her
from the time of capture. The other cargo was in general stolen by virtue of general Howe's proclamation
(which undoubtedly you have seen) appointing one C * * *
B * * * superintendant, who, by the way, was taken in
the prize, and is now confined in the Massachusetts colony,
with Mr. J * * * and sundry others, by order of the general
court to whom general Ward delivered them.

" There were a sergeant and twelve privates of the fourth,
or king's own regiment, taken prisoners on board, with the
others, making sixty-three souls. * * *

" There appeared, from the pillage of this cargo by many

of the paſſengers, the property was in him who could ſecret the moſt. For, when examining the cheſts and bedding of the priſoners, I found great quantity of goods that they had collected while on board, which were taken out of warehouſes without packing, and hove promiſcuouſly on board the veſſel. Even the ſailors had provided for their diſpoſal at pleaſure. In fact, the deſtruction of property, under cover of general Howe's proclamation, is unparalleled. * * *

"I am now diſcharging the cargo, as it is in a periſhing ſituation; and, when ſelected, and the regular courſe purſued through the admiralty, ſhall advertiſe agreeable to his excellency's inſtructions to general Ward, who was obliging enough to give me an abſtract.

"The general court of this province, finding a difficulty in making a code of laws for the admiralty-court, did not complete that inſtitution their laſt ſeſſion, when they adjourned to June; which lapſe of time will not admit my facilitating the diſpoſal of the prizes under my care, ſo early as I could wiſh, for the ſafety of part of the intereſt of the Suſanna's cargo, viz. the porter, which I fear may be ſpoiled by lying ſo long,—it not having equal body to that commonly imported for ſale;—which induces me to deſire your direction for a diſpoſal of that article either at private or public ſale."

That, ſir, is an exact copy of part of Mr. Wentworth's letter to Mr. Moylan. I now requeſt you will pleaſe to direct me, in what manner I ſhall inſtruct the agent reſpecting the complicated cargo, and whether he may be empowered to diſpoſe of the porter or any other articles on board the prizes under his care, which the delay of eſtabliſhing the court of admiralty may make liable to periſh.

I have not yet heard that there has been any trial of the prizes carried into Maſſachuſetts-Bay. This procraſtination is attended with very bad conſequences. Some of the veſſels I had fitted out are now laid up, the crews being diſſatisfied that

that they cannot get their prize-money. I have tired the Congress upon this subject: but the importance of it makes me again mention, that, if a summary way of proceeding is not resolved on, it will be impossible to get our vessels manned. I must also mention to you, sir, that captain Manly and his crew are desirous to know when they may expect their part of the value of the ordnance stores taken last fall. They are anxious to know what the amount may be. As the inventory of that cargo is in the hands of Congress, I would humbly submit it to them, whether a valuation thereof should not be made, and the captors' dividend be remitted them as soon as possible. It will give them spirit, and encourage them to be alert in looking out for other prizes.

Several officers belonging to the regiments raised in these middle colonies inform me that their men (notwithstanding their agreement) begin to murmur at the distinction of pay made between them and the regiments from the eastward. I would be glad that the Congress would attend to this in time, lest it may get to such a pitch as will make it difficult to suppress. They argue that they perform the same duty, undergo the same fatigue, and receive five dollars, when the eastern regiments receive six dollars and two-thirds per month. For my own part, I wish they were all upon the same footing: for, if the British army will not face this way, it will be necessary to detach a great part of our troops: in that case, I would, for many reasons, be sorry there should be any distinctions of regiments that are all in the pay of the United Colonies.

The deficiency of arms (in the New-York regiments especially) is very great. If I am rightly informed, there are scarce as many in colonel Ritzema's regiment as will arm one company.—Can the Congress remedy this evil? If they can, there should not a moment be lost in effecting it, as our strength at present is, in reality, on paper only. Should we think of discharging those men who are without arms, the remedy would be worse than the disease: for, by vigorous exertions, I hope arms may be procured; and I well know that the raising men is exceeding difficult, especially to be engaged during the continuance of the war, which is the footing on which colonel Ritzema's regiment is engaged.

April 26.——I had wrote thus far before I was honored with your favor of the twenty-third instant. In obedience to the order therein contained, I have directed six regiments more for Canada, which will embark as soon as vessels and other necessaries can be provided. These regiments will be commanded by general Sullivan. I shall give him instructions to join the forces in that country under general Thomas, as soon as possible.

With respect to sending more troops to that country, I am really at a loss what to advise, as it is impossible at present to know the designs of the enemy. Should they send the whole force under general Howe up the river St. Laurence to relieve Quebec and recover Canada, the troops gone and now going will be insufficient to stop their progress: and should they think proper to send that or an equal force this way from Great Britain for the purpose of possessing this city and securing the navigation of Hudson's river, the troops left here will not be sufficient to oppose them : and yet, for any thing we know, I think it not improbable they may attempt both,—both being of the greatest importance to to them,—if they have men.

I could wish indeed that the army in Canada should be more powerfully reinforced: at the same time I am conscious that the trusting this important post (which is now become the grand magazine of America) to the handful of men remaining here, is running too great a risk: The securing this post and Hudson's river is to us also of so great importance, that I cannot at present advise the sending any more troops from hence:—on the contrary, the general officers now here, whom I thought it my duty to consult, think it absolutely necessary to increase the army at this
place

place with at least ten thousand men, especially when it is considered, that, from this place only, the army in Canada must draw its supplies of ammunition, provisions, and, most probably, of men; and that all reinforcements can be sent from hence much easier than from any other place.—By the inclosed return, you will see the state of the army here, and that the number of effective men is far short of what the Congress must have expected.

I have found it necessary to order colonel Dayton's regiment from New-Jersey to march as one of the six to Canada: wherefore I must recommend it to Congress to order two companies of one of the regiments still in Pennsylvania to march to Cape-May, which can be done much sooner: for, had this destination of that regiment not taken place, it would have been very inconvenient to have detached two companies from it to that place; as the march would (according to lord Stirling's and other accounts) have been at least two hundred miles from Amboy, and they must have passed within twenty miles of Philadelphia, there being no practicable road along the sea-coast of New-Jersey for their baggage to have passed.

Dr. Potts, who is bearer hereof, was, I understand, appointed director of the hospital for these middle colonies: but the army being removed, with the general hospital, from the eastward, does in course supercede him. He is inclined to go to Canada, where he may be very useful, if a person is not already appointed for that department.—I would humbly beg leave to ask the Congress whether, in all these appointments, it would not be best to have but one chief, to whom all the others should be subordinate.

I have the honor to be, &c.   G. W.

Sir,   *New-York, April* 30, 1776.

I MEAN, through you, to do myself the honor of laying before Congress a copy of an address transmitted them some time ago by the assembly of Rhode-Island, which governor Cooke favored me with in the month of January, at the same time requesting me to interest myself in procuring a body of forces on the continental establishment, for the defence of that colony. I doubt not but the address and the subject of it have had the attention and consideration of Congress before now. But if they have not decided upon the matter, I would beg leave to mention that I have made inquiry into the situation and condition of the colony, and find it to be as stated in the address; and, with all deference to the opinion of Congress, conceive it highly necessary and expedient that they should adopt some measures for relieving their distress, and granting the aid prayed for. The importance of it in the chain of the union,—its extensive sea-coast, affording harbors for our shipping and vessels, at the same time exposing and subjecting the inhabitants to the ravages and depredations of our enemies,—the zeal and attachment which it has shewn, and which still actuates it, towards the common cause,—their incapacity to pay a sufficient number of men for its defence, should they be able to furnish them after so many engaged in other services;—these, and many other reasons which are too obvious to be mentioned, plead powerfully for the notice and attention of Congress, and seem to me to claim their support.

Having thus stated the matter to Congress for their consideration, agreeable to my promise to governor Cooke when I had the honor of seeing him on my way here,—I shall leave it with them, not doubting but they will duly weigh its importance, and give such assistance as they may think reasonable and just.—What they chiefly wish for is that the troops they have raised may be taken into continental pay, and commanding officers appointed by Congress.

I have the honor to be, &c.   G. W.

Sir, New-York, *May* 5, 1776.

I AM honored with your favor of the thirtieth ultimo, and observe what Congress have done respecting the settlement of the paymaster's accounts. This seems expedient, as he is out of office, and, I am certain, will be attended with but little if any difficulty; nothing more being necessary, than to compare the warrants with his debits, and the receipts he has given, with his credits. I wish every other settlement as easy, and that a committee was appointed to examine and audit the accounts upon which the warrants are founded, particularly those of the quarter-master and commissary generals. They are long and of high amount, consisting of a variety of charges,—of course more intricate,—and will require time and an extraordinary degree of attention to adjust and liquidate in a proper manner.—Upon this subject, I did myself the honor to write you a considerable time ago.

Having had several complaints from the officers in the eastern regiments who have been and are engaged in recruiting, about the expense attending it, and for which they have never yet been allowed any thing, though the officers in these governments have, as I am informed,—I shall be glad to know whether the allowance of ten shillings, granted to the officers for every man enlisted, by the resolve of Congress in [*January*], is general and indiscriminate, or confined to the middle districts.—If general, must I have retrospect to the time of the resolve, and pay for the services since, or only for future enlistments?

In a letter I wrote to Congress the twenty-fifth of December, I inclosed one I had received from Jacob Bailey, esquire, about opening a road from Newbury to Canada. I have received another of the fifteenth ultimo: and, from his account and the intelligence I have from others upon inquiry, I have no doubt of the practicability of the measure; and am well informed that the distance will be considerably shortened, insomuch so much that our people going from any part of the New-England governments eastward of Connecticut-river, to Canada, or returning from thence home, will perform their march in five or six days less time than by coming or going any way now used. Add to this that the road may be so conducted (as it is said) as to go to the river Missisque, from whence the water-carriage to St. John's is good, except forty odd miles,—or be carried so far to the northward, as to keep clear of the lakes altogether, and afford an easy pass into Canada at all seasons. The advantage resulting from this route being so great and important, I have advanced colonel Bailey two hundred and fifty pounds to begin with, and directed him to execute his plan. No doubt it will require a considerable advance to accomplish it: but that will be soon sunk. The expense saved, by taking off six days' pay and provisions from the soldiers returning to the eastern governments at the expiration of this campaign, will be almost if not more than equal to the charge incurred in opening it. If not,—as in all probability there will be often a necessity for sending detachments of our troops to Canada from those governments, and for others to return, it will soon be repaid.

By a letter from general Schuyler, of the twenty-seventh ultimo, I find general Thompson and his brigade were at Albany;—general Sullivan with the last (except three or four companies of colonel Wayne's regiment, not yet come) is embarked and gone, and probably will be soon there. I am apprehensive, from general Schuyler's account, that they will not proceed with the wished-for expedition, owing to a difficulty in getting teams and provender for cattle necessary to carry their baggage, and a scarcity of batteaux at the lakes for so large a number, though he is taking the utmost pains to procure them. Should they be stopped for any time, it will be exceedingly unfortunate, as their going from hence has weakened us here much, and our army in Canada will not be strengthened.

I have

I have sent with the last brigade sixty barrels of powder, and other stores and intrenching tools, a supply being asked for; also the chain for a boom at the narrows of Richelieu, and the three boxes of money brought by Mr. Hanson; and have wrote to general Schuyler to have the boom fixed as soon as possible.—The commissary too has forwarded about eight hundred barrels of pork, and is in expectation of a further quantity from Connecticut, which will go on without stopping here.

As the magazine from whence the northern and eastern armies will occasionally receive supplies of powder will probably be here, and our stock is low and inconsiderable, being much reduced by the sixty barrels sent to Canada, I shall be glad to have a quantity immediately forwarded. Our stores should be great: for if the enemy make an attack upon the town, or attempt to go up the North-river, the expenditure will be very considerable. Money too is much wanted:— the regiments that are paid have only received to the first of April, except those of Pennsylvania and Jersey which are gone to Canada: they are paid to the last of April. By a letter from general Ward, I find his chest is just exhausted; the money which was left with him for the payment of the five regiments at Boston and Beverly being almost expended by large draughts in favor of the commissary and quartermaster, and in fitting out the armed vessels.

I would here ask a question, to wit, whether, as Mr. Warren's commission is superceded by Mr. Palfrey's appointment, it will not be necessary to fix upon some person to pay the troops there: or are the payments to go through his hands? —He does not incline to do any thing in the affair without the direction of Congress.

I have inclosed you a return of the last brigade detached, and also of the forces remaining here. And as it is a matof much importance to know the whole of our strength from time to time, and to see it at one view, for regulating our movements with propriety, I wish it were a direction from
Congress

Congress to the commanding officers in the different districts to make monthly returns to the commander-in-chief of the continental army, of the state of the troops in their departments, and also of the military stores. Such direction will probably make them more attentive than they otherwise would be.—I could not get a return of the army in Canada all last year.

I beg leave to lay before Congress a copy of the proceedings of a court-martial upon lieutenant * * * * of the second regiment, and of his defence,—which I should not have troubled them with, had I not conceived the court's sentence, upon the facts stated in the proceedings, of a singular nature, to be by no means adequate to the enormity of his offence, and to be of exceeding dangerous and pernicious tendency. Upon these principles I thought it my duty to transmit the proceedings to them, in order that they may form such a judgment upon the facts stated, as they may conceive right and just, and advancive of the public good.— At the same time I would mention to Congress that I think it of material consequence that they should pass a resolve, cutting off the right of succession in the military line from one rank to another, which is claimed by many upon the happening of vacancies,—(upon which principle this offence seems to have originated in a great measure, and the extraordinary judgment in this instance to be founded)—declaring that no succession or promotion can take place upon any vacancy, without a continental commission giving and authorising it. It is of much consequence to check and entirely suppress this opinion and claim, which is becoming too prevalent, and has an obvious tendency to introduce mutiny and disorder;—or, if they conceive the claim good, and that it should take place, that they will declare it so, that the point may be settled and known in future.

I have the honor to be, &c.   G. W.

SIR,

Sir,   New-York, *May* 5, 1776.

I HAVE so often and so fully communicated my want of arms to Congress, that I should not have given them the trouble of receiving another letter upon this subject at this time, but for the particular application of colonel Wayne of Pennsylvania, who has pointed out a method by which he thinks they may be obtained.

In the hands of the committee of safety at Philadelphia, there are, according to colonel Wayne's account, not less than two or three thousand stand of arms for provincial use. From hence he thinks a number might be borrowed by Congress, provided they are replaced with continental arms as they are brought into the magazine in that city. At a crisis so important as this, such a loan might be attended with the most signal advantages,—while the defenceless state of the regiments, if no relief can be had, may be productive of fatal consequences.

To give Congress some idea of our situation with respect to arms—(and justice to my own character requires that it should be known to them, although the world at large will form their opinion of our strength from numbers, without attending to circumstances)—it may not be amiss to inclose a copy of a return which I received a few days ago from the forts in the Highlands, and add, that, by a report from colonel Ritzema's regiment, of the twenty-ninth ultimo, there appeared to be only ninety-seven firelocks and seven bayonets belonging thereto; and that all the regiments from the eastward are deficient from twenty to fifty of the former. Four of those companies at the fortifications in the Highlands belong to colonel Clinton's regiment: but in what condition the residue are on account of arms, and how colonel Wynkoop's men are provided, I cannot undertake to say, but am told, most miserably; as colonel Dayton's of New-Jersey and colonel Wayne's of Pennsylvania also are. This, sir, is a true though melancholy description of our situation. The propriety

propriety therefore of keeping arms in ſtore when men in actual pay are in want of them, and who (it is to be preſumed) will, as they ought, bear the heat and burden of the day, is ſubmitted with all due deference to the ſuperior judgment of others.

I cannot, by all the inquiries I have been able to make, learn what number of arms have been taken from the tories, where they lie, or how they are to be got at. The committee of ſafety for this colony have aſſured me that no exertions of theirs ſhall be wanting to procure arms: but our ſufferings in the mean while may prove fatal, as men without are in a manner uſeleſs. I have therefore thoughts of employing an agent whoſe ſole buſineſs it ſhall be to ride through the middle and interior parts of theſe governments, for the purpoſe of buying up ſuch arms as the inhabitants may incline to ſell, and are fit for uſe.

The deſigns of the enemy are too much behind the curtain for me to form any accurate opinion of their plan of operations for the ſummer's campaign. We are left to wander therefore in the field of conjecture: and as no place (all its conſequences conſidered) ſeemed of more importance in the execution of their grand plan, than poſſeſſing themſelves of Hudſon's river, I thought it adviſable to remove with the continental army to this city ſo ſoon as the king's troops evacuated Boſton. But if Congreſs, from their knowledge, information, or belief, think it beſt for the general good of the ſervice that I ſhould go to the northward or elſewhere, they are convinced, I hope, that they have nothing more to do than ſignify their commands.—With the greateſt reſpect, I have the honor to be, &c. G. W.

Sir, *New-York, May* 7, 1776.

AT a quarter after ſeven this evening, I received by expreſs a letter from Thomas Cuſhing, eſquire, chairman of a committee of the honorable general court, covering one to them from the committee of Salem; copies of which I do myself the honor to lay before Congress, that they may judge of the intelligence contained therein, and direct such measures to be taken upon the occasion as they may think proper and necessary.

I would observe, that, supposing captain Lee's account to be true in part, I think there must be a mistake either in the number of troops or the transport ships. If there are no more ships than what are mentioned, it is certain there cannot be so many troops. Of this, however, Congress can judge as well as myself; and I submit to them, whether, upon the whole of the circumstances, and the uncertainty of their destination (if they were seen at all), they chuse that any forces shall be detached from hence, as they will see, from the returns transmitted yesterday, that the number of men now here is but small and inconsiderable; and (what is to be regretted) no small part of these without arms.—Perhaps, by dividing and subdividing our force too much, we shall have no one post sufficiently guarded.

I shall wait their direction; and, whatever their order is, shall comply with it as soon as possible.

I have the honor to be, &c. G. W.

P. S. I have by the same express a letter from general Ward, containing a similar account to that from the Salem committee, and by way of captain Lee.

Should the commissioners arrive that are mentioned, how are they to be received and treated?—I wish the direction of Congress upon the subject, by return of the bearer.

Sir, *New-York, May* 11, 1776.

I AM now to acknowledge the receipt of your favors of the fourth and seventh instant with their several inclosures, and am exceedingly glad, that, before the resolution respecting lieutenant-colonel Ogden came to hand, I had ordered him to join his regiment, and had quelled a disagreeable

greeable spirit both of mutiny and defertion, which had taken place and feemed to be rifing to a great degree in confequence of it. In order to effect it, I had the regiment paraded, and ordered two more at the fame time under arms, convinced them of their error and ill conduct, and obtained a promife for their good behavior in future. To fuch of the men as had abfconded I gave pardons, on their affurances to return to their duty again.

In my letter of the fifth inftant which I had the honor of addreffing you, I mentioned to Congrefs the refractory and mutinous conduct of lieutenant * * * * of the fecond regiment, and laid before them a copy of the proceedings of a court-martial upon him, and of his defence, with a view that fuch meafures might be adopted as they fhould think adequate to his crime.—I would now beg leave to inform them, that, fince then, he has appeared fenfible of his mifconduct; and having made a written acknowledgment of his offence, and begged pardon for it (as by the inclofed copy will appear), I thought it beft to releafe him from his confinement, and have ordered him to join his regiment; which I hope will meet their approbation, and render any determination, as to him, unneceffary;—obferving at the fame time that I have endeavored, and, I flatter myfelf, not ineffectually, to fupport their authority, and a due fubordination in the army, I have found it of importance and highly expedient to yield many points in fact, without feeming to have done it,—and this, to avoid bringing on a too frequent difcuffion of matters, which, in a political view, ought to be kept a little behind the curtain, and not be made too much the fubjects of difquifition.—Time only can eradicate and overcome cuftoms and prejudices of long ftanding: they muft be got the better of, by flow and gradual advances.

I would here take occafion to fuggeft to Congrefs (not wifhing or meaning of myfelf to affume the fmalleft degree of power in any inftance) the propriety and neceffity of having their fentiments refpecting the filling up the vacancies

cancies and issuing commissions to officers, especially to those under the rank of field officers. Had I literally complied with the directions given upon this subject when I first engaged in the service, and which I conceived to be superceded by a subsequent resolve for forming the army upon the present establishment, I must have employed one clerk for no other business than issuing warrants of appointment, and giving information to Congress for their confirmation or refusal. It being evident from the necessity of the thing, that there will be frequent changes and vacancies in office, from death and a variety of other causes, I now submit it to them, and pray their direction whether I am to pursue that mode and all the ceremonies attending it, or to be at liberty to fill up and grant commissions at once to such as may be fit and proper persons to succeed. * * *

Before I have done, with the utmost deference and respect I would beg leave to remind Congress of my former letters and applications respecting the appointment of proper persons to superintend and take direction of such prisoners as have already fallen and will fall into our hands in the course of the war,—being fully convinced, that, if there were persons appointed who would take the whole management of them under their care, the continent would save a considerable sum of money by it, and the prisoners be better treated and provided with real necessaries than they now are;—and shall take the liberty to add that it appears to me a matter of much importance, and worthy of consideration, that particular and proper places of security should be fixed on and established in the interior parts of the different governments for their reception.

Such establishments are agreeable to the practice and usage of the English and other nations, and are founded on principles of necessity and public utility. The advantages which will arise from them are obvious and many:—I shall only mention two or three.—They will tend much to prevent escapes (which are difficult to effect when the public is once advertised

advertised that the prisoners are restrained to a few stated and well-known places, and not permitted to go from thence], and the more ingenious among them from disseminating and spreading their artful and pernicious intrigues and opinions throughout the country, which would influence the weaker and wavering part of mankind, and meet with but too favorable a hearing. Further, it will be less in their power to join and assist our enemies in cases of invasion, and will give us an opportunity always to know, from the returns of those appointed to superintend them, what number we have in possession, the force sufficient to check and suppress their hostile views in times of emergency, and the expenses necessary for their maintenance and support. Many other reasons might be adduced to prove the necessity and expediency of the measure:—I shall only subjoin one more, and then have done on the subject,—which is, that many of the towns where prisoners have been already sent, not having convenience for or the means of keeping them, complain they are burdensome; and have become careless, inattentive, and altogether indifferent whether they escape or not; and those of them that are restricted to a closer confinement (the limits of jail) are neglected, and not treated with that care and regard which Congress wish.

I have not received further intelligence of the German troops since my letter of the seventh instant, covering Mr. Cushing's dispatches. But, lest the account of their coming should be true, may it not be advisable and good policy to raise some companies of our Germans to send among them when they arrive, for exciting a spirit of disaffection and desertion?—If a few sensible and trusty fellows could get with them, I should think they would have great weight and influence with the common soldiery, who certainly have no enmity towards us, having received no injury nor cause of quarrel from us. The measure having occurred, and appearing to me expedient, I thought it prudent to mention it for the consideration of Congress.

Having

Having received a letter from general Ward, advising that Congress have accepted his resignation, and praying to be relieved,—and it being necessary that a general officer should be sent to take the command of the troops at Boston, especially if the army should arrive which is talked of, and which some consider as a probable event,—I must beg leave to recommend to Congress the appointment of some brigadier-generals, not having more here (nor so many at this time) than are essential to the government and conducting the forces and the works that are carrying on. Generals Sullivan and Thompson being ordered to Canada, I cannot spare one more general officer from hence without injuring the service greatly, and leaving the army here without a sufficient number.

Having frequent applications from the committee of safety and others, about an exchange of prisoners, and not having authority to pursue any other mode in this instance, than that marked out by a resolve of Congress some considerable time ago, I hope they will pardon me when I wish them to take under consideration such parts of my letter of the twenty-second ultimo as relate to this subject; and for their determination upon it. I shall then have it in my power to give explicit and satisfactory answers to those who shall apply.—I am, sir, &c. G. W.

Sir, New-York, *May* 15, 1776.

SINCE my last of the eleventh instant which I had the honor to address you, nothing of moment or importance has occurred; and the principal design of this is to communicate to Congress the intelligence I received last night from general Schuyler by a letter of the tenth, respecting the progress of our troops in getting towards Canada, not doubting of their impatience and anxiety to hear of it and of every thing relating to the expedition. For their more particular information and satisfaction, I have done myself the pleasure to extract the substance of his letter on this head, which is as follows:—" that general Thompson, with the last of his brigade, on the morning of tuesday se'nnight, embarked at Fort-George; and, in the evening of the next day, general Sullivan arrived at Albany;—that he had ordered an additional number of carpenters to assist in building boats; who, finishing eight every day, would have a hundred and ten complete by the twenty-first, before which he was fearful the last of general Sullivan's brigade could not embark;—that they would carry thirty men each, besides the baggage, ammunition, and intrenching tools." * * *

He also informs, " that the sixty barrels of powder had arrived, and would be forwarded that day;—that the first regiment of general Sullivan's brigade marched that morning; and that the intrenching tools and about six hundred barrels of pork were also gone on;—that he cannot possibly send more than half of the three hundred thousand dollars into Canada (being greatly in debt on the public account, and the creditors exceedingly clamorous and importunate for payment), which sum he hopes will be sufficient till the Canadians agree to take our paper currency, to which they are much averse, and of which he is exceedingly doubtful;—that he had got the chain, and would forward it that day to general Arnold, with orders to fix it at the rapids of Richelieu." He adds " that he had reviewed general Sullivan's brigade in presence of about two hundred and sixty Indians, who were greatly pleased with the order and regularity of the troops, and surprised at the number, which, the tories had industriously propagated, consisted only of three companies, and that they were kept always walking the streets, to induce them to believe their number was much greater than it really was."

I have inclosed a copy of general Schuyler's instructions to James Price, esquire, deputy commissary-general, for the regulation of his conduct in that department, which I received last night, and which general Schuyler requested

me

me to forward you.—I also beg leave to lay before Congress a copy of a letter from Samuel Stringer, director of one of the hospitals, purporting an application for an increase of surgeons'-mates, &c, an estimate of which is also inclosed; and submit it to them, what number must be sent from hence or got elsewhere. It is highly probable that many more will be wanted in Canada than are already there, on account of the late augmentation of the army: but I thought it most advisable to make his requisition known to Congress, and to take their order and direction upon it.—As to the medicines, I shall speak to Dr. Morgan (not yet arrived) as soon as he comes, and order him to forward such as may be necessary and can be possibly spared.

I have the honor to be, &c. G. W.

Sir, *New-York, May* 17, 1776.

I THIS moment received by express from general Schuyler an account of the melancholy prospect and reverse of our affairs in Canada: and presuming that the letters which accompany this will give Congress full information upon the subject, I shall only add that general Schuyler, in pursuance of orders from the honorable commissioners, has directed brigadier-general Sullivan to halt his brigade; as a further reinforcement (on account of the scarcity of provisions) would not relieve, but contribute greatly to distress our troops already in Canada. Before he received these orders, all the brigade, except Dayton's and Wayne's regiments, had left Albany: but I suppose he will be able to stop their march.

By my letter of the fifteenth, Congress will perceive the quantity of pork already gone from hence: and the commissary has assured me that he will forward a further supply as soon as it can be possibly collected. I had also directed five tons of lead to be sent to general Schuyler for the Canada expedition, before I received this unfortunate account, which was as much as could be spared for the present; you stock being inconsiderable in proportion to the demand we may reasonably expect for it); and shall do every thing in my power to relieve our affairs from their present distressed and melancholy situation in that quarter, which occurs to me and appears necessary.

I am also to acknowledge the receipt of your favors of the tenth and thirteenth instant, with their several inclosures. The money, accompanying the latter, came to the paymaster's hands safe.—I have the honor to be, &c. G. W.

Sir, *New-York, May* 18, 1776.

I DO myself the honor to transmit to you the inclosed letters and papers I received this morning in the state they now are, which contain sundry matters of intelligence of the most interesting nature. As the consideration of them may lead to important consequences and the adoption of several measures in the military line, I have thought it advisable for general Gates to attend Congress—(he will follow to-morrow, and satisfy, and explain to them some points they may wish to be informed of in the course of their deliberations)—not having an opportunity at this time to submit my thoughts to them upon these interesting accounts.

I have the honor to be, &c. G. W.

Sir, *New-York, May* 19, 1776.

THIS will be delivered you by general Gates who sets out to-day for Congress, agreeable to my letter of yesterday. I have committed to him the heads of sundry matters to lay before Congress for their consideration, which, from the interesting intelligence contained in my last, appear to me of the utmost importance, and to demand their most early and serious attention.

Sensible that I have omitted to set down many things necessary, and which probably, when deliberating, they will
with

wish to be acquainted with,—and not conceiving myself at liberty to depart from my post (though to attend them), without their previous approbation,—I have requested general Gates to subjoin such hints of his own, as he may apprehend material. His military experience and intimate acquaintance with the situation of our affairs will enable him to give Congress the fullest satisfaction about the measures necessary to be adopted at this alarming crisis; and, with his zeal and attachment to the cause of America, have a claim to their notice and favors.

When Congress shall have come to a determination on the subject of this letter, and such parts of my former letters as have not been determined on, you will be pleased to honor me with the result.—I am, sir, &c. G. W.

Sir, New-York, May 20, 1776.

YOUR favor of the sixteenth, with several resolutions of Congress therein inclosed, I had not the honor to receive till last night. Before the receipt, I did not think myself at liberty to wait on Congress, although I wished to do it; and therefore the more readily consented to general Gates's attendance, as I knew there were many matters which could be better explained in a personal interview than in whole volumes of letters. He accordingly set out for Philadelphia yesterday morning, and must have been too far advanced on his journey (as he proposed expedition) to be overtaken.

I shall, if I can settle some matters which are in agitation with the provincial Congress here, follow to-morrow or next day; and therefore, with every sentiment of regard, attachment, and gratitude to Congress for their kind attention to the means which they think may be conducive to my health, and with particular thanks to you for the politeness of your invitation to your house, conclude, dear sir, your most obedient, &c. G. W.

Sir, *Philadelphia, June* 3, 1776.

I HAVE perufed the petition preferred by the independent corps of Bofton, and beg leave, through you, to inform Congrefs that the five regiments there are extremely deficient in arms, as are many other regiments in continental pay; and fubmit it to their confideration, whether any part of the arms lately taken, under thefe circumftances, fhould be delivered to the gentlemen applying for them;—determining at the fame time, that whatever decifion they come to will be agreeable to me, and be literally complied with, by, fir, your moft obedient, &c. G. W.

Sir, *New-York, June* 7, 1776.

I DO myfelf the honor to inform Congrefs that I arrived here yefterday afternoon about one o'clock, and found all in a ftate of peace and quiet. I had not time to view the works carrying on, and thofe ordered to be begun when I went away; but have reafon to believe, from the report of fuch of the general and other officers as I had the pleafure to fee, that they have been profecuted and forwarded with all poffible diligence and difpatch.

I am much concerned for the fituation of our affairs in Canada, and am fearful, ere this, it is much worfe than was firft reported at Philadelphia. The intelligence from thence, in a letter from captain Wilkinfon of the fecond regiment, to general Greene, is truly alarming. It not only confirms the account of colonel Biddle and major Sherburne's defeat, but feems to forebode general Arnold's, with the lofs of Montreal.—I have inclofed a copy of the letter, which will but too well fhew that there is foundation for my apprehenfions.

On wednefday evening I received an exprefs from general Schuyler, with fundry papers refpecting fir John Johnfton, which I have not time to copy, as the poft is juft going off, but

but will do myself the honor of transmitting you as soon as I possibly can.

Before I left Philadelphia, I employed a person to superintend the building of the gondolas which Congress had resolved on for this place. He is arrived, and all things seem to be in a proper channel for facilitating the work: but when they are done, we shall be in much want of guns, having never received any of those taken by commodore Hopkins.

Be pleased to mention me to Congress with the utmost respect; and I am, sir, with every sentiment of regard and esteem, your and their most obedient servant, G. W.

P. S. I this minute received your favor of the fifth instant.—I am in need of commissions, and beg Congress to point out precisely the line I am to pursue in filling them up. This I mentioned in my letter of the eleventh ultimo. —I am much pleased at the fortunate captures, and the generous conduct of the owners and masters, for the tender of the money to Congress.

Sir, *June* 8, 1776.

IN my letter of yesterday which I had the honor of addressing you, and which was designed to have gone by post, but was prevented by his departure before the usual time, I mentioned my having received by express a letter and sundry papers from general Schuyler, respecting sir John Johnston, copies of which I herewith transmit you for your inspection and perusal. They will shew you what measures were planned and attempted for apprehending him, and securing the Scotch Highlanders in Tryon county.

Having heard that the troops at Boston are extremely uneasy and almost mutinous for want of pay (several months being now due), I must take the liberty to repeat a question contained in my letter of the fifth ultimo,—" what mode is to be pursued respecting it? whether is money to be sent

from

from hence by the paymaster-general, or some person subordinate to him to be appointed there for that purpose?—I expected some direction would have been given in this instance, long ere this, from what was contained in yours accompanying (or about the time of) the last remittance. I presume it has been omitted by reason of the multiplicity of important business before Congress.

In perusing the several resolves you honored me with when at Philadelphia and since my return, I find one allowing a chief engineer for the army in a separate department. The service requiring many of them, I wish Congress, if they know any persons skilled in this business, would appoint them. General Schuyler has frequently applied, and suggested the necessity of having some in Canada.—I myself know of none.

I also find there is a resolve of the third of June for taking Indians into the service, which, if literally construed, confines them to that in Canada.—Is that the meaning of Congress, or that the commander-in-chief may order their service to any place he may think necessary?

In respect to the establishing expresses between the several continental posts,—who is to do it?—the resolve does not say.—Is it expected by Congress that I should?—Whoever the work is assigned to, I think, should execute it with the utmost dispatch. The late imperfect and contradictory accounts respecting our defeat at the Cedars strongly point out the necessity there is for it. No intelligence is yet come from any officer in command there (and most probably for want of a proper channel to convey it), though this misfortune happened so long ago.

When I had the honor of being in Congress, if I mistake not, I heard a resolve read, or was told of one, allowing the New-York troops the same pay as others in the continental service. This, if any such, I do not find; and if there is not such a one, I shall be under some embarrassment, how to pay the militia to be provided by this province. The resolve providing

viding them says they are to be paid, while in service, as other troops are. But if those enlisted heretofore in this province are to receive according to the first establishment, it is a matter of doubt, what the militia are to have.

Before this comes to hand, a hand-bill, containing an account of a victory gained by general Arnold over the party that had defeated colonel Biddle and major Sherburne, will most probably have reached you. I have inquired into the authenticity of this fortunate report, and have found there is no dependence to be put in it; nor do I believe it deserving of the least credit. I shall be happy not to hear the reverse.—I have the honor to be, &c. G. W.

P. S. If Congress have come to any resolution about an allowance to induce men to re-enlist, you will please to favor me with it, as the time the rifle regiment is engaged for is just expired.

As the militia will be coming in, and they will be in much need of covering, please to have all the tents, and cloth proper for making them, that can be procured, forwarded as soon as possible.

Sir, *New-York, June* 9, 1776.

I WAS honored yesterday with your favor of the seventh, with its inclosures. When Dr. Potts arrives, I shall order him to Canada or Lake-George, as may appear most proper. It is certainly necessary that he or Dr. Stringer should go to the former.—The resolve respecting general Wooster's recall I will immediately transmit him, with directions to repair hither without delay.

The situation of our affairs in Canada, as reported by the honorable commissioners, is truly alarming; and I am sorry that my opinion of the ill consequences resulting from the short enlistment of the army should be but too well confirmed by the experience they have had of the want of discipline and order in our soldiery there. This induces me

again

again to wish Congress to determine on a liberal allowance to engage the troops already in service to re-enlist for a longer period, or during the continuance of the war: nor can I forbear expressing my opinion of the propriety of keeping the military chest always supplied with money, as evils of the most interesting nature are often produced for want of a regular payment of troops.—The neglect makes them impatient and uneasy.

I am much surprised at the scarcity of provisions there, particularly of flour; as, from several accounts I had received from thence, I was led to expect that considerable supplies of that article could be procured there. That our misfortunes may not become greater, I have wrote to the commissary to forward more provisions, in addition to those already sent.

An adjutant and quarter-master-general are indispensably necessary, with assistants. The money saved to the continent by their non-appointment will be but small and trifling, when put in competition with the loss for want of them. Colonel Fleming, who acted in the former capacity under general Montgomery, is now here: but his indisposition is such as to render him unfit, at this time, for the post:—it is an important one, and requires vigor and activity to discharge the duties of it. He will be of much service to colonel Reed, the business of whose office will increase considerably by the augmentation of the army.

It will be necessary, too, that the commissaries in Canada, and the deputy quarter-master-generals, should have several assistants and clerks: nor do I think a precise number can be fixed on, as a variety of circumstances may and must occur, to render the number, essential for doing the business in those departments, greater or less at different times. It will be better, I apprehend, to leave it indefinite, and with power to the commanding officer to allow such as may be wanted.

I am still in the dark, how the unfortunate affair ended at the

the Cedars, or on what terms the surrender was made, as the laſt letter from the commiſſioners has reference to a former, and mentions an agreement entered into, which I have not ſeen: but I know of it more than I could wiſh.

I have received from Providence, in conſequence of Mr. Morris's order, as chairman of the ſecret committee of Congreſs, two hundred and thirty-four muſkets, in part of the two hundred and forty-four directed to be ſent. The incloſed copy of a letter from Mr. Brown will account for the deficiency.

I ſhall be much obliged by your ordering a quantity of lead and flints to be immediately forwarded: our demands for both are and will be very preſſing. There are alſo wanted ſome particular and neceſſary medicines to complete our hoſpital cheſts, of which I will get Dr. Morgan to furniſh Congreſs with a liſt, when he writes or waits on them about ſome other matters neceſſary to be fixed in his department.

As general Wooſter, in all probability, will be here in a little time in compliance with the reſolve of Congreſs and my order tranſmitted to him, I wiſh to know what I am to do with him when he comes.

General Schuyler, in his letter of the thirty-firſt ultimo of which I tranſmitted you a copy yeſterday, mentions that ſundry perſons had a deſign to ſeize him as a tory, and probably ſtill have; and wiſhes Congreſs to give him ſome public mark of their approbation, if they are convinced of his zeal and attachment to the cauſe of his country.—Whether he intended that I ſhould communicate his deſire to them, or not, I am not certain: but, ſuppoſing that he did, I muſt beg leave to requeſt that you will lay the paragraph before them, that they may do, in the inſtance of his requiſition, whatever they may judge neceſſary.

I have the honor to be, &c.   G. W.

P. S. If Congreſs have agreed to the report of the committee for allowing the Indians fifty pounds for every priſoner they ſhall take at Niagara, &c, it is material I ſhould

be

be informed of it. This will be a favorable opportunity for them to embrace, to gain poffeffion of Detroit and the other pofts, whilft the enemy are engaged towards Montréal, &c.

Sir, New-York, June 10, 1776.

SINCE I did myfelf the honor of writing to you yefterday, I have had the fatisfaction of feeing, and for a few minutes converfing with, Mr. Chafe and Mr. Carroll from Canada. Their account of our troops and the fituation of affairs in that department cannot poffibly furprife you more than it has done me. But I need not touch upon a fubject which you will be fo well informed of from the fountain-head; nor fhould I have given you the trouble of a letter by this day's poft, but for the diftraction which feems to prevail in the commiffary's department, as well as others in that quarter,—the neceffity of having it under one general direction,—and the diffatisfaction of colonel Trumbull at the allowance made him by Congrefs as an equivalent for his trouble. With refpect to this particular matter, I can only fay that I think he is a man well [*calculated*] for the bufinefs, and that, where a fhilling is faved in the pay, a pound may be loft by mifmanagement in the office; and that his refignation at this time (I mean this campaign) may poffibly be attended with fatal confequences. I therefore humbly fubmit to Congrefs the propriety of handfomely rewarding thofe gentlemen who hold fuch very important, troublefome, and hazardous offices, as commiffary and quarter-mafter.

In fpeaking to the former about the fupplies neceffary for the troops to be raifed, he informed me that the quantity of falt provifions which was fhipping from hence might render his attempts to do it precarious; in confequence of which, I defired him to lay the matter before the convention of this colony, which he will do this day, but in the mean while defired Congrefs might be informed of the matter, which I cannot

cannot better do than in his own words inclosed, and submit the consideration of it to the wisdom of that honorable body.

To Congress I also submit the propriety of keeping the two continental battalions (under the command of colonels Shee and Mc Gaw) at Philadelphia, when there is the greatest probability of a speedy attack upon this place, from the king's troops. The encouragements given by governor Tryon to the disaffected, which are circulated, no one can well tell how,—the movements of these kind of people, which are more easy to perceive than describe,—the confident report, which is said to have come immediately from governor Tryon, and brought by a frigate from Halifax, that the troops at that place were embarking for this,—added to a thousand incidental circumstances, trivial in themselves, but strong from comparison,—leave not a doubt upon my mind but that troops are hourly expected at the Hook.

I had no doubt when I left this city for Philadelphia, but that some measures would have been taken to secure the suspected and dangerous persons of this government before now, and left orders for the military to give every aid to the civil power. But the subject is delicate, and nothing is done in it. We may therefore have internal as well as external enemies to contend with.

I have the honor to be, &c. G. W.

Sir, *Head-Quarters, New-York, June* 13, 1776.

I HAVE the honor of transmitting to Congress a letter which came by express last night from general Schuyler, inclosing a copy of a letter to him from colonel Kirkland. I have likewise inclosed the copy of one directed to general Putnam or the commanding officer at New-York. The representations contained in these letters have induced me, without waiting the determination of Congress, to direct general Schuyler immediately to commence a treaty with the Six-Nations,

and

and to engage them in our intereſt, upon the beſt terms he and his colleagues in commiſſion can procure: and I truſt the urgency of the occaſion will juſtify my proceeding to the Congreſs:—the neceſſity for deciſion and diſpatch in all our meaſures, in my opinion, becomes every day more and more apparent.

The expreſs, Mr. Bennet, was overtaken at Albany by general Schuyler, who had received intelligence at Fort-George that a conſiderable body of Mohawk Indians were coming down the Mohawk river under the conduct of ſir John Johnſton. The general's extreme hurry would not allow him to write: but it ſeems his intention is to collect at Albany a ſufficient force to oppoſe ſir John. I have given him my opinion that colonel Dayton's regiment ſhould be employed in that ſervice, and to ſecure the poſt where Fort-Stanwix formerly ſtood.

In conſequence of an information that ſeveral merchants were exporting ſalt pork and beef from this place, I requeſted the commiſſary to make application to the provincial Congreſs for a reſtraint to be laid on the exportation of thoſe articles, as I apprehended, not only that the enemy might receive ſupplies by the capture of our veſſels, but that our people might ſhortly experience a ſcarcity. The provincial Congreſs have accordingly made a reſolution (a copy of which is incloſed) to ſtop the exportation for fourteen days. They expect Congreſs will in the mean time frame ſome general regulations on this head. They are unwilling (they ſay) to ſubject their conſtituents to partial reſtraints.

I once mentioned to Congreſs that I thought a war-office extremely neceſſary; and they ſeemed inclined to inſtitute one for our army: but the affair ſeems to have been ſince dropped. Give me leave again to inſiſt on the utility and importance of ſuch an eſtabliſhment. The more I reflect upon the ſubject, the more I am convinced of its neceſſity, and that affairs can never be properly conducted without it.

'Tis with pleaſure I receive the reſolve incloſed in your favor

favor of the eleventh instant. One considerable ground of dissatisfaction in the army is thereby removed.

I have employed persons in building the gondolas and rafts which the Congress thought necessary for the defence of this place; and, in conjunction with the provincial Congress, have determined to sink chevaux-de-frise, one of which is already begun.

I am, with the utmost respect and esteem, &c.   G. W.

Sir,   *New-York, June 14, 1776.*

I Herewith transmit you copies of a letter from general Schuyler and its several inclosures, which I received since I had the honor of addressing you yesterday. From these you will learn that general Thomas died the second instant; and the apprehensions of our frontier friends in this colony, that our savage foes are meditating an attack against them.

I must beg leave to refer you to a paragraph in the copy of general Schuyler's letter to general Putnam or the commanding officer here, inclosed in mine of the thirteenth, where he requests a supply of clothing to be sent for the army in Canada. As there is but little or no probability of getting it here, I shall be glad to know whether there will be any chance of procuring it in Philadelphia; and, if it should be sent through the hands of the quarter-master here, to what account it is to be charged.

I was last evening favored with yours of the eleventh instant, and hope the two batallions, which Congress have ordered from Philadelphia for the defence of this place, will come provided with arms. If they do not, they will be of no service, as there are more troops here already than are armed.

From general Schuyler's letter, he has in view the taking post where Fort-Stanwix formerly stood. I wrote him, I thought it prudent, previous to that, to secure a post lower down, about the falls below the German-Flats, left the vatages should possess themselves of the country, and prevent supplies of men and provisions that may be necessary to send there in future. He says he is in want of cannon and ammunition; but has expressed himself so ambiguously, that I am at a loss to know whether he meant what he has said as an application or not,—this being the only intelligence on the subject, and the first mention of his want. I have desired him to explain the matter, and, in his future requisitions for necessaries, to be more certain and explicit as to quantity and quality. In the mean time I shall send him some intrenching tools, and inquire whether there are any cannon that can be spared from hence.

I have the honor to be, &c. G. W.

SIR, *New-York, June* 16, 1776.

I DO myself the honor to transmit to Congress a copy of a letter covering copies of other papers, which I received yesterday evening from general Sullivan. The intelligence communicated by him is pleasing and interesting, and such as must afford the greatest satisfaction, if the conduct the Canadians have discovered since his arrival among them is ingenuous and sincere.

General Sullivan mentions his having given commissions to some of the Canadians as a measure founded in necessity, and requests my approbation of it. But not considering myself empowered to say any thing upon the subject, it may not be improper for Congress to give him their opinion in this instance.

I have also inclosed copies of General Schuyler's letters received at the same time. They contain accounts respecting the Indians, variant from what was reported by Mr. Kirkland, but amounting to the same thing,—the probability of the savages attacking our frontiers.

By last night's post I had information of a capture made by our armed vessels, of one of the transports with a company

pany of Highlanders on board, bound to Boston. The inclosed extract from general Ward's letter to me will give you the intelligence more particularly.—There are accounts in the city mentioning other valuable prizes: but as general Ward has said nothing of them, I fear they want authenticity.

I beg leave to mention that a further sum of money will be wanted for our military chest by the time it can be sent. The inclosed note from the pay-master-general shews the necessity for it; and I may add, besides his estimate of draughts to be made, there are the claims of the eastern troops at Boston for three or four months' pay, not included, and now due.

Colonel Magaw is arrived with part of his batallion; and by wednesday evening the whole both of his and colonel Shee's will be here, as I am told.

As it is and may be of great importance to have a communication with the Jerseys and Long-Island, I have had several flat-bottomed boats built for the purpose, and have thoughts of getting more for Posaic and Hackinsac rivers, where they may be equally necessary for transporting our army or part of it occasionally, or succours coming to or going from it.—I have the honor to be, &c. G. W.

Sir, *New-York, June* 17, 1776.

I BEG leave to inform Congress that general Wooster has repaired to head-quarters in obedience to their resolve transmitted him; and shall be extremely glad if they will give me such further directions about him as they may conceive necessary. He is desirous of seeing his family in Connecticut, as I am informed, having been a good while from it.—I shall wait their instructions as to his future employment.

I am, sir, with sentiments of much esteem, &c. G. W.

Sir,   New-York, June 20, 1776.

I AM now to acknowledge the receipt of your favors of the fourteenth and eighteenth inftant, and the interefting refolves contained in them, with which I have been honored. The feveral matters recommended to my attention fhall be particularly regarded, and the directions of Congrefs and your requefts complied with in every inftance, as far as in my power.

The inftituting a war-office is certainly an event of great importance, and, in all probability, will be recorded as fuch in the hiftoric page. The benefits derived from it, I flatter myfelf, will be confiderable, though the plan upon which it is firft formed may not be entirely perfect. This, like other great works, in its firft edition, may not be free from error: —time will difcover its defects, and experience fuggeft the remedy, and fuch further improvements as may be neceffary; but it was right to give it a beginning, in my opinion.

The recommendation to the convention of New-York for reftraining and punifhing difaffected perfons, I am hopeful, will be attended with falutary confequences; and the prohibition againft exporting provifions appears to have been a meafure founded in found policy, left proper fupplies fhould be wanted, wherewith to fupply our armies.

I have tranfmitted general Schuyler the refolves about the Indians, and the others on which he is to act; and have requefted his ftrict attention and exertions in order to their being carried into execution with all poffible difpatch.

I note your requeft refpecting Mr. Hancock. He fhall have fuch directions as may be neceffary for conducting his office; and I am happy he will have fo early a remittance for paying the troops in his department.

The filver and paper money defigned for Canada will be highly ferviceable, and I hope will be the means of re-eftablifhing our credit there in fome degree with the Canadians, and alfo encourage our men too, who have complained in

this

this inftance. When it arrives, I will fend it forward under a proper guard.

I have communicated to major-general Gates the refolve of Congrefs for him to repair to Canada, and directed him to view Point-au-fer, that a fortrefs may be erected if he fhall judge neceffary. He is preparing for his command, and in a few days will take his departure for it. I would fain hope his arrival there will give our affairs a complexion different from what they have worn for a long time paft, and that many effential benefits will refult from it.

The kind attention Congrefs have fhewn to afford the commander-in-chief here every affiftance, by refolving that recommendatory letters be written to the conventions of New-Jerfey, New-York, and affembly of Connecticut, to authorife him to call in the militia in cafe of exigency, claims my thankful acknowledgments; and, I truft, if carried into execution, will produce many advantages in cafe it may be expedient at any time to call in early reinforcements. The delays incident to the ordinary mode may frequently render their aid too late, and prove exceedingly injurious.

I this evening received intelligence of the nineteenth inftant from captain Pond of the armed floop Schuyler, of his having taken, about fifty miles from this, on the fouth fide of Long-Ifland, a fhip and a floop bound to Sandy-Hook. The fhip, from Glafgow, with a company of the forty-fecond regiment, had been taken by one of commodore Hopkins's fleet, who took the foldiers out, and ordered her to Rhode-Ifland; after which, fhe was retaken by the Cerberus, and put under the convoy of the floop. As captain Pond informs me, there were five commiffioned officers, two ladies, and four privates on board. They are not yet arrived at head-quarters.—Inclofed is an invoice of what they have on board.

General Woofter having expreffed an inclination and wifh to wait on Congrefs, I have given him permiffion, not having any occafion for him here. He fet out this morning.

I have been up to view the grounds about Kingſbridge, and find them to admit of ſeveral places well calculated for defence; and, eſteeming it a paſs of the utmoſt importance, have ordered works to be laid out, and ſhall direct part of the two batallions from Pennſylvania to ſet about the execution immediately, and will add to their number ſeveral of the militia when they come in, to expedite them with all poſſible diſpatch. Their conſequence, as they will keep open the communication with the country, requires the moſt ſpeedy completion of them.

I have the honor to be, &c. G. W.

Sir, New-York, June 21, 1776.

I WAS this morning honored with your favor of the nineteenth inſtant, with ſundry reſolves of Congreſs, which came to hand after I had cloſed mine of the twentieth. I ſhall appoint a deputy muſter-maſter-general as ſoon as I can fix upon a proper perſon for the office, and direct him immediately to repair to Canada.

Mr. Bennet, the bearer of this, delivered me a letter to-day from general Schuyler, incloſing the proceedings of the commiſſioners of Indian affairs at a meeting at Albany in conſequence of the reſolution of Congreſs (as they ſay) which I tranſmitted, the ſeventh inſtant, for engaging the Indians in our ſervice. The gentlemen appear to me to have widely miſtaken the views of Congreſs in this inſtance, and to have formed a plan for engaging ſuch Indians as were not in contemplation. I cannot account upon what principles they have gone, as a part of their proceedings ſhews they are about to hold a conference with the Six-Nations. I ſuppoſe they eſteemed what they have done a neceſſary meaſure:—a copy of which I have the honor to incloſe you.

I ſhall now beg leave to lay before Congreſs a propoſition made to me by captain Leary of this city, in behalf of a

body

body of men who are desirous of being employed in the continental service as a troop of horse, and at the same time to offer my opinion that such a corps may be extremely useful in many respects. In a march, they may be of the utmost service in reconnoitring the enemy and gaining intelligence, and have it in their power to render many important benefits. The terms on which they are willing to engage are inclosed, which appear to me moderate and reasonable.—I am also informed that another company might readily be made up, and most probably upon the same terms. I would therefore submit the propriety and expediency of the measure to the consideration of Congress, and wish their opinion whether it will be agreeable to them that both or either of them should be formed and incorporated in this army, in manner as has been proposed by captain Leary, if it can be done.

I have the honor to be, &c. G. W.

Sir, Head-Quarters, June 21, 1776.

THIS will be delivered to you by the chevalier de Kirmovan and monsieur de Vermonet. They are French gentlemen just arrived in this place, who have made application to me to be received into the continental service. They bring letters to Dr. Franklin and some other gentlemen of the Congress. I suppose it will better appear from those letters, than from any information I can give, whether it will be proper to employ them in the capacity they are desirous of.

I am, sir, with the greatest esteem, &c. G. W.

Sir, New-York, June 23, 1776.

I Herewith transmit you an extract of a letter from general Ward which came to hand by last-night's post, containing the agreeable intelligence of their having obliged the king's ships to leave Nantasket road, and of two transports more

more being taken by our armed vessels, with two hundred and ten Highland troops on board.

I sincerely wish the same success had attended our arms in another quarter:—but it has not. In Canada, the situation of our affairs is truly alarming. The inclosed copies of generals Schuyler, Sullivan, and Arnold's letters will inform you that general Thompson has met with a repulse at Three-Rivers, and is now a prisoner in the hands of general Burgoyne, who (these accounts say) is arrived with a considerable army. Nor do they seem to promise an end of our misfortunes here:—it is greatly to be feared that the next advices from thence will be, that our shattered, divided, and broken army (as you will see by the return) have been obliged to abandon the country, and retreat, to avoid a greater calamity,—that of being cut off or becoming prisoners.—I will have done upon the subject, and leave you to draw such conclusions as you conceive, from the state of facts, are most likely to result; only adding my apprehensions that one of the latter events,—either that they are cut off, or become prisoners,—has already happened, if they did not retreat while they had an opportunity. General Schuyler and general Arnold seem to think it extremely probable: and if it has taken place, it will not be easy to describe all the fatal consequences that may flow from it. At least our utmost exertions will be necessary, to prevent the advantages they have gained being turned to our greater misfortunes.—General Gates will certainly set out to-morrow, and would have gone before now, had he not expected to receive some particular instructions from Congress, which colonel Braxton said he imagined would be given, and transmitted here.

Inclosed is a copy of a letter from general Arnold, respecting some of the Indian tribes, to general Schuyler, and of a talk had at Albany with thirteen of the Oneidas. They seemed then to entertain a friendly disposition towards us, which I wish may not be changed by the misfortunes we have sustained in Canada.

I have the honor to be, &c. G. W.

SIR,   New-York, June 27, 1776.

I THIS morning received, by express, letters from generals Schuyler and Arnold, with a copy of one from general Sullivan to the former, and also of others to general Sullivan; of all which I do myself the honor to transmit you copies. They will give you a further account of the melancholy situation of our affairs in Canada, and shew that there is nothing left to save our army there but evacuating the country.

I am hopeful general Sullivan would retreat from the Isle-aux-noix without waiting for previous orders for that purpose; as, from generals Schuyler and Arnold's letters, it is much to be feared, by remaining there any considerable time, his retreat would be cut off, or at least be a matter of extreme difficulty. I would observe to Congress that it is not in my power to send any carpenters from hence to build the gondolas and gallies general Arnold mentions, without taking them from a work equally necessary (if not more so) here, of the same kind;—and submit it to them whether it may not be advisable (as it is of great importance to us to have a number of those vessels on the lake, to prevent the enemy's passing) to withdraw the carpenters for the present from the frigates building up the North river, and detach them immediately, with all that can be got at Philadelphia, for that purpose and carrying on those here.

I have the pleasure to inform you of another capture made by our armed vessels, of a transport, on the nineteenth instant, with a company of Highland grenadiers on board. The inclosed extract of a letter from general Ward; by last night's post, contains the particulars; to which I beg leave to refer you.

I have been honored with your favors of the twenty-first and twenty-fifth instant in due order, with their important inclosures, to which I shall particularly attend.—I have transmitted general Schuyler a copy of the resolve of Congress respecting the

the Mohickan and Stockbridge Indians, and directed him to put an immediate stop to the raising the two companies.

The quarter-master-general has been called upon for stopping the tents designed for Massachusetts-Bay, and ordered to forward them immediately. He means to write to Congress upon the subject, and hopes his conduct will not appear to deserve their reprehension. Of this they will judge from his relation of the matter.

Being extremely desirous to forward the intelligence from Canada to Congress, well knowing their anxiety about our affairs there, I must defer writing upon some other matters I want to lay before them, until the next opportunity, which I hope will be to-morrow, when I will inform them fully upon the subject of rations, having desired the commissary-general to furnish me with some things necessary in that instance.

I have the honor to be, &c.   G. W.

Sir,   *New-York, June* 27, 1776.

UPON information that major * * * was travelling through the country under suspicious circumstances, I thought it necessary to have him secured. I therefore sent after him. He was taken at South-Amboy, and brought up to New-York. Upon examination, he informed me that he came from New-Hampshire, the country of his usual abode, where he had left his family; and pretended he was destined to Philadelphia on business with Congress.

As by his own confession he had crossed Hudson's-river at New-Windsor, and was taken so far out of his proper and direct route to Philadelphia, this consideration, added to the length of time he had taken to perform his journey,—his being found in so suspicious a place as Amboy,—his unnecessary stay there on pretence of getting some baggage from New-York, and an expectation of receiving money from a person here, of bad character, and in no circumstances

cumstances to furnish him out of his own stock,—the major's reputation, and his being a half-pay officer,—have increased my jealousies about him.

The business, which he informs me he has with Congress, is a secret offer of his services, to the end that, in case it should be rejected, he might have his way left open to an employment in the East Indies, to which he is assigned: and in that case he flatters himself he will obtain leave of Congress to go to Great Britain.

As he had been put upon his parole by Congress, I thought it would be improper to stay his progress to Philadelphia, should he be in fact destined thither. I therefore send him forward, but (to prevent imposition) under the care of an officer, with letters found upon him, which, from their tenor, seem calculated to recommend him to Congress.—I submit it to their consideration, whether it would not be dangerous to accept of the offer of his services.

I am, sir, with the greatest respect, &c. G. W.

Sir, *New-York, June* 28, 1776.

IN compliance with the request of Congress contained in your favor of the twenty-fifth instant, and my promise of yesterday, I do myself the honor to inform you that the cost of a ration, according to the commissary-general's estimate, from the first of July to the first of December, will be from eight-pence to eight-pence halfpenny, York currency.

Having discharged the obligation I was under in this instance, and finding that many applications have been made for victualling the flying camp, I would, with all possible deference, wish Congress to consider the matter well before they come to any determination upon it. Who the gentlemen are that have made offers upon this occasion, I know not: consequently my objections to their appointment cannot proceed from personal dislike; nor have I it in view to serve Mr. Trumbull the commissary-general, by wishing him to have the direction of the whole fupplies for his emolument; becaufe whatever rations are taken from him fave him the trouble of fupplying provifions to the amount, without diminifhing his pay,—that being fixed and certain:—but what influences me is a regard to the public good. I am morally certain, if the bufinefs is taken out of Mr. Trumbull's hands and put into another's, that it may, and will in all probability, be attended with great and many inconveniences. It is likely, during the continuance of the war between us and Great Britain, that the army here, or part of it, and the troops compofing the flying camp, will be frequently joined, and under the neceffity of affording each other mutual aid. If this event is probable (and moft certainly it is), the fame confufion and diforder will refult from having two commiffaries, or one commiffary and one contractor in the fame army in the fame department, as did between Mr. Trumbull and Mr. Livingfton on the coming of the former to New-York. I cannot difcriminate the two cafes; and not forefeeing that any good confequences will flow from the meafure, but that many bad ones will,—fuch as clafhing of interefts,—a contention for ftores, carriages,—and many other caufes that might be mentioned if hurry of bufinefs would permit,—I confefs I cannot perceive the propriety of appointing a different perfon, or any but the commiffary.

I would alfo add, that few armies, if any, have been better fupplied than the troops under Mr. Trumbull's care in this inftance; which, I fhould fuppofe, ought to have confiderable weight, efpecially as we have ftrong reafons to believe that a large fhare of the misfortunes our arms have fuftained in Canada fprang from a want of proper and neceffary fupplies of provifions.

Mr. Trumbull too (I am informed) has already made provifion in New-Jerfey for the flying camp which will be ftationed there, and employed proper perfons in that colony to tranfact the bufinefs incident to his department, in obedience to my orders, and in full confidence that it was to come under his management.

My great desire to see the affairs of this important post, on which so much depends, go on in an easy, smooth and uninterrupted course, has led me to say thus much upon the subject, and will, I hope, (if I am unhappy enough to differ in opinion with Congress), plead my excuse for the liberty I have taken.

I would also beg leave to mention to Congress the necessity there is of some new regulations being entered into, respecting the chaplains of this army. They will remember that applications were made to increase their pay, which was conceived too low for their support; and that it was proposed (if it could not be done for the whole) that the number should be lessened, and one be appointed to two regiments, with an additional allowance. This latter expedient was adopted, and, while the army continued all together at one encampment, answered well, or at least did not produce many inconveniences. But the army now being differently circumstanced from what it then was,—part here, part at Boston, and a third part detached to Canada,—has introduced much confusion and disorder in this instance; nor do I know how it is possible to remedy the evil, but by affixing one to each regiment, with salaries competent to their support. No shifting, no change from one regiment to another can answer the purpose; and in many cases it could never be done though the regiments should consent,—as where detachments are composed of unequal numbers, or ordered from different posts. Many more inconveniences might be pointed out: but these, it is presumed, will sufficiently shew the defect of the present establishment, and the propriety of an alteration. What that alteration shall be, Congress will please to determine.

Congress, I doubt not, will have heard of the plot that was forming among many disaffected persons in this city and government for aiding the king's troops upon their arrival.

No

No regular plan seems to have been digested: but several persons have been enlisted, and sworn to join them. The matter, I am in hopes, by a timely discovery, will be suppressed and put a stop to. Many citizens and others, among whom is the mayor, are now in confinement. The matter has been traced up to governor Tryon; and the mayor appears to have been a principal agent, or go-between him and the persons concerned in it. The plot had been communicated to some of the army, and part of my guard engaged in it. T * * * H * * *, one of them, has been tried, and, by the unanimous opinion of a court-martial, is sentenced to die,—having enlisted himself, and engaged others. The sentence, by the advice of the whole council of general officers, will be put in execution to-day at eleven o'clock. The others are not tried.—I am hopeful this example will produce many salutary consequences, and deter others from entering into the like traitorous practices.

The inclosed copy of a resolve of the provincial Congress will shew that some of the disaffected on Long-Island have taken up arms.—I have, agreeable to their request, sent a party after them, but have not as yet been able to apprehend them,—having concealed themselves in different woods and morasses.

General Gates set out on tuesday with a fine wind which has been fair ever since, and would soon arrive at Albany.

I this moment received a letter from lieutenant Davison, of the Schuyler armed sloop, a copy of which I have inclosed; to which I beg leave to refer you for the intelligence communicated by him.

I could wish general Howe and his armament not to arrive yet, as not more than a thousand militia have yet come in, and our whole force (including the troops at all the detached posts, and on board the armed vessels, which are comprehended in our returns) is but small and inconsiderable, when compared with the extensive lines they are to defend, and (most probably) the army that he brings. I have no further intelligence about him than what the lieutenant mentions: but it is extremely probable his accounts and conjectures are true.

I have the honor to be, &c.   G. W.

P. S. I have inclosed a general return:— and it may be certainly depended on, that general Howe and fleet have sailed from Halifax. Some of the men, on board the prizes mentioned in the lieutenant's letter, were on board the Greyhound, and saw general Howe.

Sir,   New-York, June 29, 1776.

I WAS last night honored with your favor of the twenty-sixth instant, and, agreeable to your request, shall pay proper attention to the resolves it inclosed.

I observe the augmentation Congress have resolved to make to the forces destined for the northern department, and the bounty to be allowed such soldiers as will enlist for three years. I hope many good consequences will result from these measures; and that, from the latter, a considerable number of men may be induced to engage in the service.

I should esteem myself extremely happy to afford the least assistance to the Canada department in compliance with the desire of Congress and your requisition, were it in my power: but it is not. The return which I transmitted yesterday will but too well convince Congress of my incapacity in this instance, and point out to them that the force I now have is trifling, considering the many and important posts that are necessary, and must be supported, if possible. But few militia have yet come in, the whole being about twelve hundred, including the two batalions of this city, and one company from the Jerseys. I wish the delay may not be attended with disagreeable consequences, and their aid may not come too late, or when it might be wanted. I have wrote,— I have done every thing I could, to call them in: but they

               have

have not come, though I am told that they are generally willing.

The accounts communicated yesterday through lieutenant Davison's letter are partly confirmed, and, I dare say, will turn out to be true on the whole. For two or three days past, three or four ships have been dropping in; and I just now received an express from an officer appointed to keep a look-out on Staten-Island, that forty-five arrived at the Hook to-day:—some say more;—and I suppose the whole fleet will be in, within a day or two. I am hopeful, before they are prepared to attack, that I shall get some reinforcements.—Be that as it may, I shall attempt to make the best disposition I can of our troops, in order to give them a proper reception, and to prevent the ruin and destruction they are meditating against us.

As soon as the express arrived last night, I sent the letters for the northern colonies to the quarter-master-general, with orders to forward them immediately.

When monsieur Wiebert comes—(I have not seen him yet)—I shall employ him as Congress have directed. The terms upon which he offers his service seem to promise something from him. I wish he may answer, and be skilled in the business he says he is acquainted with.

I have the honor to be, &c. G. W.

SIR, *New-York, June* 30, 1776.

I HAD the pleasure of receiving your favor of the twenty-ninth early this morning, with which you have been pleased to honor me, together with the resolves for a further augmentation of our army.

The batallion of Germans, which Congress have ordered to be raised, will be a corps of much service: and I am hopeful that such persons will be appointed officers, as will complete their enlistments with all possible expedition.

I shall

I shall communicate to colonel Stevenson and one of his field-officers what you have requested, and direct them to repair immediately to Philadelphia. It is an unlucky circumstance that the term of enlistment of these three companies, and of the rifle batallion, should expire at this time, when a hot campaign is, in all probability, about to commence.

Canada, it is certain, would have been an important acquisition, and well worth the expenses incurred in the pursuit of it. But as we could not reduce it to our possession, the retreat of our army with so little loss, under such a variety of distresses, must be esteemed a most fortunate event. It is true, the accounts we have received do not fully authorise us to say that we have sustained no loss: but they hold forth a probable ground for such conclusion.—I am anxious to hear it confirmed.

I have the honor of transmiting you an extract of a letter received last night from general Ward.—If the scheme the privateers had in view, and the measures he had planned, have been carried into execution, the Highland corps will be tolerably well disposed of: but I fear the fortunate event has not taken place.

In general Ward's letter, was inclosed one from lieutenant-colonel Campbell, who was made prisoner with the Highland troops. I have transmitted you a copy. This will give you a full and exact account of the number of prisoners that were on board the four transports; and will prove, beyond a possibility of doubt, that the evacuation of Boston by the British troops was a matter neither known nor expected when he received his orders. Indeed so many facts had concurred before to settle the matter, that no additional proofs were necessary.

When I had the honor of addressing you yesterday, I had only been informed of the arrival of forty-five of the fleet in the morning. Since that, I have received authentic intelligence from sundry persons (among them, from general Greene) that a hundred and ten sail came in before night, that were counted, and that more were seen about dusk in the offing.—I have no doubt but the whole that sailed from Halifax are now at the Hook.

Just as I was about to conclude my letter, I received one from a gentleman upon the subject of calling the five regiments from Boston to the defence of Canada or New-York, and to have militia raised in their lieu.—I have sent you a copy, and shall only observe, that I know the author well: his hand-writing is quite familiar to me: he is a member of the general court, very sensible, of great influence, and a warm and zealous friend to the cause of America.—The expedient proposed by him is submitted to Congress.

I have the honor to be, &c. G. W.

Sir, *New-York, July 3, 1776.*

SINCE I had the honor of addressing you, and on the same day, several ships more arrived within the Hook, making the number that came in then a hundred and ten; and there remains no doubt of the whole of the fleet from Halifax being now here. Yesterday evening fifty of them came up the bay and anchored on the Staten Island side. Their views I cannot precisely determine; but am extremely apprehensive, as part of them only came, that they mean to surround the island, and secure the stock upon it. I had consulted with a committee of the provincial Congress upon the subject, before the arrival of the fleet; and they appointed a person to superintend the business, and to drive the stock off. I also wrote to brigadier-general Heard, and directed him to the measure, lest it might be neglected; but am fearful it has not been effected.

Our reinforcement of militia is yet but small:—I cannot ascertain the amount, not having got a return. However, I trust, if the enemy make an attack, they will meet with a repulse, as I have the pleasure to inform you that an agreeable

spirit

spirit and willingness for action seem to animate and pervade the whole of our troops.

As it is difficult to determine what objects the enemy may have in contemplation, and whether they may not detach some part of their force to Amboy, and to ravage that part of the country, if not extend their views farther, I submit it to Congress whether it may not be expedient for them to repeat and press home their requests to the different governments that are to provide men for the flying camp, to furnish their quotas with all possible dispatch. It is a matter of great importance, and will be of serious consequence, to have the camp established in case the enemy should be able to possess themselves of this river, and cut off the supplies of troops that might be necessary on certain emergencies to be sent from hence.

I must entreat your attention to an application I made some time ago for flints. We are extremely deficient in this necessary article, and shall be greatly distressed if we cannot obtain a supply. Of lead we have a sufficient quantity for the whole campaign, taken off the houses here.

Esteeming it of infinite advantage to prevent the enemy from getting fresh provisions, and horses for their waggons, artillery, &c, I gave orders to a party of our men on Staten-Island (since writing to general Heard) to drive the stock off without waiting for the assistance or direction of the committees there, lest their slow mode of transacting business might produce too much delay;—and have sent this morning to know what they have done.—I am this morning informed by a gentleman, that the committee of Elizabeth-town sent their company of light-horse on monday to effect it, and that some of their militia were to give their aid yesterday. He adds that he was credibly told last night by a party of the militia coming to this place, that yesterday they saw a good deal of stock driving off the island, and crossing to the Jerseys.—If the business is not executed before now, it will be impossible to do it.

I have the honor to be, &c. G. W.

Sir, New-York, July 4, 1776.

THIS will be handed to you by colonel Stevenson, whom I have ordered, with the captains of the two rifle companies from Maryland, to wait on Congress. They will point out such measures as they conceive most likely to advance the raising of the new rifle batallion, and the persons they think worthy of promotion, that have served in the three companies here, agreeable to the inclosed list. I am not acquainted with them myself, but from their report and recommendation which I doubt not to be just; and that, if Congress will please to inquire of them, they will mention other proper persons for officers.

Only about forty of the three old companies have re-enlisted, whom I shall form into one for the present, and place under an officer or two, till a further and complete arrangement is made of the whole batallion.

I have the honor to be, &c. G. W.

Sir, New-York, July 4, 1776.

WHEN I had the honor to address you on the thirtieth ultimo, I transmitted a copy of a letter I had received from a gentleman, a member of the honorable general court [*of Massachusetts*], suggesting the improbability of succours coming from thence in any reasonable time, either for the defence of this place, or to reinforce our troops engaged in the Canada expedition. I am sorry to inform you, that, from a variety of intelligence, his apprehensions appear to be just, and to be fully confirmed: nor have I reason to expect but that the supplies from the other two governments, Connecticut and

and New-Hampshire, will be extremely slow and greatly deficient in number.

As it now seems beyond question, and clear to demonstration, that the enemy mean to direct their operations and bend their most vigorous efforts against this colony, and will attempt to unite their two armies,—that under general Burgoyne, and the one arrived here,—I cannot but think the expedient proposed by that gentleman is exceedingly just; and that the continental regiments, now in the Massachusetts-Bay, should be immediately called from thence, and be employed where there is the strongest reason to believe their aid will be indispensably necessary. The expediency of the measure I shall submit to the consideration of Congress, and will only observe, as my opinion, that there is not the most distant prospect of an attempt being made, where they now are, by the enemy; and, if there should, that the militia that can be assembled upon the shortest notice will be more than equal to repel it. They are well armed, resolute, and determined, and will instantly oppose any invasion that may be made in their own colony.

I shall also take the liberty again to request Congress to interest themselves in having the militia raised, and forwarded with all possible expedition, as fast as any considerable number of them can be collected, that are to compose the flying camp. This I mentioned in my letter yesterday, but think proper to repeat it, being more and more convinced of the necessity. The camp will be in the neighborhood of Amboy: and I shall be glad that the conventions, or committees of safety, of those governments from whence they come, may be requested to give me previous notice of their marching, that I may form some plan, and direct provision to be made for their reception.

The disaffection of the people at that place and others not far distant is exceedingly great; and, unless it is checked and overawed, it may become more general, and be very alarming. The arrival of the enemy will encourage it. They, or at least a part of them, are already landed on Staten-Island which is quite contiguous; and about four thousand were marching about it yesterday, as I have been advised, and are leaving no arts un-essayed to gain the inhabitants to their side, who seem but too favorably disposed. It is not unlikely that in a little time they may attempt to cross to the Jersey side, and induce many to join them either from motives of interest or fear, unless there is a force to oppose them.

As we are fully convinced that the ministerial army we shall have to oppose this campaign will be great and numerous, and well know that the utmost industry will be used, as it already has been, to excite the savages and every body of people to arms against us whom they can influence, it certainly behoves us to strain every nerve to counteract their designs. I would therefore submit it to Congress, whether (especially as our schemes for employing the western Indians do not seem to be attended with any great prospect of success, from general Schuyler's accounts) it may not be advisable to take measures to engage those of the eastward, the St. John's, Nova-Scotia, Penobscot, &c, in our favor. I have been told that several might be got, perhaps five or six hundred or more, readily to join us. If they can, I should imagine it ought to be done. It will prevent our enemies from securing their friendship; and further they will be of infinite service in annoying and harrassing them, should they ever attempt to penetrate the country. Congress will be pleased to consider the measure: and if they determine to adopt it, I conceive it will be necessary to authorise and request the general court of the Massachusetts-Bay to carry it into execution. Their situation and advantages will enable them to negotiate a treaty and an alliance better than it can be done by any persons else.

I have been honored with your two favors of the first instant; and, agreeable to the wishes of Congress, shall put monsieur Wiebert in the best place I can to prove his abilities.

ties in the art he professes. I shall send him up immediately to the works erecting towards Kingsbridge under the direction of general Mifflin, whom I shall request to employ him.

I this moment received a letter from general Greene, an extract of which I have inclosed. The intelligence it contains is of the most important nature, and evinces the necessity of the most spirited and vigorous exertions on our part.

The expectation of the fleet under admiral Howe is certainly the reason the army already come have not begun their hostile operations. When that arrives, we may look for the most interesting events; and such as, in all probability, will have considerable weight in the present contest. It behoves us to be prepared in the best manner: and I submit it again to Congress, whether the accounts given by their prisoners do not shew the propriety of calling the several continental regiments from the Massachusetts government, raising the flying camp with all possible dispatch, and engaging the eastern Indians.

July 5.——General Mercer arrived here on tuesday, and, the next morning, was ordered to Paulus-Hook to make some arrangements of the militia as they came in, and the best disposition he could to prevent the enemy crossing from Staten-Island, if they should have any such views. The distressed situation of the inhabitants of Elizabethtown and Newark has since induced me, upon their application, to give up all the militia from the Jerseys, except those engaged for six months. I am hopeful they will be able to repel any incursions that may be attempted. Generals Mercer and Livingston are concerting plans for that purpose. By a letter from the latter last night, I am informed the enemy are throwing up small works at all the passes on the north side of Staten-Island, which it is probable they mean to secure.

None of the Connecticut militia are yet arrived: so that the reinforcement we have received is very inconsiderable.

A letter from general Schuyler, with sundry inclosures (of which N° 1, 2, and 3, are exact copies), this moment came to hand, and will no doubt claim, as it ought to do, the immediate attention of Congress. The evils which must inevitably follow a disputed command are too obvious and alarming to admit a moment's delay in your decision thereupon: and, although I do not presume to advise in a matter, now, of this delicacy, yet as it appears evident that the northern army has retreated to Crown-Point, and mean to act upon the defensive only, I cannot help giving it as my opinion that one of the major-generals in that quarter would be more usefully employed here, or in the flying camp, than there: for it becomes my duty to observe, if another experienced officer is taken from hence in order to command the flying camp, that your grand army will be entirely stripped of generals who have seen service,—being in a manner already destitute of such. My distress on this account,—the appointment of general Whitcomb to the eastern regiments,—a conviction in my own breast that no troops will be sent to Boston,—and the certainty of a number coming to this place,—occasioned my postponing, from time to time, sending any general officer from hence to the eastward heretofore: and now I shall wait the sentiments of Congress relative to the five regiments in Massachusetts-Bay, before I do any thing in this matter.

The commissary-general has been with me this morning, concerning the other matter contained in general Schuyler's letter respecting the business of that department. He has, I believe, (in order to remove difficulties), recalled Mr. Avery, but seems to think it necessary in that case that Mr. Livingston should be left to himself, as he cannot be responsible for persons not of his own appointment.—This matter should also be clearly defined by Congress.—I have already given my opinion of the necessity of these matters being under one general direction, in so full and clear a manner, that I shall not take up the time of Congress to repeat it in this place.

I have the honor to be, &c.   G. W.

Sir,   *New-York, July* 8, 1776.

 CONGRESS having resolved to raise a regiment of Germans to counteract the designs of our enemies, I must beg leave to recommend to their notice John David Wilpert, now a first lieutenant in colonel Shee's batallion, to the office of captain in said regiment. I am personally acquainted with him, and know that he joined the Virginia forces under my command in the year 1754, and continued in service the whole war, during which he conducted himself as an active, vigilant, and brave officer. He is a German; and his merit, as a soldier, entitles him much to the office he wishes for.—I have the honor to be, &c.   G. W.

Sir,   *New-York, July* 10, 1776.

 I AM now to acknowledge the receipt of your two favors of the fourth and sixth instant, which came duly to hand, with their important inclosures.

 I perceive that Congress have been employed in deliberating on measures of the most interesting nature. It is certain that it is not with us to determine in many instances what consequences will flow from our councils: but yet it behoves us to adopt such, as, under the smiles of a gracious and all-kind providence, will be most likely to promote our happiness. I trust the late decisive part they have taken is calculated for that end, and will secure us that freedom and those privileges, which have been and are refused us, contrary to the voice of nature and the British constitution. Agreeable to the request of Congress, I caused " THE DECLARATION" to be proclaimed before all the army under my immediate command; and have the pleasure to inform them that the measure seemed to have their most hearty assent,—the expressions and behavior, both of officers and men, testifying their warmest approbation of it. I have transmitted a copy to General Ward at Boston,

Boston, requesting him to have it proclaimed to the continental troops in that department.

It is with great pleasure that I hear the militia from Maryland, the Delaware government, and Pennsylvania, will be in motion every day to form the flying camp. It is of great importance, and should be accomplished with all possible dispatch. The readiness and alacrity, with which the committee of safety of Pennsylvania and the other conferees have acted in order to forward the associated militia of that state to the Jerseys for service till the men to compose the flying camp arrive, strongly evidence their regard to the common cause, and that nothing on their part will be wanting to support it. I hope, and I doubt not, that the associated militia, impressed with the expediency of the measure, will immediately carry it into execution, and furnish in this instance a proof of the continuance of that zeal which has so eminently marked their conduct. I have directed the commissary to make the necessary provision for their reception, who will also supply the army for the flying camp with rations.— A proper officer will be appointed to command it.

In pursuance of the power given me by Congress, and the advice of my general officers, I have wrote to general Ward, and desired him forthwith to detach three of the fullest regiments from the Massachusetts-Bay to join the northern army,— esteeming it a matter of the greatest importance to have a sufficient force there to prevent the enemy passing the lake and making an impression in that quarter.—The gondolas and gallies will be of great service; and I am hopeful the carpenters you have sent from Philadelphia, and that will go from the eastward on your application, will be able to build a sufficient number in time to answer every exigency.

I have requested governor Cooke, if the duck mentioned in Mr. Greene's letter is proper for tents, to have it made up as early as possible, and forwarded here. I have also desired him to send the flints and small-arms, as I have general

Ward

Ward those of the latter that were taken out of the Scotch transports,—our deficiency in these necessary articles being still great.

Observing that Congress have particularly mentioned a bounty of ten dollars to be paid to men of some corps directed to be raised in two or three instances since their resolve of the twenty-sixth of June allowing such bounty; I have been led to doubt how that resolve is to be construed; whether it is a general regulation, and extends to all men that will engage for three years,—for instance, the soldiers of the present army, if they will enlist for that time. If it is, and extends to them, it will be necessary to forward a large sum of money:—many perhaps would engage.

I also observe, by their resolve of the twenty-fifth of June for raising four regiments of militia in the eastern governments to augment the troops in the northern department, that the assemblies of those governments are empowered to appoint paymasters to the said regiments. This appears to me a regulation of great use, and I could wish that it was made general, and one allowed to every regiment in the service. Many advantages would result from it

The Connecticut militia begin to come in: but from every account the batallions will be very incomplete,—owing, they say, to the busy season of the year. That government, lest any inconvenience might result from their militia not being here in time, ordered three regiments of their light-horse to my assistance, part of which have arrived. But, not having the means to support them (and, if it could be done, the expense would be enormous), I have thanked the gentlemen for their zeal, and the attachment they have manifested upon this occasion, and informed them that I cannot consent to their keeping their horses,—at the same time wishing them to stay themselves.—I am told they or part of them mean to do so.

General Mercer is now in the Jerseys, for the purpose of receiving and ordering the militia coming for the flying camp;

camp: and I have sent over our chief engineer to view the ground within the neighborhood of Amboy, and to lay out some necessary works for the encampment, and such as may be proper at the different passes in Bergen-Neck, and other places on the Jersey shore opposite Staten-Island, to prevent the enemy making impressions, and committing depredations on the property of the inhabitants.

The intelligence we have from a few deserters that have come over to us, and from others, is that general Howe has between nine and ten thousand men, who are chiefly landed on the island, posted in different parts, and securing the several communications from the Jerseys with small works and intrenchments, to prevent our people from paying them a visit;—that the islanders have all joined them, seem well disposed to favor their cause, and have agreed to take up arms in their behalf. They look for admiral Howe's arrival every day with his fleet and a large reinforcement; are in high spirits, and talk confidently of success, and carrying all before them when he comes. I trust, through divine favor and our own exertions, they will be disappointed in their views: and, at all events, any advantages they may gain will cost them very dear. If our troops will behave well (which I hope will be the case, having every thing to contend for, that freemen hold dear), they will have to wade through much blood and slaughter before they can carry any part of our works, if they carry them at all,—and, at best, be in possession of a melancholy and mournful victory.—May the sacredness of our cause inspire our soldiery with sentiments of heroism, and lead them to the performance of the noblest exploits!—With this wish, I have the honor to be, &c. G. W.

SIR, *New-York, July 11, 1776.*

I WAS honored with your favor of the eighth instant by yesterday-morning's post, with the several resolves to
which

which you referred my attention. I shall duly regard them, and attempt their execution as far as I am able.

By virtue of the discretionary power that Congress were pleased to vest me with, and by advice of such of my general officers as I have had an opportunity of consulting, I have ordered the two remaining continental regiments in the Massachusetts-Bay to march immediately for the defence of this place, in full confidence that nothing hostile will be attempted against that state in the present campaign.

I have wrote to the general court of Massachusetts-Bay, and transmitted a copy of the resolve for employing the eastern Indians, entreating their good offices in this instance, and their exertions to have them forthwith engaged and marched to join this army. I have desired five or six hundred of them to be enlisted for two or three years, if they will consent to it,—subject to an earlier discharge, if it shall be thought necessary,—and upon the same terms as the continental troops, if better cannot be had,—though I am hopeful they may.

In my letter of yesterday I mentioned the arrival of part of the Connecticut light-horse to assist in the defence of this place, and my objection to their horses being kept. Four or five hundred of them are now come in : and, in justice to their zeal and laudable attachment to the cause of their country, I am to inform you that they have consented to stay as long as occasion may require, though they should be at the expense of maintaining their horses themselves. They have pastured them out about the neighborhood of Kingsbridge (being unwilling to send them away) at the rate of half a dollar per week each, meaning to leave it entirely with Congress either to allow or refuse it, as they shall judge proper. I promised to make this representation, and thought it my duty; and will only observe that the motives which induced them at first to set out were good and praise-worthy, and were, to afford the most speedy and early succour, which they apprehended would be wanted before the militia arrived. Their services may be extremely important,—

being

being moſt of them, if not all, men of reputation and of property.

The ſubject of the incloſed copy of a letter from governor Trumbull I beg leave to ſubmit to the conſideration of Congreſs. They will perceive from his repreſentation the diſquieting apprehenſions that have ſeized on the minds of the people ſince the retreat of the northern army, and how expoſed the northern frontiers of New-York and New-Hampſhire are to the ravages and incurſions of the Indians. How far it may be expedient to raiſe the batallion he conceives neceſſary to prevent the calamities and diſtreſſes he points out, they will determine, upon what he has ſaid, and the neceſſity that may appear to them for the meaſure ;—whatI have done, being only to lay the matter before them in compliance with his wiſhes.

I have alſo incloſed a memorial from the ſurgeons'-mates, ſetting forth the inadequacy of their pay to their ſervices and maintenance, and praying that it may be increaſed. I ſhall obſerve that they have a long time complained in this inſtance, and that ſome additional allowance may not be unneceſſary.

As I am truly ſenſible the time of Congreſs is much taken up with a variety of important matters, it is with unwillingneſs and pain I ever repeat a requeſt after having once made it, or take the liberty of enforcing any opinion of mine after it is once given : but as the eſtabliſhing of ſome office for auditing accounts is a matter of exceeding importance to the public intereſt, I would beg leave once more to call the attention of Congreſs to an appointment competent to the purpoſe. Two motives induce me to urge the matter ; firſt, a conviction of the utility of the meaſure ;—ſecondly, that I may ſtand exculpated if hereafter it ſhould appear that money has been improperly expended, and neceſſaries for the army obtained upon unreaſonable terms.

For me, whoſe time is employed from the hour of my riſing till I retire to bed again, to go into an examination of

the

the accounts of such an army as this with any degree of precision and exactness, without neglecting other matters of equal importance, is utterly impracticable. All that I have been able to do (and that, in fact, was doing nothing), was, when the commissary, and quarter-master, and director-general of the hospital (for it is to these the great advances are made) applied for warrants,—to make them at times produce a general account of their expenditures. But this answers no valuable purpose. It is the minutiæ that must be gone into,—the propriety of each charge examined,—the vouchers looked into;—and, with respect to the commissary-general, his victualling returns and expenditures of provisions should be compared with his purchases: otherwise a person in this department, if he was inclined to be knavish, might purchase large quantities with the public money, and sell one half of it again for private emolument; and yet his accounts upon paper would appear fair, and be supported with vouchers for every charge.

I do not urge this matter from a suspicion of any unfair practices in either of the departments before-mentioned; and sorry should I be if this construction was put upon it,—having a high opinion of the honor and integrity of these gentlemen. But there should nevertheless be some control as well upon their discretion as honesty:—to which may be added, that accounts become perplexed and confused by long standing, and the errors therein not so discoverable as if they underwent an early revision and examination. I am well apprised that a treasury-office of accounts has been resolved upon, and an auditor-general for settling all public accounts: but, with all deference and submission to the opinion of Congress, these institutions are not calculated to prevent the inconveniences I have mentioned; nor can they be competent to the purposes, circumstanced as they are.

We have intelligence from a deserter that came to us, that, on wednesday morning, the Asia, Chatham, and Greyhound men-of-war weighed anchor, and (it was said) intended to pass up the North-river above the city, to prevent
the

the communication with the Jerseys. They did not attempt it, nor does he know what prevented them.—A prisoner belonging to the tenth regiment, taken yesterday, informs that they hourly expected admiral Howe and his fleet. He adds that a vessel has arrived from them, and the prevailing opinion is, that an attack will be made immediately on their arrival.

By a letter from general Ward, I am informed that the small-pox has broke out at Boston, and infected some of the troops. I have wrote to him to place the invalids under an officer, to remain till they are well; and to use every possible precaution to prevent the troops from thence bringing the infection. The distresses and calamities we have already suffered by this disorder in one part of our army, I hope, will excite his utmost care that they may not be increased.

I have the honor to be, &c.   -   G. W.

Sir,   *New-York, July* 12, 1776.

THE design of this is to inform Congress, that, about half after three o'clock this evening, two of the enemy's ships of war, one of forty and the other of twenty guns, with three tenders, weighed anchor in the bay opposite Staten-Island, and, availing themselves of a brisk and favorable breeze, with a flowing tide, ran past our batteries up the North-river, without receiving any certain damage that I could perceive, notwithstanding a heavy and incessant cannonade was kept up from our several batteries here, as well as from that at Paulus-Hook. They, on their part, returned and contined the fire as they ran by.—I dispatched an express to brigadier-general Mifflin at our encampment towards the upper end of the island; but have not heard whether they have got by, or received any damage.

The account transmitted by this morning's post, respecting the arrival of one of the fleet, seems to be confirmed. Several ships have come in to-day: among them, one this evening, with a Saint-George's flag at her fore-top-mast-
                                                                                           head

head, which we conclude to be admiral Howe from the circumstance of the flag, and the several and general salutes that were paid. It is probable they will all arrive in a day or two, and immediately begin their operations.

As it will be extremely necessary that the flying camp should be well provided with powder and ball, and it may be impracticable to send supplies from hence on account of our hurry and engagements (besides, the communication may be uncertain), I must beg the attention of Congress to this matter, and request that they will forward with all possible expedition such a quantity of musket-powder and lead (if balls of different sizes cannot be had), as will be sufficient for the militia to compose that camp.

By an express this minute arrived from general Mifflin, the ships have passed his works.

I am, in haste, with sentiments of great regard, &c. G. W.
A quarter past eight, P. M.

SIR,   *New-York, July* 14, 1776.

MY last of friday evening, which I had the honor of addressing you, advised that two of the enemy's ships of war and three tenders had run above our batteries here and the works at the upper end of the island. I am now to inform you, that, yesterday forenoon, receiving intelligence from general Mifflin that they had passed the Tappan-Sea, and were trying to proceed higher up,—by advice of R. R. Livingston, esquire, and other gentlemen, I dispatched expresses to general Clinton of Ulster, and the committee of safety for Duchess-county, to take measures for securing the passes in the Highlands, lest they might have designs of seizing them, and have a force concealed for the purpose. I wrote the evening before to the commanding officer of the two garrisons there to be vigilant and prepared against any attempts they or any disaffected persons might make against them, and to forward expresses all the way to Albany, that provision and other veſſels might be ſecured and prevented falling into their hands.

The information given general Mifflin was rather premature, as to their having gone paſt the Sea.—A letter from the committee of Orange-county, which came to hand this morning, ſays they were there yeſterday, and that a regiment of their militia was under arms, to prevent their landing and making an incurſion. The meſſenger who brought it, and to whom it refers for particulars, adds that a party of them, in two or three boats, had approached the ſhore, but were forced back by our people firing at them. Since the manœuvre of friday, there have been no other movements in the fleet.

General Sullivan, in a letter of the ſecond inſtant, informs me, of his arrival with the army at Crown-Point, where he is fortifying and throwing up works. He adds that he has ſecured all the ſtores except three cannon left at Chamblee, which in part is made up by taking a fine twelve-pounder out of the lake.—The army is ſickly,—many with the ſmall-pox; and he is apprehenſive the militia, ordered to join them, will not eſcape the infection.—An officer he had ſent to reconnoitre had reported that he ſaw at Saint John's about a hundred and fifty tents,—twenty at Saint Roy's, and fifteen at Chamblee; and works at the firſt were buſily carrying on.

I have incloſed a general return of the army here, which will ſhew the whole of our ſtrength. All the detached poſts are included.

A letter from the eaſtward, by laſt-night's poſt, to Mr. Hazard, poſt-maſter in this city, adviſes that two ſhips had been taken and carried into Cape-Ann,—one from Antigua, conſigned to general Howe, with four hundred and thirty-nine puncheons of rum,—the other a Jamaica-man, with four hundred hogſheads of ſugar, two hundred puncheons of rum, thirty-nine bales of cotton, pimento, fuſtic, &c, &c. Each mounted two guns, ſix-pounders.

About

About three o'clock this afternoon I was informed that a flag from lord Howe was coming up, and waited with two of our whale-boats, until directions should be given. I immediately convened such of the general officers as were not upon other duty, who agreed in opinion that I ought not to receive any letter directed to me as a private gentleman: but if otherwise, and the officer desired to come up to deliver the letter himself, as was suggested, he should come under a safe-conduct. Upon this, I directed colonel Reed to go down and manage the affair under the above general instruction.

'On his return, he informed me, that, after the common civilities, the officer acquainted him that he had a letter from lord Howe to Mr. Washington, which he shewed under a superscription, " *To George Washington, esquire.*"—Colonel Reed replied there was no such person in the army, and that a letter intended for the general could not be received under such a direction.—The officer expressed great concern,—said it was a letter rather of a civil than military nature,—that lord Howe regretted he had not arrived sooner,—that he (lord Howe) had great powers.—The anxiety to have the letter received was very evident, though the officer disclaimed all knowledge of its contents. However, colonel Reed's instructions being positive, they parted.—After they had got some distance, the officer with the flag again put about, and asked under what direction Mr. Washington chose to be addressed:—to which colonel Reed answered, his station was well known, and that certainly they could be at no loss how to direct to him.—The officer said they knew it and lamented it;. and again repeated his wish that the letter could be received.—Colonel Reed told him a proper direction would obviate all difficulties, and that this was no new matter,—this subject having been fully discussed in the course of the last year; of which lord Howe could not be ignorant:—upon which they parted.

I would not upon any occasion sacrifice essentials to punctilio:

tilio: but in this inſtance, the opinion of others concurring with my own, I deemed it a duty to my country and my appointment, to inſiſt upon that reſpect, which, in any other than a public view, I would willingly have waved. Nor do I doubt, but, from the ſuppoſed nature of the meſſage, and the anxiety expreſſed, they will either repeat their flag, or fall upon ſome mode to communicate the import and [*contents*] of it.

I have been duly honored with your two letters,—that of the tenth by Mr. Anderſon,—and the eleventh, with its incloſures. I have directed the quarter-maſter to provide him with every thing he wants to carry his ſcheme into execution. It is an important one, and I wiſh it ſucceſs; but am doubtful that it will be better in theory than practice.

The paſſage of the ſhips of war and tenders up the river is a matter of great importance, and has excited much conjecture and ſpeculation. To me two things have occurred, as leading them to this proceeding,—firſt a deſign to ſeize on the narrow paſſes on both ſides of the river, giving almoſt the only land-communication with Albany, and of conſequence with our northern army; for which purpoſe they might have troops concealed on board, which they deemed competent of themſelves, as the defiles are narrow,—or that they would be joined by many diſaffected perſons in that quarter. Others have added a probability of their having a large quantity of arms on board, to be in readineſs to put into the hands of the tories immediately on the arrival of the fleet, or rather at the time they intend to make their attack.—The ſecond is, to cut off entirely all intercourſe between this and Albany by water, and the upper country, and to prevent ſupplies of every kind going and coming.

Theſe matters are truly alarming, and of ſuch importance, that I have wrote to the provincial congreſs of New-York, and recommended to their ſerious conſideration the adoption of every poſſible expedient to guard againſt the two firſt; and have ſuggeſted the propriety of their employing the militia,

litia, or some part of them, in the counties in which these defiles are, to keep the enemy from possessing them, till further provision can be made; and to write to the several leading persons on our side in that quarter, to be attentive to all the movements of the ships and the disaffected, in order to discover and frustrate whatever pernicious schemes they have in view.

In respect to the second conjecture of my own, and which seems to be generally adopted, I have the pleasure to inform Congress, that, if their design is to keep the armies from provision, the commissary has told me upon inquiry, he has forwarded supplies to Albany (now there, and above it) sufficient for ten thousand men for four months;—that he has a sufficiency here for twenty thousand men for three months, and an abundant quantity secured in different parts of the Jerseys for the flying camp, besides having about four thousand barrels of flour in some neighboring part of Connecticut. Upon this head, there is but little occasion for any apprehensions, at least for a considerable time.

I have the honor to be, &c.   G. W.

P. S. I have sent orders to the commanding officer of the Pennsylvania militia to march to Amboy, as their remaining at Trenton can be of no service.

Sir,   *New-York, July* 15, 1776.

THIS will be handed you by Mr. Griffin, who has also taken upon him the charge and delivery of two packets containing sundry letters which were sent to Amboy yesterday by a flag, and forwarded to me to-day by general Mercer.—The letter addressed to governor Franklin came open to my hands.

I was this morning honored with yours of the thirteenth instant, with its important and necessary inclosures; and, in obedience to the commands of Congress, have transmitted general Howe the resolves intended for him. Those for general Burgoyne I inclofed and fent to general Schuyler, with directions immediately to forward them to him.

The inhuman treatment of the whole, and murder of part of our people, after their furrender and capitulation, was certainly a flagrant violation of that faith which ought to be held facred by all civilifed nations, and founded in the moft favage barbarity. It highly deferved the fevereft reprobation; and I truft the fpirited meafures Congrefs have adopted upon the occafion will prevent the like in future: but if they fhould not, and the claims of humanity are difregarded, juftice and policy will require recourfe to be had to the law of retaliation, however abhorrent and difagreeable to our natures in cafes of torture and capital punifhments.

I have the honor to be, &c.   G. W.

Sir,   *New-York, July* 17, 1776.

I WAS this morning honored with yours of the fifteenth inftant, with fundry refolves.

I perceive the meafures Congrefs have taken to expedite the raifing of the flying camp, and providing it with articles of the greateft ufe. You will fee by a poftfcript to my letter of the fourteenth, I had wrote to the commanding officer of the Pennfylvania militia, ordering them to be marched from Trenton to Amboy, as their remaining there could not anfwer the leaft public good. For, having confulted with fundry gentlemen, I was informed, if the enemy mean to direct their views towards Pennfylvania or penetrate the Jerfeys, their route will be from near Amboy, and either by way of Brunfwic or Boundbrook,—the lower road from South-Amboy being through a woody fandy country. Befides, they will be then able to throw in fuccour here, and to receive it from hence in cafes of emergency.

The Connecticut light-horfe, mentioned in my letter of the eleventh, notwithftanding their then promife to continue here for the defence of this place, are now difcharged, and about to return home,—having peremptorily refused all kind of fatigue duty, or even to mount guard, claiming an exemption as troopers. Though their assistance is much needed, and might be of essential service in case of an attack, yet I judged it advisable, on their application and claim of such indulgences, to discharge them; as granting them would set an example to others, and might produce many ill consequences. The number of men included in the last return, by this, is lessened about five hundred.

I last night received a letter from general Schuyler, with several inclosures, copies of which I have herewith transmitted. They will give Congress every information I have respecting our northern army and the situation of our affairs in that quarter;—to which I beg leave to refer their attention.—I cannot but express my surprise at the scarcity of provision which general Schuyler mentions, after what the commissary assured me, and which formed a part of my letter of the fourteenth. He still assures me of the same.—This is a distressing circumstance, as every article of provision, and every thing necessary for that department, can have no other now than a land-conveyance, the water-communication from hence to Albany being entirely cut off.

Congress will please to consider the inclosure, N° 6, about raising six companies out of the inhabitants about the lakes, to prevent the incursions of the Indians. The general officers, in their minutes of council, have determined it a matter of much importance;—and their attention to the price of goods furnished the soldiery may be extremely necessary. They have complained much upon this head.

The retreat from Crown-Point seems to be considered in opposite views by the general and field officers. The former (I am satisfied) have weighed the matter well; and yet the reasons assigned by the latter against it appear strong and forcible.—I hope whatever is done will be for the best. * * *

By a letter from the committee of Orange-county, received this

this morning, the men-of-war and tenders were yesterday at Haversham-bay, about forty miles above this. A number of men, in four barges from the tenders, attempted to land, with a view (they suppose) of taking some sheep and cattle, that had been previously removed.—A small number of militia that were collected obliged them to retreat, without their doing any damage with their cannon.—They were sounding the water up towards the Highlands; by which it is probable they will attempt to pass with part of the fleet, if possible.

Yesterday evening a flag came from general Howe with a letter addressed " *To George Washington, esquire, &c, &c, &c.*"—It was not received, upon the same principle that the one from lord Howe was refused.

I have the honor to be, &c.   G. W.

SIR,   *New-York, July* 19, 1776.

I HAVE been duly honored with your favors of the fixteenth and seventeenth, with the several resolves they contained; to the execution of which, so far as shall be in my power, I will pay proper attention.

In my letter of the seventeenth I transmitted you a copy of one from general Schuyler, and of its several inclosures.— I confess the determination of the council of general officers on the seventh, to retreat from Crown-Point, surprised me much: and the more I consider it, the more striking does the impropriety appear. The reasons assigned against it by the field-officers, in their remonstrance, coincide greatly with my own ideas and those of the other general officers I have had an opportunity of consulting with, and seem to be of considerable weight,—I may add, conclusive.—I am not so fully acquainted with the geography of that country and the situation of the different posts, as to pronounce a peremptory judgment upon the matter: but, if my ideas are right, the

possession

poffeffion of Crown-Point is effential, to give us the fuperiority and maftery upon the lake.

That the enemy will poffefs it as foon as abandoned by us, there can be no doubt: and if they do, whatever gallies or force we keep on the lake will be unqueftionably in their rear. —How they are to be fupported there, or what fuccour can be drawn from them there, is beyond my comprehenfion.—Perhaps it is only meant that they fhall be employed on the communication between that and Ticonderoga. If this is the cafe, I fear the views of Congrefs will not be anfwered, nor the falutary effects be derived from them, that were intended.

I have mentioned my furprife to general Schuyler, and would, by the advice of the general officers here, have directed that that poft fhould be maintained, had it not been for two caufes,—an apprehenfion that the works have been deftroyed, and that, if the army fhould be ordered from Ticonderoga, or the poft oppofite to it (where I prefume they are), to repoffefs it, they would have neither one place nor another fecure and in a defenfible ftate:—the other, left it might increafe the jealoufy and diverfity of opinions which feem already too prevalent in that army, and eftablifh a precedent for the inferior officers to fet up their judgments whenever they would, in oppofition to thofe of their fuperiors,—a matter of great delicacy, and that might lead to fatal confequences, if countenanced;—though in the prefent inftance I could wifh their reafoning had prevailed.

If the army has not removed, what I have faid to general Schuyler may perhaps bring on a reconfideration of the matter; and it may not be too late to take meafures for maintaining that poft. But of this I have no hope.

In confequence of the refolve of Congrefs for three of the eaftern regiments to reinforce the northern army, I wrote to general Ward, and, by advice of my general officers, directed them to march to Norwich, and there to embark for Albany; conceiving that two valuable purpofes might refult therefrom,—firft, that they would fooner join the army by

purfuing

purfuing this route, and be faved from the diftrefs and fatigue that muft attend every long march through the country at this hot and uncomfortable feafon;—and fecondly, that they might give fuccour here, in cafe the enemy fhould make an attack about the time of their paffing. But the enemy having now, with their fhips of war and tenders, cut off the water-communication from hence to Albany, I have wrote this day and directed them to proceed by land acrofs the country.—If Congrefs difapprove the route, or wifh to give any orders about them, you will pleafe to certify me thereof, that I may take meafures accordingly.

Inclofed I have the honor to tranfmit you copies of a letter and fundry refolutions which I received yefterday from the convention of this ftate. By them you will perceive they have been acting upon matters of great importance, and are exerting themfelves in the moft vigorous manner to defeat the wicked defigns of the enemy, and fuch difaffected perfons as may incline to affift and facilitate their views.— In compliance with their requeft, and on account of the fcarcity of money for carrying their falutary views into execution, I have agreed to lend them, out of the fmall ftock now in hand (not more than fixty thoufand dollars), twenty thoufand dollars, in part of what they want; which they promife fpeedily to replace.—Had there been money fufficient for paying the whole of our troops, and no more, I could not have done it. But as it was otherwife, and by no means proper to pay a part and not the whole, I could not forefee any inconveniences that would attend the loan;— on the contrary, that it might contribute in fome degree to forward their fchemes.—I hope my conduct in this inftance will not be difapproved.

I inclofed governor Trumbull a copy of their letter and of their feveral refolves, to-day, by colonel Broom and Mr. Duer, two members of the convention, who are going to wait on him; but did not think myfelf at liberty to urge or requeft his intereft in forming the camp of fix thoufand men, as the levies, directed by Congress to be furnished the third of June, for the defence of this place, by that government, are but little more than one-third come in. At the same time, the proposition I think a good one, if it could be carried into execution. In case the enemy should attempt to effect a landing above Kingsbridge, and to cut off the communication between this city and the country, an army to hang on their rear would distress them exceedingly.

I have the honor to be, &c.   G. W.

The inclosed paper should have been sent before, but was omitted through hurry.

P. S. After I had closed my letter, I received one from general Ward, a copy of which is herewith transmitted.—I have wrote him to forward the two regiments now at Boston, by the most direct road, to Ticonderoga, as soon as they are well, with the utmost expedition; and consider their having had the small-pox, as a fortunate circumstance. When the three arrive which have marched for Norwich, I shall immediately send one of them on, if Congress shall judge it expedient;—of which you will please to inform me.

Sir,   *New-York, July* 21, 1776.

I HAVE just time to acknowledge the receipt of your favor of the nineteenth. The interesting intelligence of the success of our arms in the southern department gives me the highest satisfaction. Permit me to join my joy to the congratulations of Congress upon this event.—To-morrow I will write more fully.

Two o'clock, P. M. I this moment had report made me, that ten ships were seen in the offing, coming in,—I suppose, part of admiral Howe's fleet.

I have the honor to be, &c.   G. W.

Sir,   *New-York, July* 22, 1776.

YOUR favors of the eighteenth and nineteenth, with which you have been pleafed to honor me, have been duly received, with the feveral refolves alluded to.

When, the letter and declaration, from lord Howe to Mr. Franklin and the other late governors, come to be publifhed, I fhould fuppofe the warmeft advocates for dependence on the Britifh crown muft be filent, and be convinced beyond all poffibility of doubt, that all that has been faid about the commiffioners was illufory, and calculated exprefsly to deceive and unguard, not only the good people of our own country, but thofe of the Englifh nation that were averfe to the proceedings of the king and miniftry. Hence we fee the caufe why a fpecification of their powers was not given the mayor and city of London, on their addrefs requefting it. That would have been dangerous, becaufe it would then have been manifeft that the line of conduct they were to purfue would be totally variant from that they had induftrioufly propagated, and amufed the public with.—The uniting the civil and military offices in the fame perfons, too, muft be conclufive to every thinking one, that there is to be but little negotiation of the civil kind.

I have inclofed, for the fatisfaction of Congrefs, the fubftance of what paffed beween myfelf and lieutenant-colonel Patterfon, adjutant-general, at an interview had yefterday in confequence of a requeft from general Howe the day before;—to which I beg leave to refer them for particulars.

Colonel Knox of the train having often mentioned to me the neceffity of having a much more numerous body of artillerifts than what there now is, in cafe the prefent conteft fhould continue longer,—and knowing the deficiency in this inftance, and their extreme ufefulnefs,—I defired him to commit his ideas upon the fubject to writing, in order that I might tranfmit them to Congrefs for their confideration. Agreeable to my requeft, he has done it; and the propriety

of

of his plan is now submitted for their decision. It is certain that we have not more at this time than are sufficient for the several extensive posts we now have,—including the draughts which he speaks of, and which, I presume (not only from what he has informed me, but from the nature of the thing), can never be qualified to render the same service as if they were regularly appointed and formed into a corps for that particular purpose.

I beg leave to remind Congress that some time ago I laid before them the proposals of some persons here for forming a company of light-horse; and the president's answer, a little time after, intimated that the plan seemed to be approved of.—As those who wanted to make up the troop are frequently pressing me for an answer, I could wish to be favored with the decision of Congress upon the subject.

By a letter from general Schuyler, of the fourteenth instant, dated at Albany, he informs me, that, the day before, some desperate designs of the tories in that quarter had been discovered, the particulars of which he could not divulge, being under an oath of secrecy;—however, that such measures had been taken, as to promise a prevention of the intended mischief; and that four of the conspirators (among them, a ringleader) were apprehended about one o'clock that morning, not far from the town. What the plot was, or who were concerned in it, is a matter I am ignorant of as yet.

With my best regards to Congress, I have the honor to be your and their most obedient servant, G. W.

P. S. Congress will please to observe what was proposed respecting the exchange of Mr. Lovell, and signify their pleasure in your next.—The last week's return is also inclosed.

Sir, *New-York, July 22, 1776.*

CONGRESS having been pleased to appoint Mr. Wilper to the command of a company in the German battalion tallion now raising, I have directed him to repair to Philadelphia for their orders. From my acquaintance with him, I am persuaded his conduct as an officer will merit their approbation: and, thanking them for their kind attention to my recommendation of him, I have the honor to be, with sentiments of the highest respect, &c. G. W.

Sir, New-York, *July* 23, 1776.

I WAS honored with your favor of the twentieth by yesterday's post, since which, and my letter, nothing of moment has occurred.

The ships, mentioned in my letter of the twenty-first to have been in the offing, got in that day, and are supposed to be part of the Scotch fleet, having landed some Highlanders yesterday.

Inclosed I have the honor to transmit you copies of a letter and sundry resolutions which I received last night from the convention of this state. They will inform you of the computed number of inhabitants and stock upon Nassau-Island, and their sentiments on the impracticability of removing the latter; and also of the measures they think necessary and likely to secure them.

I have also inclosed a letter from Mr. Faesh to lord Stirling upon the subject of a cannon-furnace for the use of the states. Congress will see his plan and proposals, and determine upon them as they shall judge proper.

I am, sir, with every sentiment of respect, &c. G. W.

Sir, New-York, *July* 23, 1776.

SINCE I had the pleasure of writing you by this morning's post, I was favored with a letter from governor Trumbull, a copy of which is inclosed, and to which I beg leave to refer you.—In regard to the stock he mentions, I wrote to him, requesting that they might be removed from the islands on which they were, as I conceived it of great importance

importance to diftrefs the enemy as much as poffible in the article of frefh provifion.—I wifh the other governments may follow his example, and have it removed from the iflands belonging to them refpectively.

When the fhips of war and tenders went up the river, it was thought expedient that application fhould be made for the Connecticut row-gallies and thofe belonging to Rhode-Ifland, in order to attempt fomething for their deftruction. As foon as they arrive we fhall try to employ them in fome ufeful way,—but in what, or how fuccefsfully, I cannot at prefent determine.

Congrefs will pleafe to obferve what Mr. Trumbull fays refpecting the continental regiment raifing under colonel Ward. If they incline to give any orders about their deftination, you will pleafe to communicate them by the earlieft opportunity, as their march will be fufpended till they are known.

The orders Mr. Trumbull has given to the officers of their cruifers, to ftop provifion-veffels, feem to be neceffary. We have too much reafon to believe that fome have gone voluntarily to the enemy, and that there are many perfons who would continue to furnifh them with large fupplies: and, however upright the intentions of others may be, it will be a matter of the utmoft difficulty, if not an impoffibility, for any to efcape falling into their hands now, as every part of the coaft (it is probable) will fwarm with their fhips of war and tenders. I had propofed writing to the convention of this ftate upon the fubject before I received his letter; and am now more perfuaded of the neceffity of their taking fome fteps to prevent further exportations down the Sound. In my next I fhall inform them of the intelligence received from Mr. Trumbull, and recommend the matter to their attention.—I have the honor to be, &c.   G. W.

P. S. It appears abfolutely neceffary that the exportation of provifion fhould be ftopped. Our army is large, and otherwife may want. Nor can individuals be injured, as
they

they have a ready-money market for every thing they have to difpofe of in that way.

Sir, New-York, July 25, 1776.

DISAGREEABLE as it is to me and unpleafing as it may be to Congrefs to multiply officers, I find myfelf under the unavoidable neceffity of afking an increafe of my aides-de-camp. The augmentation of my command,—the increafe of my correfpondence,—the orders to give,—the inftructions to draw,—cut out more bufinefs than I am able to execute in time with propriety. The bufinefs of fo many different departments centring with me, and by me to be handed on to Congrefs for their information,—added to the intercourfe I am obliged to keep up with the adjacent ftates, —and incidental occurrences,—all of which require confidential and not hack writers to execute,—renders it impoffible, in the prefent ftate of things, for my family to difcharge the feveral duties expected of me, with that precifion and difpatch that I could wifh.—What will it be then, when we come into a more active fcene, and I am called upon from twenty different places perhaps at the fame inftant?

Congrefs will do me the juftice to believe (I hope) that it is not my inclination or wifh to run the continent to any unneceffary expenfe; and thofe who better know me will not fufpect that fhew and parade can have any influence on my mind in this inftance. A conviction of the neceffity of it, for the regular difcharge of the truft repofed in me, is the governing motive for the application; and, as fuch, is fubmitted to Congrefs by, fir, your moft obedient, &c. G. W.

Sir, New-York, July 27, 1776.

I WAS yefterday morning honored with your favor of the twenty-fourth inftant with its feveral inclofures, to which I fhall pay the ftricteft attention.

The confidence Congress are pleased to repose in my judgment demands my warmest acknowledgments, and they may rest assured it shall be invariably employed, so far as shall be in my power, to promote their views and the public weal. * * *

Since my last, nothing material has occurred.—Yesterday evening report was made that eight ships were seen in the offing, standing towards the Hook. The men-of-war and tenders are still up the river. They have never attempted to pass the Highland fortifications; and, a day or two ago, quitted their station, and fell down the river eight or ten miles. The vigilance and activity of the militia opposite where they were have prevented their landing and doing much injury.—One poor peasant's cot they plundered and then burnt.

I would wish to know whether the allowance given to officers, the seventeenth of January, of a dollar and one-third for every man they enlist, Congress mean to extend to the officers who enlist for the new army for three years. At first it may appear wrong, or rather exorbitant, supposing that many will be recruited out of the regiments now in service, and under them: but the allowance will be of great use; as it will interest the officers, and call forth their exertions which otherwise would be faint and languid. Indeed I am fearful, from the inquiries I have made, that their utmost exertions will be attended with but little success. It is objected that the bounty of ten dollars is too low; and argued, —" if the states, furnishing men for five or six months, allow considerably more, why should that be accepted when the term of enlistment is to be for three years?"—I heartily wish a bounty in land had been or could be given, as was proposed some time ago. I think it would be attended with salutary consequences.

In consequence of my application to governor Trumbull, he has sent me two row-gallies; and I expect another from him. None from governor Cooke are yet come; nor have

I heard from him on the subject.—One is complete here.—The fire-ships are going on under Mr. Anderson's direction, but rather slowly; and I am preparing some obstructions for the channel nearly opposite the works at the upper end of this island.—When all things are ready, I intend to try, if it shall seem practicable, to destroy the ships and tenders above, and to employ the gallies, if they can be of advantage.

The militia for the flying camp come in but slowly. By a return from general Mercer yesterday, they are but little more than three thousand. If they were in, or can be there shortly, and the situation of the enemy remains the same, I would make some efforts to annoy them, keeping our posts here well guarded, and not putting too much to the hazard, or in any manner to the risk.

I have the honor to be, &c. G. W.

SIR, *New-York, July* 29, 1776.

YOUR favor of the twenty-fourth I received on saturday evening, and, agreeable to your request, shall expunge the preamble to the resolution subjecting the property of subjects to the British crown to forfeiture and confiscation.

Our stock of musket-powder is entirely made up in cartridges. I therefore request that Congress will order four or five tons more of that sort to be immediately forwarded; it being not only necessary that we should have more for that purpose, but also some stock to remain in barrels.

Yesterday evening Hutchinson's and Sergeant's regiments from Boston arrived; also two row-gallies from Rhode-Island.—I am fearful the troops have not got entirely clear of the small-pox. I shall use every possible precaution to prevent the infection spreading; and, for that purpose, have ordered them to an encampment separate and detached from the rest.

By saturday's report from Long-Island camp, five ships, a brig,

brig, and five schooners, had got into the Hook;—by yesterday's, two ships more, and a sloop, were standing in.— What they are, I have not been able to learn.

I have transmitted a general return herewith, by which Congress will perceive the whole of our force at the time it was made.

I have inclosed you an account of sundry prizes, which was transmitted to several gentlemen here by saturday's post: The two last prizes I did not see mentioned in the letters shewn me; and I fear the report of the second provision-vessel is premature.—I was also this minute informed that captain Biddle had taken a ship with sugars for Britain, and, in bringing her in, unfortunately lost her on Fisher's-Island.

I have the honor to be, &c. G. W.

Sir, New-York, *July* 30, 1776.

I WAS this morning honored with your two favors of yesterday's date; and, agreeable to your request, have given Mr. Palfrey liberty to negotiate your claim with Mr. Brimer, and wish it may be satisfied agreeably to you.

I last night received a letter from general Schuyler, a copy of which I do myself the honor to transmit you. You will thereby perceive his reasons for leaving Crown-Point, and preferring the post the council of officers determined to take opposite to Ticonderoga.—I am totally unacquainted with those several posts and the country about them, and therefore cannot determine on the validity of his observations, or think myself at liberty to give any direction in the matter.

Congress will please to observe what he says of their distress for money. From hence he can have no relief, there being only about three of four thousand dollars in the paymaster's hands according to his return this morning,—and all but two months' pay due to the army, besides many other demands.—I could wish that proper supplies of money could be always kept:—the want may occasion consequences of an alarming nature.

By a letter from him, of a prior date to the copy inclosed, he tells me that a Mr. Ryckman, who has just returned through the country of the Six-Nations, reports that the Indians who were at Philadelphia have gone home with very favorable ideas of our strength and resources. This he heard in many of their villages:—a lucky circumstance, if it will either gain their friendship or secure their neutrality.

In my letter of the twenty-seventh I informed Congress of my views and wishes to attempt something against the troops on Staten-Island. I am now to acquaint them, that, by the advice of general Mercer and other officers at Amboy, it will be impracticable to do any thing upon a large scale, for want of craft, and as the enemy have the entire command of the water all round the island.—I have desired general Mercer to have nine or ten flat-bottomed boats built at Newark-bay and Elizabethtown, with a design principally to keep up the communication across Hackinsac and Passaic rivers, which I deem a matter of great importance, and extremely necessary to be attended to.

Since I wrote you yesterday, eleven ships more, four brigs, and two sloops, have come into the Hook. I have not yet received intelligence what any of the late arrivals are: but I suppose we shall not long remain in a state of uncertainty.

Having reason to believe that lord Howe will readily come into an exchange of such prisoners as may be more immediately under his command, and that something will be offered on this subject within a day or two, or rather come in answer to the propositions I have made general Howe, I should be glad to have Congress's interpretation of the resolve of the twenty-second instant, empowering the commanders to exchange, &c;—whether, by the word '*sailor*,' they mean sailors generally, as well those taken in the vessels of private adventurers by the enemy, as those belonging
to

to the continental cruisers, or vessels in the continent's employ; or whether they only design to extend the exchange to the latter,—those in their particular employ.

I would also observe, that, heretofore, sailors belonging to merchant ships that have fallen into our hands, and those employed merely as transports, have not generally been considered as prisoners.—I submit it to Congress whether it may not be now necessary to pass a resolve declaring their sentiments on this subject, and, in general, who are to be treated as prisoners of war, that are taken on board vessels belonging to the subjects of the British crown, &c.—The result of their opinion upon the first question proposed, you will be pleased to transmit me by the earliest opportunity.

I have inclosed, for the consideration of Congress, a memorial and petition by captain Holdridge, praying to be relieved against the loss of money stolen from him,—not conceiving myself authorised to grant his request. The certificate which attends it proves him a man of character; and his case is hard, on his state of it.—Whether making the loss good may not open a door to others, and give rise to applications not so just as his may be, I cannot determine.—That seems to be the only objection to relieving him.

I am informed by general Putnam that there are some of the Stockbridge Indians here (I have not seen them myself) who express great uneasiness at their not being employed by us, and have come to inquire into the cause. I am sensible Congress had them not in contemplation when they resolved that Indians might be engaged in our service. However, as they seem so anxious,—as they were led to expect it, from what general Schuyler and the other commissioners did,—as we are under difficulties in getting men, and there may be danger of their (or some of them) taking an unfavorable part,—I beg leave to submit it as my opinion, under all these circumstances, that they had better be employed.

I have the honor to be, &c. G. W.

Sir,   *New-York, August* 2, 1776,

YOUR favor of the thirtieth ultimo, with its several inclosures, I was honored with by wednesday's post.

Congress having been pleased to leave with me the direction of colonel Ward's regiment, I have wrote to governor Trumbull, and requested him to order their march to this place, being fully satisfied that the enemy mean to make their grand push in this quarter, and that the good of the service requires every aid here that can be obtained. I have also wrote to colonel Elmore, and directed him to repair hither with his regiment.—When it comes, I shall fill up commissions for such officers as appear with their respective companies.

Colonel Holman, with a regiment from the Massachusetts state, is arrived. Colonel Cary from thence is also here, waiting the arrival of his regiment which he hourly expects. He adds, when he left New-London he heard that the third regiment from the Massachusetts was almost ready, and would soon be in motion.

The enemy's force is daily augmenting and becoming stronger by new arrivals. Yesterday, general Greene reports that about forty sail, including tenders, came into the Hook. What they are, or what those have brought that have lately got in, I remain un-informed. However, I think it probable they are part of lord Howe's fleet, with the Hessian troops:—it is time to look for them.

I have the honor to be, &c.   G. W.

P. S. I am extremely sorry to inform Congress our troops are very sickly.

Sir,   *New-York, August* 5, 1776.

I WAS honored with your favor of the thirty-first ultimo on friday, with its several inclosures; and return you my thanks for the agreeable intelligence you were pleased

to

to communicate, of the arrival of one of our ships with such valuable articles as arms and ammunition; also of the capture made by a privateer.

The mode for the exchange of prisoners, resolved on by Congress, is acceded to by general Howe, so far as it comes within his command. A copy of my letter and his answer upon this subject I have the honor to inclose you; to which I beg leave to refer Congress.

The inclosed copy of a letter from colonel Tupper, who had the general command of the gallies here, will inform Congress of the engagement between them and the ships of war up the North-river on saturday evening, and of the damage we sustained. What injury was done to the ships, I cannot ascertain. It is said they were hulled several times by our shot. All accounts agree that our officers and men, during the whole of the affair, behaved with great spirit and bravery. The damage done the gallies shews beyond question that they had a warm time of it.—The ships still remain up the river; and, before any thing further can be attempted against them (should it be thought advisable), the gallies must be repaired.

I have also transmitted Congress a copy of a letter I received by saturday's post from governor Cooke, to which I refer them for the intelligence it contains. The seizure of our vessels by the Portuguese is, I fear, an event too true. Their dependence upon the British crown for aid against the Spaniards must force them to comply with every thing required of them.—I wish the Morris may get safe in with her cargo.—As to the ships captain Buchlin saw on the twenty-fifth ultimo, they are probably arrived: for yesterday twenty-five sail came into the Hook.

By a letter from general Ward, of the twenty-ninth ultimo, he informs me that two of our armed vessels, the day before, had brought into Marblehead a ship bound from Halifax to Staten-Island. She had in about fifteen hundred and nine pounds' worth of British goods, besides a good many belonging to tories. A Halifax paper, found on board her, I have inclosed, as also an account sent me by Mr. Hazard, transmitted him by some of his friends, as given by the tories taken in her. Their intelligence, I dare say, is true respecting the arrival of part of the Hessian troops.—General Ward in his letter mentions, that, the day this prize was taken, captain Burke, in another of our armed vessels, had an engagement with a ship and a schooner which he thought were transports, and would have taken them, had it not been for an unlucky accident in having his quarter-deck blown up. Two of his men were killed, and several more were wounded.

The hulks and chevaux-de-frise, that have been preparing to obstruct the channel, have got up to the place they are intended for, and will be sunk as soon as possible.

I have transmitted Congress a general return of the army in and about this place on the third instant, by which they will perceive the amount of our force.

Before I conclude, I would beg leave to remind Congress of the necessity there is of having some major-generals appointed for this army, the duties of which are great, extensive, and impossible to be discharged as they ought and the good of the service requires, without a competent number of officers of this rank. I mean to write more fully upon the subject: and, as things are drawing fast to an issue, and it is necessary to make every proper disposition and arrangement that we possibly can, I pray that this matter may be taken into consideration, and claim their early attention.—I well know what has prevented appointments of this sort for some time past: but the situation of our affairs will not justify longer delays in this instance.—By the first opportunity, I shall take the liberty of giving you my sentiments more at large upon the propriety and necessity of the measure.

I have the honor to be, &c. G. W.

Sir,   New-York, August 7, 1776.

IN my letter of the fifth which I had the honor of addressing you, I begged leave to recall the attention of Congress to the absolute necessity there is for appointing more general officers,—promising at the same time, by the first opportunity, to give my sentiments more at large upon the subject.

Confident I am that the postponing this measure has not proceeded from motives of frugality: otherwise I should take the liberty of attempting to prove that we put too much to the hazard by such a saving.—I am but too well apprised of the difficulties that occur in the choice. They are, I acknowledge, great; but at the same time it must be allowed they are of such a nature as to present themselves whenever the subject is thought of. Time on the one hand does not remove them; on the other, delay may be productive of fatal consequences

This army, though far short as yet of the numbers intended by Congress, is by much too unwieldy for the command of any one man, without several major-generals to assist. For it is to be observed that a brigadier-general at the head of his brigade is no more than a colonel at the head of a regiment, except that he acts upon a larger scale. Officers of more general command are at all times wanted for the good order and government of an army, especially when the army is composed chiefly of raw troops: but in an action they are indispensably necessary.—At present there is but one major-general for this whole department and the flying camp; whereas, at this place alone, less than three cannot discharge the duties with that regularity they ought to be.

If these major-generals are appointed, as undoubtedly they will, out of the present brigadiers, you will want for this place three brigadiers at least.—The northern department will require one, if not two (as general Thompson is a prisoner, and the baron Woedtke reported to be dead or in a state a state not much better), there being at present only one brigadier-general (Arnold) in all that department.—For the eastern governments there ought to be one, or a major-general, to superintend the regiments there, and to prevent impositions that might otherwise be practised.—These make the number wanted to be six or seven: and who are to be appointed, Congress can best judge.

To make brigadiers of the oldest colonels would be the least exceptionable way: but it is much to be questioned whether by that mode the ablest men would be appointed to office. And I would observe, though the rank of the colonels of the eastern governments was settled at Cambridge last year, it only respected themselves, and is still open as to officers of other governments. To pick a colonel here and a colonel there through the army according to the opinion entertained of their abilities, would no doubt be the means of making a better choice, and nominating the fittest persons: but then the senior officers would get disgusted, and, more than probable, with their connexions, quit the service.—That might prove fatal at this time.—To appoint gentlemen as brigadiers, that had not served in this army (in this part of it at least), would not wound any one in particular, but hurt the whole equally, and must be considered in a very discouraging light by every officer of merit.—View the matter therefore in any point of light you will, there are inconveniencies on the one hand, and difficulties on the other, which ought to be avoided.—Would they be remedied by appointing the oldest colonels from each state?—If this mode should be thought expedient, the inclosed list gives the names of the colonels, from New-Hampshire to Pennsylvania inclusive, specifying those who rank first, as I am told, in the several colony lists.

I have transmitted a copy of a letter from Mr. John Glover, setting forth the nature and grounds of a dispute between him and a Mr. Bradford respecting their agency. Not conceiving myself authorised, nor having the smallest inclination to interfere

terfere in any degree in the matter, it is referred to Congress, who will determine and give direction upon it in such manner as they shall judge best. I will only observe that Mr. Glover was recommended to me as a proper person for an agent when we first fitted out armed vessels, and was accordingly appointed one; and, so far as I know, discharged his office with fidelity and industry.

I received yesterday evening a letter from general Schuyler, containing lieutenant McMichael's report, who had been sent a scout to Oswego. A copy of the report I have inclosed for the information of Congress, left general Schuyler should have omitted it in his letter which accompanies this. He was at the German-Flats when he wrote, which was the second instant, and the treaty with the Indians not begun; nor had the whole expected then arrived. But of these things he will have advised you more fully, I make no doubt.

The paymaster informs me he received a supply of money yesterday. It came very seasonably: for the applications and clamors of the troops had become incessant and distressing beyond measure.—There is now two months' pay due to them.—I have the honor to be, &c. G. W.

SIR,

SINCE closing the letter which I had the honor to write you this morning, two deserters have come in, who left the Solebay man-of-war last evening. One of them is a native of New-York. Their account is that they were in the engagement with colonel Moultrie at Sullivan's Island on the ninth of July—(the particulars they give nearly correspond with the narrative sent by general Lee);—that they left Carolina three weeks ago as a convoy to forty-five transports having on board general Clinton, lord Cornwallis, and the whole southern army consisting of about three thousand men, all of whom were landed last week on Staten-Island in tolerable health;—that, on sunday, thirteen transports, part

of

of lord Howe's fleet, and having on board Hessians and Highlanders, came to Staten-Island;—that the remainder of the fleet, which was reported to have, in the whole, twelve thousand men, had parted with these troops off the banks of Newfoundland, and were expected to come in every moment;—that they were getting their heavy carriages and cannon on board, had launched eight gondolas with flat bottoms, and two rafts or stages to carry cannon.

These men understand that the attack will soon be made if the other troops arrive;—that they give out they will lay the Jerseys waste with fire and sword;—that the computed strength of their army will be thirty thousand men. They further add, that, when they left Carolina, one transport got on shore, so that they were not able to give her relief; upon which, she surrendered, with five companies of Highlanders, to general Lee, who, after taking every thing valuable out of her, burnt her;—that the admiral turned general Clinton out of his ship after the engagement, with a great deal of abuse;— great differences between the principal naval and military gentlemen;—that the ships, left in Carolina, are now in such a weakly distressed condition, they would fall an easy prey.

I am, sir, with great respect, &c.   G. W.

Head-Quarters, New-York, August 7, 1776, one o'clock, P. M.

The ships are changing their position, and the men-of-war forming into a line: but I still think they will wait the arrival of the remaining Hessians before any general attack will be made.—Monday's return will shew our strength here.

SIR,   *New-York, August* 8, 1776.

BY yesterday-morning's post, I was honored with your favor of the second instant, with sundry resolutions of Congress, to which I shall pay strict attention.

As the proposition for employing the Stockbridge Indians has been approved, I have wrote to Mr. Edwards, one of the commissioners, and who lives among them, requesting him to engage them or, such as are willing, to enter the service. I have directed him to indulge them with liberty to join this or the northern army, or both, as their inclination may lead.

I wish the salutary consequences may result from the regulation respecting seamen taken, that Congress have in view. From the nature of this kind of people, and the privileges granted on their entering into our service, I should suppose many of them will do it.—We want them much.

I yesterday transmitted the intelligence I received from the deserters from the Solebay man-of-war.—The inclosed copy of a letter by last night's post, from the honorable Mr. Bowdoin, with the information of a captain Kennedy lately taken, corroborate their accounts respecting the Hessian troops. Indeed his report makes the fleet and armament, to be employed against us, greater than what we have heard they would be. However there remains no doubt of their being both large and formidable, and such as will require our most vigorous exertions to oppose them. Persuaded of this, and knowing how much inferior our numbers are and will be to theirs when the whole of their troops arrive,—of the important consequences that may and will flow from the appeal that will soon be made,—I have wrote to Connecticut and New-Jersey, for all the succour they can afford, and also to the convention of this state.—What I may receive, and in what time, the event must determine. But I would fain hope, the situation and the exigency of our affairs will call forth the most strenuous efforts and early assistance of those who are friends to the cause. I confess there is but too much occasion for their exertions. I confidently trust they will not be withheld.

I have inclosed a copy of a letter from Mr. Bowdoin respecting the eastern Indians. Congress will thereby perceive that they profess themselves to be well attached to our interest,—and the summary of the measures taken to engage them in our service. I have the treaty at large between the honorable

honorable council of the Massachusetts, on behalf of the United States, with the delegates of the Saint-John's and Mickmac tribes. The probability of a copy's being sent already, and its great length, prevent one coming herewith. If Congress have not had it forwarded to them, I will send a copy by the first opportunity after notice that it has not been received.

August 9.——By a report received from general Greene last night, at sunset and a little after, about a hundred boats were seen bringing troops from Staten-Island to the ships, three of which had fallen down towards the Narrows, having taken in soldiers from thirty of the boats. He adds, that, by the best observations of several officers, there appeared to be a general embarkation.

I have wrote to general Mercer for two thousand men from the flying camp. Colonel Smallwood's batallion, as part of them, I expect this forenoon: but where the rest are to come from, I know not, as, by the general's last return, not more than three or four hundred of the new levies had got in.

In my letter of the fifth I inclosed a general return of the army under my immediate command: but I imagine the following state will give Congress a more perfect idea, though not a more agreeable one, of our situation. For the several posts on New-York, Long and Governor's islands, and Paulus-Hook, we have, fit for duty, ten thousand five hundred and fourteen,—sick present, three thousand and thirty-nine—sick absent, six hundred and twenty-nine,—on command, two thousand nine hundred and forty-six,—on furlough, ninety-seven,—total, seventeen thousand two hundred and twenty-five. In addition to these, we are only certain of colonel Smallwood's batallion in case of an immediate attack. Our posts too are much divided, having waters between many of them, and some distant from others, fifteen miles. These circumstances, sufficiently distressing of themselves, are much aggravated by the sickness that prevails through the army.

Every

Every day more or less are taken down; so that the proportion of men that may come in cannot be considered as a real and serviceable augmentation on the whole.

These things are melancholy; but they are nevertheless true.—I hope for better.—Under every disadvantage, my utmost exertions shall be employed to bring about the great end we have in view: and, so far as I can judge from the professions and apparent disposition of my troops, I shall have their support. The superiority of the enemy and the expected attack do not seem to have depressed their spirits. These considerations lead me to think, that, though the appeal may not terminate so happily in our favor as I could wish, yet they will not succeed in their views without considerable loss. Any advantage they may get, I trust, will cost them dear.

Eight o'clock, A. M.

By the reverend Mr. Madison and a Mr. Johnson, two gentlemen of Virginia, who came from Staten-Island yesterday, where they arrived the day before in the packet with colonel Guy Johnson, I am informed that nothing material had taken place in England when they left it;—that there had been a change in the French ministry, which, many people thought, foreboded a war;—that it seemed to be believed by many that Congress would attempt to buy off the foreign troops, and that it might be effected without great difficulty. Their accounts from Staten-Island nearly correspond with what we had before: they say that every preparation is making for an attack;—that the force now upon the island is about fifteen thousand;—that they appear very impatient for the arrival of the foreign troops, but a very small part having got in. Whether they would attempt any thing before they come, they are uncertain: but they are sure they will as soon as they arrive, if not before.—They say, from what they could collect from the conversation of officers, &c, they mean to hem us in by getting above us, and cutting off all communication with the country.

That

That this is their plan, seems to be corroborated and confirmed by the circumstance of some ships of war going out at different times within a few days past, and other vessels. It is probable that a part are to go round and come up the Sound.

Mr. Madison says lord Howe's powers were not known when he left England;—that general Conway moved, before his departure, that they might be laid before the commons; and had his motion rejected by a large majority.

I have the honor to be, &c.   G. W.

Sir,   *New-York, August* 12, 1776.

I HAVE been duly honored with your favors of the eighth and tenth instant, with their several inclosures. I shall pay attention to the resolution respecting lieutenant Josiah, and attempt to relieve him from his rigorous usage.—Your letters to such of the gentlemen as were here have been delivered. The rest will be sent by the first opportunity.

Since my last, of the eighth and ninth, the enemy have made no movements of consequence. They remain nearly in the same state; nor have we any further intelligence of their designs. They have not been yet joined by the remainder of the fleet with the Hessian troops.

Colonel Smallwood and his batallion got in on friday; and colonel Miles is also here with two batallions more of Pennsylvania riflemen.

The convention of this state have been exerting themselves to call forth a portion of their militia to an encampment forming above Kingsbridge, to remain in service for the space of one month after their arrival there; and also half of those in King and Queen's counties, to reinforce the troops on Long-Island till the first of September, unless sooner discharged. General Morris too is to take post with his brigade on the Sound and Hudson's-river for ten days, to annoy

annoy the enemy in case they attempt to land; and others of their militia are directed to be in readiness, in case their aid should be required. Upon the whole, from the information I have from the convention, the militia ordered are now in motion, or will be in a little time, and will amount to about three thousand or more. From Connecticut, I am not certain what succours are coming. By one or two gentlemen who have come from thence, I am told some of the militia were assembling, and, from the intelligence they had, would march this week.

By a letter from governor Trumbull, of the fifth, I am advised that the troops from that state, destined for the northern army, had marched for Skenesborough.—General Ward too, by a letter of the fourth, informs me that the two regiments would march from Boston last week, having been cleansed and generally recovered from the small-pox. I have also countermanded my orders to colonel Elmore, and directed him to join the northern army, having heard, after my orders to Connecticut for his marching hither, that he and most of his regiment were at Albany or within its vicinity.—General Ward mentions that the council of the Massachusetts state will have in from two to three thousand of their militia to defend their lines and different posts, in lieu of the regiments ordered from thence agreeable to the resolution of Congress.

The inclosed copy of a resolve of this state, passed the tenth instant, will discover the apprehension they are under of the defection of the inhabitants of King's county from the common cause, and of the measures they have taken thereupon. I have directed general Greene to give the committee such assistance as he can, and they may require, in the execution of their commission; though at the same time I wish the information the convention have received upon the subject may prove groundless.

I would beg leave to mention to Congress, that, in a letter I received from general Lee, he mentions the valuable consequences

sequences that would result from a number of cavalry being employed in the southern department. Without them (to use his own expressions) he can answer for nothing:—with one thousand, he would ensure the safety of those states.— I should have done myself the honor of submitting this matter to Congress before at his particular request, had it not escaped my mind.—From his acquaintance with that country, and the nature of the grounds, I doubt not he has weighed the matter well, and presume he has fully represented the advantages that would arise from the establishment of such a corps:—all I mean, is, in compliance with his requisition, to mention the matter, that such consideration may be had upon it (if not already determined) as it may be deserving of.

I have transmitted a general return, whereby Congress will perceive the whole of our strength, except the two batallions under colonel Miles, which, coming since it was made out, are not included.

I have inclosed a letter just come to hand from Martinique. Congress will please to consider of the purport, favoring me with their answer and a return of the letter.

This moment (ten o'clock) report is made by general Greene that a man-of-war came in yesterday, and that sixty sail of ships are now standing in.—No doubt, they are a further part of the Hessian fleet.

I have the honor to be, &c. G. W.

Sir, *New-York, August* 12, 1776.

THIS will be handed to you by colonel * * * from the northern army, whom the inclosed letter and proceedings of a general court-martial will shew to have been in arrest, and tried for sundry matters charged against him. As the court-martial was by order of the commander in that department,—the facts committed there,—the trial there,— I am much at a loss to know why the proceedings were referred

ferred to me to approve or disapprove. As my interfering in the matter would carry much impropriety with it, and shew a want of regard to the rules and practice in such instances,—and as colonel * * * is going to Philadelphia,—I have submitted the whole of the proceedings to the consideration of Congress for their decision upon his case,—perfectly convinced that such determination will be had therein, as will be right and just.

have the honor to be, &c. G. W.

Sir, *New-York, August* 13, 1776.

AS there is reason to believe that but little time will elapse before the enemy make their attack, I have thought it advisable to remove all the papers in my hands, respecting the affairs of the states, from this place. I hope the event will shew the precaution was unnecessary: but yet prudence required that it should be done, lest by any accident they might fall into their hands. They are all contained in a large box, nailed up, and committed to the care of lieutenant-colonel Reed, brother of the adjutant-general, to be delivered to Congress, in whose custody I would beg leave to deposit them until our affairs shall be so circumstanced as to admit of their return.

The enemy, since my letter of yesterday, have received a further augmentation of thirty-six ships to their fleet, making the whole that have arrived since yesterday morning, ninety-six.

I have the honor to be, &c. G. W.

P. S. I would observe that I have sent off the box privately, that it might raise no disagreeble ideas; and have enjoined colonel Reed to secrecy.

Sir, New-York, *August* 14, 1776.

SINCE I had the honor of addressing you on monday, nothing of importance has occurred here, except that the enemy have received an augmentation to their fleet, of ninety-six ships:—some reports make them more. In a letter I wrote you yesterday by lieutenant-colonel Reed, I advised you of this: but presuming it may not reach you so soon as this will, I have thought proper to mention the intelligence again.

Inclosed I have the honor to transmit a copy of the examination of a deserter sent me this morning by general Mercer, to which I beg leave to refer Congress for the latest accounts I have from the enemy. Whether the intelligence he has given is literally true, I cannot determine: but as to the attack, we daily expect it.

Your favor of the tenth, with its inclosures, was duly received; and I have instructed the several officers who were promoted, to act in their stations as you requested, though their commissions were not sent.

As we are in extreme want of tents and covering for this army,—a great part of those at the out-posts having nothing to shelter them, nor houses to go into,—I submit it to Congress whether it may not be prudent to remand those that were lately sent to Boston, where there are no troops at present; and, if there were, the necessity for them would not be great, as the town, and barracks at several of the posts, would be sufficient to receive them.

The inclosed letter from lieutenant-colonel Henshaw will discover to Congress his views and wishes, which they will consider and determine on, in whatever way they think right and conducive to the public good;—meaning only to lay his letter before them.

I take the liberty of mentioning that colonel Varnum of Rhode-Island has been with me this morning to resign his commission, conceiving himself to be greatly injured in not

having

having been noticed in the late arrangement and promotion of general officers.—I remonstrated against the impropriety of the measure at this time; and he has consented to stay till affairs wear a different aspect from what they do at present.

Eleven o'clock.—By a report just come to hand from general Greene, twenty ships more are coming in.

I have the honor to be, &c. G. W.

SIR, *New-York, August* 14, 1776.

THIS will be delivered you by captain Moeballe, a Dutch gentleman from Surinam, who has come to the continent with a view of entering into the service of the states, as you will perceive by the inclosed letters from Mr. Browne of Providence, and general Greene. What other letters and credentials he has, I know not; but, at his request, have given him this line to Congress, to whom he wishes to be introduced, and where he will make his pretensions known.

I have ordered the quarter-master immediately to write to Mr. Browne for the Russia duck he mentions, with directions to have it instantly made into tents there,—being in great distress for want of a sufficient number to cover our troops.

I have the honor to be, &c. G. W.

SIR, *New-York, August* 15, 1776.

AS the situation of the two armies must engage the attention of Congress, and lead them to expect that each returning day will produce some important events, this is meant to inform them that nothing of moment has yet cast up. In the evening of yesterday there were great movements among their boats; and, from the number that appeared to be passing and repassing about the Narrows, we were induced to believe they intended to land a part of their force upon Long-Island: but, having no report from general Greene, I presume they have not done it.

I have the honor to be, &c. G. W.

P. S. Your favor of the thirteenth was received by yesterday's post.—I wrote on monday by the return express, as you supposed.

Sir, New-York, August 16, 1776.

I BEG leave to inform you, that, since I had the pleasure of addressing you yesterday, nothing interesting between the two armies has happened. Things remain nearly in the situation they then were.

It is with peculiar regret and concern that I have an opportunity of mentioning to Congress the sickly condition of our troops. In some regiments there are not any of the field-officers capable of doing duty: in others the duty is extremely difficult for want of a sufficient number. I have been obliged to nominate some till Congress transmit the appointments of those they wish to succeed to the several vacancies occasioned by the late promotions. This, being a matter of some consequence, I presume will have their early attention, and that they will fill up the several vacancies also mentioned in the list I had the honor of transmitting some few days ago to the board of war.

I am, sir, with the utmost respect, &c. G. W.

Sir, New-York, August 17, 1776.

THE circumstances of the two armies having undergone no material alteration since I had the honor of writing to you last, I have nothing particular or important to communicate respecting them.

In my letter of yesterday I forgot to mention the arrival of lord Dunmore here. By the examination of a captain Hunter (who escaped from the enemy, and came to Amboy on the fourteenth) tranfmitted me by general Roberdeau, I am certainly informed his lordfhip arrived on the thirteenth. The examination does not fay any thing about the fhips he brought with him: it only extends to his force, which it mentions to be weak.

I before now expected the enemy would have made their attack; nor can I account for their deferring it, unlefs the intelligence, given by captain Hunter and another perfon who efcaped about the fame time, is the caufe,—to wit, that they are waiting the arrival of another divifion of the Heffian troops, which (they fay) is ftill out.—Whether that is the reafon of the delay, I cannot undertake to determine: but I fhould fuppofe things will not long remain in their prefent ftate.—I have inclofed a copy of general Roberdeau's letter, and of the examination of thofe two perfons, which will fhew Congrefs all the information they have given upon thefe fubjects.

I am juft now advifed by Mr. Aires who came from Philadelphia to build the row-gallies, that two of our fire-veffels attempted laft night to burn the enemy's fhips and tenders up the river. He fays that they burned one tender, and one of them boarded the Phœnix, and was grappled with her for near ten minutes; but fhe cleared herfelf.—We loft both of the veffels.—His account is not fo particular as I could wifh; however, I am certain the attempt has not fucceeded to our wifhes. In a little time it is probable the matter will be more minutely reported.

I have the honor to be, &c. G. W.

SIR, *New-York, Auguft* 18, 1776.

I HAVE been honored with your favor of the fixteenth with the inclofure, and am forry it is not in my power to tranfmit Congrefs a copy of the treaty as they require, having fent it away with the other papers that were in my hands.

The resolution they have entered into respecting the foreign troops, I am persuaded, would produce salutary effects, if it could be properly circulated among them. I fear it will be a matter of difficulty. However I will take every measure that shall appear probable to facilitate the end.

I have the honor to inclose you, for the perusal and consideration of Congress, sundry papers marked N° 1 to N° 7 inclusive, the whole of which, except N° 2 and 7 (my answers to lord Drummond and general Howe) I received yesterday evening by a flag, and to which I beg leave to refer Congress.

I am exceedingly at a loss to know the motives and causes inducing a proceeding of such a nature at this time, and why lord Howe has not attempted some plan of negotiation before, as he seems so desirous of it. If I may be allowed to conjecture and guess at the cause, it may be that part of the Hessians have not arrived, as mentioned in the examination transmitted yesterday,—or that general Burgoyne has not made such progress as was expected, to form a junction of their two armies,—or, what I think equally probable, they mean to procrastinate their operations for some time, trusting that the militias which have come to our succour will soon become tired and return home, as is but too usual with them.—Congress will make their observations upon these several matters, and favor me with the result as soon as they have done.—They will observe my answer to lord Drummond, who (I am pretty confident) has not attended to the terms of his parole, but has violated it in several instances. It is with the rest of the papers: but, if my memory serves me, he was not to hold any correspondence directly or indirectly with those in arms against us, or to go into any port or harbor in America, where the enemy themselves were or had a fleet, or to go on board their ships.

The treaty with the Indians is in the box which lieutenant-colonel Reed, I presume, has delivered before this. If Congress are desirous of seeing it, they will be pleased to have

have the box opened. It contains a variety of papers, and all the affairs of the army, from my firft going to Cambridge, till it was fent away.

This morning, the Phœnix and Rofe men of-war, with two tenders, availing themfelves of a favorable and brifk wind, came down the river, and have joined the fleet. Our feveral batteries fired at them in their paffage, but without any good effect that I could perceive.

I have the honor to be, &c. G. W.

Sir, New-York, Auguft 19, 1776.

I HAVE nothing of moment to communicate to Congrefs, as things are in the fituation they were when I had laft the honor of addreffing them.

By a letter from general Ward, of the twelfth, I find that Whitcomb's regiment, on the eighth, and Phinney's, on the ninth, marched from Bofton for Ticonderoga.

Governor Trumbull alfo, in a letter of the thirteenth, advifes me that Ward's regiment in the fervice of the ftates was on the march to this army, and that he and his council of fafety had in the whole ordered fourteen militia regiments to reinforce us. Three of them have arrived, and amount to about a thoufand and twenty men. When the whole come in, we fhall be on a much more refpectable footing than we have been: but I greatly fear, if the enemy defer their attempt for any confiderable time, they will be extremely impatient to return home; and if they fhould, we fhall be reduced to diftrefs again.

He alfo adds that captain Van Buren, who had been fent for that purpofe, had procured a fufficient fupply of failcloth for the veffels to be employed on the lake, and a part of the cordage, in that ftate; and had a profpect of getting the remainder.

As there will be a difficulty in all probability to circulate the papers defigned for the foreign troops, and many mifcarriages

carriages may happen before it can be effected, it may be proper to furnish me with a larger quantity than what I already have.

Inclosed I have the honor to transmit you a general return of our whole force at this time, in which are comprehended the three regiments of militia above mentioned. I am sorry it should be so much weakened by sickness. The return will shew you how it distresses us.

I have the honor to be, &c.   G. W.

P. S. The post just now arrived has brought a further supply of papers for the Hessians, which makes my requisition unnecessary.

Sir,   *New-York, August* 20, 1776.

I WAS yesterday morning favored with yours of the seventeenth, accompanied by several resolutions of Congress, and commissions for officers appointed to the late vacancies in this army.

I wrote some days ago to general Schuyler to propose to generals Carleton and Burgoyne an exchange of prisoners in consequence of a former resolve of Congress authorising their commanders in each department to negotiate one. That of major Meigs for major French, and captain Dearborn's for any officer of equal rank, I submitted to general Howe's consideration, by letter, on the seventeenth, understanding their paroles had been sent him by general Carleton; but have not yet received his answer upon the subject.

In respect to the exchange of the prisoners in Canada, if a proposition on that head has not been already made (and I believe it has not), the inclosed copy of general Carleton's orders (transmitted me under seal by major Bigelow, who was sent with a flag to general Burgoyne from Ticonderoga, with the proceedings of Congress on the breach of capitulation at the Cedars, and the inhuman treatment of our people afterwards) will shew it is unnecessary, as he has determined

mined to send them to their own provinces, there to remain as prisoners; interdicting at the same time all kind of intercourse between us and his army, except such as may be for the purpose of imploring the king's mercy.—The assassination he mentions, of brigadier-general Gordon, is a fact entirely new to me, and what I never heard of before.—I shall not trouble Congress with my strictures upon this * * * performance, * * * only observing that its design is somewhat artful, and that each boatman with major Bigelow was furnished with a copy.

I have also transmitted Congress a copy of the major's journal, to which I beg leave to refer them for the intelligence reported by him on his return from the truce.

By a letter from general Greene yesterday evening, he informed me he had received an express from Hog-Island inlet, advising that five of the enemy's small vessels had appeared at the mouth of the creek, with some troops on board;— also that he had heard two periaguas were off Oyster-bay,— the whole supposed to be after live stock;—and, to prevent their getting it, he had detached a party of horse, and two hundred and twenty men, among them twenty riflemen. I have not received further intelligence upon the subject.

I am also advised by the examination of a captain Button (master of a vessel that had been taken) transmitted me by general Mercer, that the general report among the enemy's troops, when he came off, was, that they were to attack Long-Island, and to secure our works there if possible, at the same time that another part of their army was to land above this city. This information is corroborated by many other accounts, and is probably true: nor will it be possible to prevent them landing on the island, as its great extent affords a variety of places favorable for that purpose, and the whole of our works on it are at the end opposite to the city. However, we shall attempt to harrass them as much as possible, which will be all that we can do.

I have the honor to be, &c. - G. W.

Sir, New-York, August 21, 1776.

INCLOSED I have the honor to transmit you a copy of my letter to lord Howe (as well on the subject of a general exchange of prisoners in the naval line, as that of lieutenant Josiah in particular) and of his lordship's answer, which, for its matter and manner, is very different from general Carleton's orders which were forwarded yesterday.

The situation of the armies being the same as when I had the pleasure of addressing you last, I have nothing special to communicate on that head, nor more to add, than that I am, with all possible respect, &c. G. W.

Sir, New-York, August 22, 1776.

I DO myself the honor to transmit Congress a copy of a letter I received yesterday evening by express from governor Livingston, also copies of three reports from colonel Hand.

Though the intelligence reported by the spy on his return to governor Livingston has not been confirmed by the event he mentions (an attack last night), there is every reason to believe that one is shortly designed. The falling down of several ships yesterday evening to the Narrows, crowded with men,—those succeeded by many more this morning,—and a great number of boats parading around them (as I was just now informed) with troops,—are all circumstances indicating an attack: and it is not improbable it will be made to-day. It could not have happened last night, by reason of a most violent gust.

We are making every preparation to receive them; and I trust, under the smiles of providence, with our own exertions, that my next, if they do attack, will transmit an account that will be pleasing to every friend of America, and of the rights of humanity.

I have the honor to be, &c. G. W.

Sir,   New-York, *August* 23, 1776.

I BEG leave to inform Congress, that, yesterday morning and in the course of the preceding night, a considerable body of the enemy, amounting by report to eight or nine thousand, and these all British, landed from the transport-ships mentioned in my last, at Gravesend-bay on Long-Island, and have approached within three miles of our lines, having marched across the low cleared grounds near the woods at Flat-bush, where they are halted, from my last intelligence.

I have detached from hence six batallions as a reinforcement to our troops there, which are all that I can spare at this time, not knowing but the fleet may move up with the remainder of their army, and make an attack here, on the next flood-tide. If they do not, I shall send a further reinforcement, should it be necessary; and have ordered five batallions more to be in readiness for that purpose.

I have no doubt but a little time will produce some important events. I hope they will be happy.—The reinforcement detached yesterday went off in high spirits; and I have the pleasure to inform you that the whole of the army, that are effective and capable of duty, discover the same, and great cheerfulness.—I have been obliged to appoint major-general Sullivan to the command on the island, owing to general Greene's indisposition:—he has been extremely ill for several days, and still continues bad.

By wednesday evening's post I received a letter from general Ward, inclosing a copy of the invoice of the ordnance-stores taken by captain Manly, with the appraisement of the same (made in pursuance of my direction, founded on the order of Congress), which I do myself the honor of transmitting.—You will also receive the treaty between the commissioners and the Indians of the Six-Nations, and others, at the German-Flats, which general Schuyler requested me to forward, by his letter of the eighteenth instant.

I have the honor to be, &c.   G. W.

Sir, New-York, August 24, 1776.

THE irregularity of the post prevents your receiving the early and constant intelligence it is my wish to communicate. This is the third letter which you will probably receive from me by the same post. The first was of little or no consequence: but that of yesterday gave you the best information I had been able to obtain, of the enemy's landing and movements upon Long-Island.—Having occasion to go over thither yesterday, I sent my letter to the post-office at the usual hour, being informed that the rider was expected every moment, and would go out again directly: but in the evening when I sent to inquire, none had come in.

I now inclose you a report made to me by general Sullivan after I left Long-Island yesterday. I do not conceive that the enemy's whole force was in motion, but a detached party rather. I have sent over four more regiments, with boats, to be ready either to reinforce the troops under general Sullivan, or to return to this place, if the remainder of the fleet at the watering-place should push up to the city; which hitherto (I mean, since the landing upon Long-Island) they have not had in their power to do, on account of the wind which has either been a-head or too small when the tide has served. I have nothing further to trouble the Congress with at present, than that I am theirs and your most obedient humble servant, G. W.

Sir, New-York, August 26, 1776.

I HAVE been duly honored with your favors of the twentieth and twenty-fourth, and am happy to find my answer to lord Drummond has met the approbation of Congress. Whatever his views were, most certainly his conduct respecting his parole is highly reprehensible.

Since my letter of the twenty-fourth, almost the whole of the enemy's fleet have fallen down to the Narrows; and, from this circumstance, and the striking of their tents at their several encampments on Staten-Island from time to time previous to the departure of the ships from thence, we are led to think they mean to land the main body of their army on Long-Island, and to make their grand push there. I have ordered over considerable reinforcements to our troops there, and shall continue to send more as circumstances may require. There has been a little skirmishing and irregular firing kept up between their and our advanced guards, in which colonel Martin of the Jersey levies has received a wound in his breast, which, it is apprehended, will prove mortal; a private has had his leg broke by a cannon-ball, and another has received a shot in the groin from their musketry. This is all the damage they have yet done us:—what they have sustained, is not known.

The shifting and changing the regiments have undergone of late has prevented their making proper returns, and of course put it out of my power to transmit a general one of the army. However, I believe our strength is much the same as it was when the last was made, with the addition of nine militia regiments come from the state of Connecticut, averaging about three hundred and fifty men each. These are nine of the fourteen regiments mentioned in my letter of the nineteenth.—Our people still continue to be very sickly.

The papers designed for the foreign troops have been put into several channels, in order that they might be conveyed to them; and, from the information I had yesterday, I have reason to believe many have fallen into their hands.

I have inclosed a copy of lord Drummond's second letter (in answer to mine) which I received since I transmitted his first, and which I have thought necessary to lay before Congress, that they may possess the whole of the correspondence between us, and see how far he has exculpated himself from the charge alleged against him. The log-book he mentions to have sent colonel Moylan proves nothing in his favor. That shews he had been at Bermuda, and from thence to some other island, on his passage from which to this place,

place, the vessel he was in was boarded by a pilot who brought her into the Hook, where he found the British fleet, which his lordship avers he did not expect were there, having understood their destination was to the southward.

I have the honor to be, &c. G. W.

[*The following letter is from one of the general's aides, whose signature will also appear to a few of the subsequent letters in this volume.*]

Sir, *New-York, Aug. 27, 1776, 8 o'clock, P. M.*

I THIS minute returned from our lines on Long-Island, where I left his excellency the general. From him I have it in command to inform Congress, that yesterday he went there, and continued till evening, when, from the enemy's having landed a considerable part of their forces,—and many of their movements,—there was reason to apprehend they would make in a little time a general attack.—As they would have a wood to pass through before they could approach the lines, it was thought expedient to place a number of men there on the different roads leading from where they were stationed, in order to harrass and annoy them in their march.—This being done, early this morning a smart engagement ensued between the enemy and our detachments, which, being unequal to the force they had to contend with, have sustained a pretty considerable loss : at least many of our men are missing. Among those that have not returned, are generals Sullivan and lord Stirling. The enemy's loss is not known certainly : but we are told by such of our troops as were in the engagement and have come in, that they had many killed and wounded.—Our party brought off a lieutenant, sergeant, and corporal, with twenty privates, prisoners.

While these detachments were engaged, a column of the enemy descended from the woods, and marched towards the centre

centre of our lines with a design to make an impression, but were repulsed. This evening they appeared very numerous about the skirts of the woods, where they have pitched several tents: and his excellency inclines to think they mean to attack and force us from our lines by way of regular approaches, rather than in any other manner.

To-day, five ships of the line came up towards the town, where they seemed desirous of getting, as they turned a long time against an unfavorable wind: and on my return this evening, I found a deserter from the twenty-third regiment, who informed me that they design, as soon as the wind will permit them to come up, to give us a severe cannonade, and to silence our batteries, if possible.

I have the honor to be, in great haste, sir, your most obedient, ROBERT H. HARRISON.

SIR, *Long-Island, Aug. 29, 1776, half after 4, A. M.*

I WAS last night honored with your favor of the twenty-seventh, accompanied by sundry resolutions of Congress. Those respecting the officers, &c, that may be wounded in the service of the states, are founded much in justice, and (I should hope) may be productive of many salutary consequences. As to the encouragement to the Hessian officers, I wish it may have the desired effect. Perhaps it might have been better, had the offer been sooner made.

Before this, you will probably have received a letter from Mr. Harrison, of the twenty-seventh, advising of the engagement between a detachment of our men and the enemy on that day.—I am sorry to inform Congress that I have not yet heard either of general Sullivan or lord Stirling, who (they would observe) were among the missing after the engagement: nor can I ascertain our loss. I am hopeful, part of our men will yet get in: several did yesterday morning.— That of the enemy is also uncertain: the accounts are various. I incline to think they suffered a good deal. Some deserters say five hundred were killed and wounded.

There was some skirmishing, the greatest part of yesterday, between parties from the enemy and our people: in the evening it was pretty smart. The event I have not yet learned.

The weather of late has been extremely wet. Yesterday it rained severely the whole afternoon, which distressed our people much,—not having a sufficiency of tents to cover them, and what we have, not being got over yet. I am in hopes they will all be got to-day, and that they will be more comfortably provided, though the great scarcity of these articles distresses us beyond measure, not having any thing like a sufficient number to protect our people from the inclemency of the weather;—which has occasioned much sickness, and the men to be almost broken down.

I have the honor to be, &c. G. W.

SIR, *New-York, August* 31, 1776.

INCLINATION as well as duty would have induced me to give Congress the earliest information of my removal and that of the troops, from Long-Island and its dependencies, to this city, the night before last: but the extreme fatigue which myself and family have undergone, as much from the weather since as the engagement on the twenty-seventh, rendered me and them entirely unfit to take pen in hand. Since monday, scarce any of us have been out of the lines till our passage across the East-river was effected yesterday morning; and, for forty-eight hours preceding that, I had hardly been off my horse, and never closed my eyes; so that I was quite unfit to write or dictate till this morning.

Our retreat was made without any loss of men or ammunition, and in better order than I expected from troops in the

the situation ours were.. We brought off all our cannon and stores, except a few heavy pieces, which, in the condition the earth was by a long-continued rain, we found, upon trial, impracticable. The wheels of the carriages sinking up to the hobs rendered it impossible for our whole force to drag them.—We left but little provisions on the island, except some cattle which had been driven within our lines, and which, after many attempts to force across the water, we found impossible to effect, circumstanced as we were.

I have inclosed a copy of the council of war held previous to the retreat, to which I beg leave to refer Congress for the reasons, or many of them, that led to the adoption of that measure.

Yesterday evening and last night, a party of our men were employed in bringing our stores, cannon, tents, &c, from Governor's-Island, which they nearly completed. Some of the heavy cannon remain there still, but (I expect) will be got away to-day.

In the engagement on the twenty-seventh, generals Sullivan and Stirling were made prisoners. The former has been permitted, on his parole, to return for a little time. From my lord Stirling I had a letter by general Sullivan (a copy of which I have the honor to transmit) that contains his information of the engagement with his brigade. It is not so full and certain as I could wish:—he was hurried most probably, as his letter was unfinished:—nor have I been yet able to obtain an exact account of our loss:—we suppose it from seven hundred to a thousand killed and taken.

General Sullivan says lord Howe is extremely desirous of seeing some of the members of Congress; for which purpose he was allowed to come out, and to communicate to them what has passed between him and his lordship. I have consented to his going to Philadelphia, as I do not mean, or conceive it right, to withhold, or prevent him from giving, such information as he possesses in this instance.

I am much hurried and engaged in arranging and making

new difpofitions of our forces; the movements of the enemy requiring them to be immediately had;—and therefore have only time to add, that I am, with my beft regards to Congrefs, their and your moft obedient, &c. G. W.

Sir, New-York, September 2, 1776.

AS my intelligence of late has been rather unfavorable, and would be received with anxiety and concern, peculiarly happy fhould I efteem myfelf, were it in my power at this time to tranfmit fuch information to Congrefs, as would be more pleafing and agreeable to their wifhes:—but, unfortunately for me,—unfortunately for them,—it is not.

Our fituation is truly diftreffing. The check our detachment fuftained on the twenty-feventh ultimo has difpirited too great a proportion of our troops, and filled their minds with apprehenfion and defpair. The militia, inftead of calling forth their utmoft efforts to a brave and manly oppofition in order to repair our loffes, are difmayed, intractable, and impatient to return. Great numbers of them have gone off,—in fome inftances, almoft by whole regiments, by half ones, and by companies at a time. This circumftance, of itfelf, independent of others, when fronted by a well-appointed enemy fuperior in number to our whole collected force, would be fufficiently difagreeable:—but, when their example has infected another part of the army,—when their want of difcipline, and refufal of almoft every kind of reftraint and government, have produced a like conduct but too common to the whole, and an entire difregard of that order and fubordination neceffary to the well doing of an army, and which had been inculcated before, as well as the nature of our military eftablifhment would admit of,—our condition is ftill more alarming: and with the deepeft concern I am obliged to confefs my want of confidence in the generality of the troops.

All thefe circumftances fully confirm the opinion I ever entertained,

entertained, and which I more than once in my letters took the liberty of mentioning to Congress, that no dependence could be put in a militia, or other troops than those enlisted and embodied for a longer period than our regulations heretofore have prescribed. I am persuaded, and as fully convinced as I am of any one fact that has happened, that our liberties must of necessity be greatly hazarded if not entirely lost, if their defence is left to any but a permanent standing army,—I mean, one to exist during the war. Nor would the expense, incident to the support of such a body of troops as would be competent to almost every exigency, far exceed that which is daily incurred by calling in succour, and new enlistments, which, when effected, are not attended with any good consequences. Men who have been free, and subject to no control, cannot be reduced to order in an instant : and the privileges and exemptions, they claim and will have, influence the conduct of others; and the aid derived from them is nearly counterbalanced by the disorder, irregularity, and confusion they occasion.

I cannot find that the bounty of ten dollars is likely to produce the desired effect. When men can get double that sum to engage for a month or two in the militia, and that militia frequently called out, it is hardly to be expected.— The addition of land might have a considerable influence on a permanent enlistment.

Our number of men at present fit for duty is under twenty thousand : they were so by the last returns and best accounts I could get after the engagement on Long-Island; since which, numbers have deserted. I have ordered general Mercer to send the men intended for the flying camp to this place, about a thousand in number, and to try with the militia, if practicable, to make a diversion upon Staten-Island.

Till of late, I had no doubt in my own mind, of defending this place : nor should I have yet, if the men would do their duty : but this I despair of. It is painful, and extremely grating

grating to me, to give such unfavorable accounts: but it would be criminal to conceal the truth at so critical a juncture. Every power I possess shall be exerted to serve the cause; and my first wish is, that, whatever may be the event, the Congress will do me the justice to think so.

If we should be obliged to abandon the town, ought it to stand as winter-quarters for the enemy?—They would derive great conveniences from it on the one hand; and much property would be destroyed on the other.—It is an important question, but will admit of but little time for deliberation. At present I dare say the enemy mean to preserve it if they can. If Congress therefore should resolve upon the destruction of it, the resolution should be a profound secret, as the knowledge of it will make a capital change in their plans.—I have the honor to be, &c. G. W.

Sir, *New-York, September* 4, 1776.

SINCE I had the honor of addressing you on the second, our affairs have not undergone a change for the better, nor assumed a more agreeable aspect than what they then wore. The militia, under various pretences, of sickness, &c, are daily diminishing; and in a little time, I am persuaded, their number will be very inconsiderable.

On monday night a forty-gun ship passed up the Sound between Governor's and Long-Island, and anchored in Turtlebay. In her passage she received a discharge of cannon from our batteries, but without any damage; and, having a favorable wind and tide, soon got out of their reach. Yesterday morning I dispatched major Crane of the artillery, with two twelve-pounders and a howitzer, to annoy her; who, hulling her several times, forced her from that station, and to take shelter behind an island, where she still continues. There are several other ships of war in the Sound, with a good many transports or store-ships which came round Long-Island, so that that communication is entirely cut off.

off.—The admiral, with the main body of the fleet, is close in with Governor's-Island.

Judging it expedient to guard against every contingency as far as our peculiar situation will admit, and that we may have resources left if obliged to abandon this place, I have sent away and am removing above Kingsbridge all our stores that are unnecessary, and that will not be immediately wanted.

I have inclosed several original letters from some of our officers prisoners at Quebec, which fell into general Gates's hands, and were transmitted by him to general Schuyler who sent them to me. General Gates adds, that the persons who brought them said general Burgoyne had sent messages to the inhabitants upon the lakes, inviting their continuance on their farms, and assuring them that they should remain in security.

The post-master having removed his office from the city to Dobbs's-ferry, as it is said, makes it extremely inconvenient, and will be the means of my not giving such constant and regular intelligence as I could wish.—Cannot some mode be devised, by which we may have a pretty constant and certain intercourse and communication kept up? It is an interesting matter, and of great importance; and, as such, I am persuaded, will meet with due attention from Congress.

I have transmitted the copy of general Gates's letter as sent me by general Schuyler, from which Congress will discover all the information I have respecting general Burgoyne's message, and my latest intelligence from Ticonderoga, with the returns of the army there.—Those of the army here it is impossible to obtain, till the hurry and bustle we are now in are a little over.

I have the honor to be, &c. G. W.

P. S. Congress will perceive, by general Gates's letter, his want of musket-cartridge-paper. It is impossible to supply him from hence. They will therefore be pleased to order what he wants (if it can be procured) to be immediately sent him from Philadelphia.

SIR, *New-York, September* 6, 1776.

I WAS last night honored with your favor of the third, with sundry resolutions of Congress: and perceiving it to be their opinion and determination that no damage shall be done the city in case we are obliged to abandon it, I shall take every measure in my power to prevent it.

Since my letter of the fourth, nothing very material has occurred, unless it is that the fleet seem to be drawing more together, and all getting close in with Governor's-Island. Their designs we cannot learn; nor have we been able to procure the least information of late, of any of their plans or intended operations.

As the enemy's movements are very different from what we expected,—and, from their large encampments a considerable distance up the Sound, there is reason to believe they intend to make a landing above or below Kingsbridge, and thereby to hem in our army, and cut off the communication with the country,—I mean to call a council of general officers to-day or to-morrow, and endeavor to digest and fix upon some regular and certain system of conduct to be pursued in order to baffle their efforts and counteract their schemes; and also to determine of the expediency of evacuating or attempting to maintain the city and the several posts on this island. The result of their opinion and deliberations I shall advise Congress of by the earliest opportunity, which will be by express, having it not in my power to communicate any intelligence by post, as the office is removed to so great a distance, and entirely out of the way.

I have inclosed a list of the officers who are prisoners, and from whom letters have been received by a flag.—We know there are others not included in the list.

General

General Sullivan having informed me that general Howe was willing that an exchange of him for general Prescot should take place, it will be proper to send general Prescot immediately, that it may be effected.

As the militia regiments in all probability will be impatient to return, and become pressing for their pay, I shall be glad of the direction of Congress, whether they are to receive it here or from the conventions or assemblies of the respective states to which they belong. On the one hand, the settlement of their abstracts will be attended with trouble and difficulty: on the other, they will go away much better satisfied, and be more ready to give their aid in future, if they are paid before their departure.

Before I conclude, I must take the liberty of mentioning to Congress the great distress we are in for want of money. Two months' pay (and more to some batallions) is now due to the troops here, without any thing in the military chest to satisfy it. This occasions much dissatisfaction, and almost a general uneasiness. Not a day passes without complaints and the most importunate and urgent demands on this head.—As it may injure the service greatly, and the want of a regular supply of cash produce consequences of the most fatal tendency, I entreat the attention of Congress to this subject, and that we may be provided as soon as can be with a sum equal to every present claim.

I have wrote to general Howe, proposing an exchange of general M'Donald for lord Stirling, and shall be extremely happy to obtain it, as well as that of general Sullivan for general Prescot,—being greatly in want of them, and under the necessity of appointing, pro tempore, some of the colonels to command brigades.

I have the honor to be, &c.   G. W.

P. S. As two regiments from North-Carolina and three regiments more from Virginia are ordered here,—if they could embark at Norfolk, &c, and come up the bay with security, it would expedite their arrival, and prevent the men from a

long

long fatiguing march. This however should not be attempted if the enemy have vessels in the bay, which might probably intercept them.

Sir,   New-York, September 7, 1776.

THIS will be delivered you by captain Martindale and lieutenant Turner, who were taken last fall in the armed brig Washington, and who, with Mr. Childs the second lieutenant, have lately effected their escape from Halifax. Captain Martindale and these two officers have applied to me for pay from the first of January till this time: but, not conceiving myself authorised to grant it, however reasonable it may be, as they were only engaged till the last of December,—at their instance I have mentioned the matter to Congress, and submit their case to their consideration.

I have the honor to be, &c.   G. W.

Sir,   New-York, Head-Quarters, Sept. 8, 1776.

SINCE I had the honor of addressing you on the sixth instant, I have called a council of the general officers, in order to take a full and comprehensive view of our situation, and thereupon form such a plan of future defence as may be immediately pursued, and subject to no other alteration than a change of operations on the enemy's side may occasion.

Before the landing of the enemy on Long-Island, the point of attack could not be known, or any satisfactory judgment formed of their intentions. It might be on Long-Island, on Bergen, or directly on the city. This made it necessary to be prepared for each, and has occasioned an expense of labor which now seems useless, and is regretted by those who form a judgment from after-knowledge. But I trust, men of discernment will think differently, and see that by such works and preparations we have not only delayed the operations of the campaign till it is too late to effect any capital incurfion into the country, but have drawn the enemy's forces to one point and obliged them to [*difclofe*] their plan, fo as to enable us to form our defence on fome certainty.

It is now extremely obvious from all intelligence,—from their movements, and every other circumftance,—that having landed their whole army on Long-Ifland (except about four thoufand on Staten-Ifland), they mean to inclofe us on the ifland of New-York by taking poft in our rear while the fhipping effectually fecure the front; and thus, either by cutting off our communication with the country, oblige us to fight them on their own terms, or furrender at difcretion, —or by a brilliant ftroke endeavor to cut this army in pieces, and fecure the collection of arms and ftores, which they well know we fhall not be able foon to replace.

Having therefore their fyftem unfolded to us, it became an important confideration how it could be moft fuccefsfully oppofed. On every fide there is a choice of difficulties; and every meafure on our part (however painful the reflexion is from experience) to be formed with fome apprehenfion that all our troops will not do their duty. In deliberating on this great queftion, it was impoffible to forget, that hiftory, our own experience, the advice of our ableft friends in Europe, the fears of the enemy, and even the declarations of Congrefs, demonftrate, that on our fide the war fhould be defenfive—(it has ever been called a war of pofts);—that we fhould on all occafions avoid a general action, nor put any thing to the rifk, unlefs compelled by a neceffity into which we ought never to be drawn.

The arguments on which fuch a fyftem was founded were deemed unanfwerable; and experience has given her fanction. With thefe views, and being fully perfuaded that it would be prefumption to draw out our young troops into open ground againft their fuperiors both in number and difcipline, I have never fpared the fpade and pickaxe. I confefs I have not found that readinefs to defend even ftrong

pofts

posts at all hazards, which is necessary to derive the greatest benefit from them. The honor of making a brave defence does not seem to be a sufficient stimulus when success is very doubtful, and the falling into the enemy's hands probable: but I doubt not, this will be gradually attained.—We are now in a strong post, but not an impregnable one, nay acknowledged by every man of judgment to be untenable, unless the enemy will make the attack upon lines when they can avoid it, and their movements indicate that they mean to do so.

To draw the whole army together in order to arrange the defence proportionate to the extent of lines and works, would leave the country open for an approach, and put the fate of this army and its stores on the hazard of making a successful defence in the city, or the issue of an engagement out of it. On the other hand, to abandon a city which has been by some deemed defensible, and on whose works much labor has been bestowed, has a tendency to dispirit the troops and enfeeble our cause. It has also been considered as the key to the northern country. But as to that, I am fully of opinion that the establishing of strong posts at Mount-Washington on the upper part of this island, and on the Jersey side opposite to it, with the assistance of the obstructions already made (and which may be improved) in the water, not only the navigation of Hudson's-river, but an easier and better communication may be more effectually secured between the northern and southern states. This, I believe, every one acquainted with the situation of the country will readily agree to; and it will appear evident to those who have an opportunity of recurring to good maps.

These and many other consequences, which will be involved in the determination of our next measure, have given our minds full employ, and led every one to form a judgment as the various objects presented themselves to his view.

The post at Kingsbridge is naturally strong, and is pretty well fortified: the heights about it are commanding, and might

might soon be made more so. These are important objects, and I have attended to them accordingly. I have also removed from the city all the stores and ammunition except what was absolutely necessary for its defence, and made every other disposition that did not essentially interfere with that object,—carefully keeping in view, until it should be absolutely determined on full consideration, how far the city was to be defended at all events.

In resolving points of such importance, many circumstances peculiar to our own army also occur. Being only provided for a summer's campaign, their clothes, shoes, and blankets, will soon be unfit for the change of weather which we every day feel. At present we have not tents for more than two-thirds, many of them old and worn out; but if we had a plentiful supply, the season will not admit of continuing in them long.—The case of our sick is also worthy of much consideration. Their number, by the returns, forms at least one-fourth of the army. Policy and humanity require they should be made as comfortable as possible.

With these and many other circumstances before them, the whole council of general officers met yesterday in order to adopt some general line of conduct to be pursued at this important crisis. I intended to have procured their separate opinions on each point; but time would not admit. I was therefore obliged to collect their sense more generally than I could have wished.—All agreed the town would not be tenable if the enemy resolved to bombard and cannonade it: but the difficulty attending a removal operated so strongly, that a course was taken between abandoning it totally and concentring our whole strength for its defence: nor were some a little influenced in their opinion, to whom the determination of Congress was known, against an evacuation totally, as they were led to suspect Congress wished it to be maintained at every hazard.

It was concluded to arrange the army under three divisions;—five thousand to remain for the defence of the city;

city;—nine thousand to Kingsbridge and its dependencies, as well to possess and secure those posts, as to be ready to attack the enemy who are moving eastward on Long-Island, if they should attempt to land on this side;—the remainder to occupy the intermediate space, and support either;—that the sick should be immediately removed to Orangetown, and barracks prepared at Kingsbridge with all expedition to cover the troops.

There were some general officers, in whose judgment and opinion much confidence is to be reposed, that were for a total and immediate removal from the city,—urging the great danger of one part of the army being cut off before the other can support it, the extremities being at least sixteen miles apart;—that our army, when collected, is inferior to the enemy;—that they can move with their whole force to any point of attack, and consequently must succeed by weight of numbers, if they have only a part to oppose them;—that, by removing from hence, we deprive the enemy of the advantage of their ships, which will make at least one half of the force to attack the town;—that we should keep the enemy at bay, put nothing to the hazard, but at all events keep the army together, which may be recruited another year;—that the unspent stores will also be preserved; and, in this case, the heavy artillery can also be secured. But they were over-ruled by a majority, who thought for the present a part of our force might be kept here, and attempt to maintain the city a while longer.

I am sensible a retreating army is encircled with difficulties; that the declining an engagement subjects a general to reproach; and that the common cause may be affected by the discouragement it may throw over the minds of many. Nor am I insensible of the contrary effects, if a brilliant stroke could be made with any probability of success, especially after our loss upon Long-Island. But, when the fate of America may be at stake on the issue,—when the wisdom of cooler moments and experienced men have decided that

we

we should protract the war if possible,—I cannot think it safe or wise to adopt a different system when the season for action draws so near a close.

That the enemy mean to winter in New-York, there can be no doubt:—that, with such an armament, they can drive us out, is equally clear.—The Congress having resolved that it should not be destroyed, nothing seems to remain, but to determine the time of their taking possession. It is our interest and wish to prolong it as much as possible, provided the delay does not affect our future measures.

The militia of Connecticut is reduced, from six thousand, to less than two thousand, and in a few days will be merely nominal. The arrival of some Maryland troops, &c, from the flying camp, has in a great degree supplied the loss of men: but the ammunition they have carried away will be a loss sensibly felt. The impulse for going home was so irresistible, it answered no purpose to oppose it. Though I would not discharge, I have been obliged to acquiesce; and it affords one more melancholy proof, how delusive such dependencies are.

Inclosed I have the honor to transmit a general return, the first I have been able to procure for some time; also a report of captain Newell from our works at Horn's-hook or Hell-gate. Their situation is extremely low, and the Sound so very narrow, that the enemy have them much within their command.—I have the honor to be, &c. G. W.

P. S. The inclosed information this minute came to hand.—I am in hopes we shall henceforth get regular intelligence of the enemy's movements.

SIR, *New-York, September* 11, 1776.

I WAS yesterday honored with your favor of the eighth instant, accompanied by sundry resolutions of Congress, to which I shall pay the strictest attention, and, in the instances required, make them the future rule of my conduct.

The mode of negotiation purfued by lord Howe I did not approve of: but as general Sullivan was fent out upon the bufinefs, and with a meffage to Congrefs, I could not conceive myfelf at liberty to interfere in the matter, as he was in the character of a prifoner, and totally fubject to their power and direction.

The lift of prifoners, before omitted through hurry, is now inclofed; though it will probably have reached Congrefs before this.—I fhall write by the firft opportunity for major Hawfackfe to repair to Philadelphia—(he is in the northern army);—and will alfo mention the feveral appointments in confequence of colonel St. Clair's promotion.

As foon as generals Prefcot and M'Donald arrive, I fhall take meafures to advife general Howe of it, that the propofed exchange for general Sullivan and lord Stirling may be carried into execution.

Since my letter of the eighth, nothing material has occurred, except that the enemy have poffeffed themfelves of Montezore's-ifland, and landed a confiderable number of troops upon it. This ifland lies in the mouth of Haerlem-river, which runs out of the Sound into the North-river, and will give the enemy an eafy opportunity of landing either on the low grounds of Morrifania, if their views are to feize and poffefs the paffes above Kingfbridge, or on the plains of Haerlem, if they defign to intercept and cut off the communication between our feveral pofts. I am making every difpofition and arrangement that the divided ftate of our troops will admit of, and which appear moft likely and the beft calculated to oppofe their attacks; for I prefume there will be feveral.—How the event will be, God only knows: but you may be affured that nothing in my power, circumftanced as I am, fhall be wanting, to effect a favorable and happy iffue.

By my letter of the eighth you would perceive that feveral of the council were for holding the town, conceiving it practicable for fome time. Many of them now, upon feeing

our

our divided state, have altered their opinion, and allow the expediency and necessity of concentring our whole force, or drawing it more together. Convinced of the propriety of this measure, I am ordering our stores away, except such as may be absolutely necessary to keep as long as any troops remain; that, if an evacuation of the city becomes inevitable (which certainly must be the case), there may be as little to remove as possible.

The inclosed packet contains several letters for particular members of Congress and for some gentlemen in Philadelphia. They came to hand yesterday, and were brought from France by a captain Levez lately arrived at Bedford in the Massachusetts state. I must request the favor of you to open the packet, and to have the letters put in a proper channel of conveyance to the gentlemen they are addressed to.

I have the honor to be, &c. G. W.

Sir, *Head-Quarters, New-York, Sept.* 12, 1776.

HIS excellency being called from head-quarters to-day on business of importance which prevents his writing, I therefore do myself the honor to inform Congress of what has happened since his letter of yesterday.

Last evening the enemy transported a number of men from Buchanan's to Montezore's island, and, by their several movements, more strongly indicate their intention to land somewhere about Haerlem or Morrisania,—most likely, at both at the same time. This morning one of the ships that have been for some time in the Sound moved down towards Hell-gate; but, the tide leaving her, she could not get near enough to bring her guns to bear upon our fortification. If she means to attack it, it is probable she will warp in the next tide. Their batteries have kept up a pretty constant fire against ours at that place, but without any considerable effect. This morning they opened a new one.

I do

I do not recollect any other material occurrence, and shall only add, that I have the honor to be, &c. R. H. HARRISON.

SIR,   New-York, September 14, 1776.

I HAVE been duly honored with your favor of the tenth, with the resolution of Congress which accompanied it, and thank them for the confidence they repose in my judgment respecting the evacuation of the city. I could wish to maintain it, because I know it to be of importance: but I am fully convinced that it cannot be done, and that an attempt for that purpose, if persevered in, might and most certainly would be attended with consequences the most fatal and alarming in their nature.

Sensible of this, several of the general officers, since the determination of the council mentioned in my last, petitioned that a second council might be called to reconsider the propositions which had been before them upon the subject. Accordingly I called one on the twelfth, when a large majority not only determined a removal of the army prudent, but absolutely necessary,—declaring they were entirely convinced from a full and minute inquiry into our situation, that it was extremely perilous; and, from every movement of the enemy, and the intelligence received, their plan of operations was to get in our rear, and, by cutting off the communication with the main, oblige us to force a passage through them on the terms they wish, or to become prisoners in some short time for want of necessary supplies of provision.

We are now taking every method in our power to remove the stores, &c, in which we find almost insuperable difficulties. They are so great and so numerous, that I fear we shall not effect the whole before we meet with some interruption.—I fully expected that an attack somewhere would have been made last night. In that I was disappointed; and happy shall I be, if my apprehensions of one to-night, to-night, or in a day or two, are not confirmed by the event. If it is deferred a little while longer, I flatter myself all will be got away, and our force be more concentred, and of course more likely to resist them with success.

Yesterday afternoon, four ships of war, two of forty and two of twenty eight guns, went up the East-river, passing between Governor's and Long-Island, and anchored about a mile above the city, opposite Mr. Stivansent's, where the Rose man-of-war was lying before. The design of their going not being certainly known, gives rise to various conjectures,—some supposing they are to cover the landing of a party of the enemy above the city,—others that they are to assist in destroying our battery at Horn's-hook, that they may have a free and un-interrupted navigation in the Sound. It is an object of great importance to them, and what they are industriously trying to effect by a pretty constant cannonade and bombardment.

Before I conclude, I would beg leave to mention to Congress, that the pay now allowed to nurses for their attendance on the sick is by no means adequate to their services; the consequence of which is, that they are extremely difficult to procure : indeed they are not to be got ; and we are under the necessity of substituting in their place a number of men from the respective regiments, whose service by that means is entirely lost in the proper line of their duty, and but little benefit rendered to the sick. The officers I have talked with upon the subject all agree that they should be allowed a dollar per week, and that for less they cannot be had.

Our sick are extremely numerous, and we find their removal attended with the greatest difficulty. It is a matter that employs much of our time and care ; and what makes it more distressing is the want of proper and convenient places for their reception.—I fear their sufferings will be great and many. However, nothing on my part, that humanity or policy can require, shall be wanting to make them comfortable, so far as the state of things will admit of.

I have the honor to be, &c. G. W.

Head-Quarters at Col. Roger Morris's House, Sept. 16, 1776.
SIR,

ON saturday about sunset, six more of the enemy's ships, one or two of which were men-of-war, passed between Governor's-island and Red-hook, and went up the East-river to the station taken by those mentioned in my last. In half an hour I received two expresses,—one from colonel Serjeant at Horn's-hook [Hell-gate] giving an account that the enemy, to the amount of three or four thousand, had marched to the river, and were embarking for Barns's or Montezore's island, where numbers of them were then encamped;—the other from general Mifflin, that uncommon and formidable movements were discovered among the enemy; which being confirmed by the scouts I had sent out, I proceeded to Haerlem, where it was supposed (or at Morrisania opposite to it) the principal attempt to land would be made. However, nothing remarkable happened that night: but in the morning they began their operations. Three ships of war came up the North-river as high as Bloomingdale, which put a total stop to the removal, by water, of any more of our provision, &c; and about eleven o'clock those in the East-river began a most severe and heavy cannonade, to scour the grounds, and cover the landing of their troops between Turtle-bay and the city, where breastworks had been thrown up to oppose them.

As soon as I heard the firing, I rode with all possible dispatch towards the place of landing, when, to my great surprise and mortification, I found the troops that had been posted in the lines retreating with the utmost precipitation, and those ordered to support them (Parsons and Fellows's brigades)

brigades) flying in every direction, and in the greateſt confuſion, notwithſtanding the exertions of their generals to form them. I uſed every means in my power to rally and get them into ſome order: but my attempts were fruitleſs and ineffectual; and on the appearance of a ſmall party of the enemy, not more than ſixty or ſeventy, their diſorder increaſed, and they ran away in the greateſt confuſion, without firing a ſingle ſhot.

Finding that no confidence was to be placed in theſe brigades, and apprehending that another party of the enemy might paſs over to Haerlem plains and cut off the retreat to this place, I ſent orders to ſecure the heights in the beſt manner with the troops that were ſtationed on and near them; which being done, the retreat was effected with but little or no loſs of men, though of a conſiderable part of our baggage,—occaſioned by this diſgraceful and daſtardly conduct. Moſt of our heavy cannon, and a part of our ſtores and proviſions which we were about removing, was unavoidably left in the city, though every means (after it had been determined in council to evacuate the poſt) had been uſed to prevent it.

We are now encamped with the main body of the army on the heights of Haerlem, where I ſhould hope the enemy would meet with a defeat in caſe of an attack, if the generality of our troops would behave with tolerable bravery. But experience, to my extreme affliction, has convinced me that this is rather to be wiſhed for than expected. However, I truſt that there are many who will act like men, and ſhew themſelves worthy of the bleſſings of freedom.

I have ſent out ſome reconnoitring parties to gain intelligence, if poſſible, of the diſpoſition of the enemy, and ſhall inform Congreſs of every material event by the earlieſt opportunity.—I have the honor to be, &c.

Head-Quarters at Col. R. Morris's House, Sept. 18, 1776.
SIR,

AS my letter of the sixteenth contained intelligence of an important nature, and such as might lead Congress to expect that the evacuation of New-York and retreat to the heights of Haerlem, in the manner they were made, would be succeeded by some other interesting event, I beg leave to inform them that as yet nothing has been attempted upon a large and general plan of attack.

About the time of the post's departure with my letter, the enemy appeared in several large bodies upon the plains about two and a half miles from hence. I rode down to our advanced posts, to put matters in a proper situation if they should attempt to come on. When I arrived there I heard a firing, which, I was informed, was between a party of our rangers under the command of lieutenant-colonel Knolton, and an advanced party of the enemy. Our men came in and told me that the body of the enemy, who kept themselves concealed, consisted of about three hundred as near as they could guess. I immediately ordered three companies of colonel Weedon's regiment from Virginia, under the command of major Leitch, and colonel Knolton with his rangers composed of volunteers from different New-England regiments, to try to get in their rear, while a disposition was making as if to attack them in front, and thereby draw their whole attention that way.

This took effect as I wished on the part of the enemy. On the appearance of our party in front, they immediately ran down the hill, took possession of some fences and bushes, and a smart firing began, but at too great a distance to do much execution on either side. The parties under colonel Knolton and major Leitch unluckily began their attack too soon, as it was rather in flank than in rear.—In a little time major Leitch was brought off wounded, having received three balls through his side; and, in a short time after, colonel
Knolton

Knolton got a wound which proved mortal. Their men however perfevered, and continued the engagement with the greateft refolution.

Finding that they wanted a fupport, I advanced part of colonel Griffith's and colonel Richardfon's Maryland regiments, with fome detachments from the eaftern regiments who were neareft the place of action. Thefe troops charged the enemy with great intrepidity, and drove them from the wood into the plain, and were pufhing them from thence (having filenced their fire in a great meafure) when I judged it prudent to order a retreat, fearing the enemy (as I have fince found was really the cafe) were fending a large body to fupport their party.

Major Leitch, I am in hopes, will recover: but colonel Knolton's fall is much to be regretted, as that of a brave and good officer.—We had about forty wounded: the number of flain is not yet afcertained: but it is very inconfiderable.

By a fergeant who deferted from the enemy and came in this morning, I find that their party was greater than I imagined. It confifted of the fecond batallion of light infantry, a batallion of the royal Highlanders, and three companies of Heffian riflemen, under the command of brigadier-general Leflie. The deferter reports that their lofs in wounded and miffing was eighty-nine, and eight killed. In the latter, his account is too fmall, as our people difcovered and buried double that number.—This affair, I am in hopes, will be attended with many falutary confequences, as it feems to have greatly infpirited the whole of our troops.—The fergeant further adds that a confiderable body of men are now encamped from the Eaft to the North-river, between the feven and eight-mile ftones, under the command of general Clinton.—General Howe, he believes, has his quarters at Mr. Apthorp's houfe.—I have the honor to be, &c. G. W.

P. S. I fhould have wrote to Congrefs by exprefs before now, had I not expected the poft every minute; which, I flatter

flatter myself, will be a sufficient apology for my delaying it.—The late losses we have sustained in our baggage and camp necessaries have added much to our distress which was very great before. I must therefore take the liberty of requesting Congress to have forwarded as soon as possible such a supply of tents, blankets, camp-kettles, and other articles, as can be collected.—We cannot be overstocked.

Head-Quarters at Col. R. Morris's House, Sept. 19, 1776.
Sir,

SINCE I had the honor of addressing you yesterday, nothing material has occurred. However, it is probable in a little time the enemy will attempt to force us from hence, as we are informed they are bringing many of their heavy cannon towards the heights and the works we have thrown up. They have also eight or nine ships of war in the North-river, which (it is said) are to cannonade our right flank when they open their batteries against our front. Every disposition is making on our part for defence: and Congress may be assured that I shall do every thing in my power to maintain the post so long as it shall appear practicable, and conducive to the general good.

I have the honor to be, &c. G. W.

Head-Quarters, Heights of Haerlem, Sept. 20, 1776.
Sir,

I HAVE been honored with your favor of the sixteenth with its inclosures.—To prevent the injury and abuses which would arise from the militia and other troops carrying away ammunition and continental property, I have published the substance of the resolves upon the subject in general orders.

Since my letter of yesterday, nothing of importance has cast up.—The enemy are forming a large and extensive encampment in the plains mentioned in my last, and are busily employed

employed in transporting their cannon and stores from Long-Island. As they advance them this way, we may reasonably expect their operations will not long be deferred.

Inclosed are sundry letters, &c, to which Congress will be pleased to pay such regard as they may think them deserving of.—The letter from monsieur • • • •••• came open under cover of one to me.—Those from colonel Hand and colonel Ward contain a list of vacancies in their regiments, and of the persons they esteem proper to fill them. The former, I believe, returned no list before: the latter says he never got any commissions.—Generals Howe and Erskine's proclamations shew the measures that have been pursued, to force and seduce the inhabitants of Long-Island from their allegiance to the states, and to assist in their destruction.

As the period will soon arrive, when the troops composing the present army (a few excepted) will be disbanded according to the tenor of their enlistments, and the most fatal consequences may ensue if a suitable and timely provision is not made in this instance, I take the liberty of suggesting to Congress not only the expediency but the absolute necessity there is that their earliest attention should be had to this subject. In respect to the time that troops should be engaged for, I have frequently given my sentiments; nor have I omitted to express my opinion of the difficulties that will attend raising them, nor of the impracticability of effecting it without the allowance of a large and extraordinary bounty.

It is a melancholy and painful consideration to those who are concerned in the work and have the command, to be forming armies constantly, and to be left by troops just when they begin to deserve the name, or perhaps at a moment when an important blow is expected. This, I am informed, will be the case at Ticonderoga with part of the troops there, unless some system is immediately come into, by which they can be induced to stay. General Schuyler tells me in a letter received yesterday, that De Haas's, Maxwell's, well's, and Wind's regiments stand engaged only till the beginning of next month, and that the men, he is fearful, will not remain longer than the time of their enlistment.

I would also beg leave to mention to Congress, that the season is fast approaching when clothes of every kind will be wanted for the army. Their distress is already great, and will be increased as the weather becomes more severe. Our situation is now bad, but is much better than that of the militia that are coming to join us from the states of the Massachusetts-Bay and Connecticut in consequence of the requisition of Congress. They, I am informed, have not a single tent or a necessary of any kind; nor can I conceive how it will be possible to support them. These circumstances are extremely alarming, and oblige me to wish Congress to have all the tents, clothing of every kind, and camp necessaries, provided and forwarded, that are to be procured. These eastern reinforcements have not a single necessary, not a pan or a kettle,—in which we are now greatly deficient.—It is with reluctance that I trouble Congress with these matters: but to whom can I resort for relief unless to them? The necessity therefore, which urges the application, will excuse it, I am persuaded.

I have not been able to transmit Congress a general return of the army this week, owing to the peculiar situation of our affairs, and the great shifting and changing among the troops. As soon as I can procure one, a copy shall be forwarded to Congress.

I have the honor to be, &c. G. W.

P. S.—*September* 21, 1776.—Things with us remain in the situation they were yesterday.

SIR, *Head-Quarters, Haerlem Heights, Sept.* 22, 1776.

I HAVE nothing in particular to communicate to Congress respecting the situation of our affairs: it is much the same as when I had the honor of addressing you last.

On friday night, about eleven or twelve o'clock, a fire broke out in the city of New-York, near the new or Saint Paul's church, as it is said, which continued to burn pretty rapidly till after sunrise the next morning. I have not been informed how the accident happened, nor received any certain account of the damage. Report says many of the houses between the Broadway and the river were consumed.

I have the honor to be, &c. G. W.

Sir, *Head-Quarters, Haerlem Heights, Sept.* 24, 1776.

THE post being about to depart, I have only time to add that no event of importance has taken place on this side Hudson's-river since my last of the twenty-second instant.

The inclosed letter, received last night from general Greene who now commands in the Jerseys, will give Congress all the information I have respecting the evacuation of Paulus-Hook and the landing of the enemy to possess it.

I this minute obtained a copy of the general return of our force, the first I have been able to procure for some time past, which I do myself the honor of transmitting for the satisfaction of Congress.

I am, sir, with the greatest respect, &c. G. W.

P. S. The thirteen militia regiments from Connecticut being reduced to a little more than seven hundred men rank and file fit for duty, I have thought proper to discharge the whole, to save the states the immense charge that would arise for officers' pay. There are many militia, too, that have just come in, and on their way from that state, none of whom are provided with a tent, or a single camp utensil. This distresses me beyond measure.

Colonel Morris's on the Heights of Haerlem, Sept. 24, 1776.
Sir,

FROM the hours allotted to sleep I will borrow a few moments to convey my thoughts on sundry important

matters

matters to Congress. I shall offer them with the sincerity which ought to characterise a man of candor, and with the freedom which may be used in giving useful information without incurring the imputation of presumption.

We are now, as it were, upon the eve of another dissolution of our army. The remembrance of the difficulties which happened upon the occasion last year,—the consequences which might have followed the change if proper advantages had been taken by the enemy,—added to a knowledge of the present temper and situation of the troops,—reflect but a very gloomy prospect upon the appearances of things now, and satisfy me beyond the possibility of doubt, that, unless some speedy and effectual measures are adopted by Congress, our cause will be lost.

It is in vain to expect that any or more than a trifling part of this army will again engage in the service on the encouragement offered by Congress. When men find that their townsmen and companions are receiving twenty, thirty, and more dollars, for a few months' service (which is truly the case), it cannot be expected, without using compulsion: and to force them into the service would answer no valuable purpose. When men are irritated, and the passions inflamed, they fly hastily and cheerfully to arms: but after the first emotions are over * * *, a soldier, reasoned with upon the goodness of the cause he is engaged in and the inestimable rights he is contending for, hears you with patience, and acknowledges the truth of your observations, but adds that it is of no more importance to him than others. The officer makes you the same reply, with this further remark, that his pay will not support him, and he cannot ruin himself and family to serve his country, when every member of the community is equally interested, and benefited by his labors. * * *

It becomes evidently clear then, that, as this contest is not likely to be the work of a day,—as the war must be carried on systematically,—and to do it you must have good officers,

officers,—there are, in my judgment, no other possible means to obtain them but by establishing your army upon a permanent footing, and giving your officers good pay. This will induce gentlemen and men of character to engage: and, till the bulk of your officers are composed of such persons as are actuated by principles of honor and a spirit of enterprise, you have little to expect from them. They ought to have such allowances as will enable them to live like and support the characters of gentlemen. * * * Besides, something is due to the man who puts his life in [*your*] hands, hazards his health, and forsakes the sweets of domestic enjoyment.—Why a captain in the continental service should receive no more than five shillings currency per day for performing the same duties that an officer of the same rank in the British service receives ten shillings sterling for, I never could conceive, especially when the latter is provided with every necessary he requires upon the best terms, and the former can scarce procure them at any rate.—There is nothing that gives a man consequence and renders him fit for command, like a support that renders him independent of every body but the state he serves.

With respect to the men, nothing but a good bounty can obtain them upon a permanent establishment: and for no shorter time than the continuance of the war, ought they to be engaged; as facts incontestably prove that the difficulty and cost of enlistments increase with time.—When the army was first raised at Cambridge, I am persuaded the men might have been got, without a bounty, for the war. After this, they began to see that the contest was not likely to end so speedily as was imagined, and to feel their consequence by remarking, that, to get in the militia in the course of the last year, many towns were induced to give them a bounty.

Foreseeing the evils resulting from this, and the destructive consequences which unavoidably would follow short enlistments, I took the liberty in a long letter (date not now recollected, as my letter-book is not here) to recommend the

enlistments

enliftments for and during the war, affigning fuch reafons for it as experience has fince convinced me were well founded. At that time, twenty dollars would, I am perfuaded, have engaged the men for this term. But it will not do to look back: and, if the prefent opportunity is flipped, I am perfuaded that twelve months more will increafe our difficulties four-fold. I fhall therefore take the freedom of giving it as my opinion, that a good bounty be immediately offered, aided by the proffer of at leaft a hundred or a hundred and fifty acres of land, and a fuit of clothes and blanket to each non-commiffioned officer and foldier; as I have good authority for faying, that, however high the men's pay may appear, it is barely fufficient, in the prefent fcarcity and dearnefs of all kinds of goods, to keep them in clothes, much lefs afford fupport to their families.

If this encouragement then is given to the men, and fuch pay allowed the officers as will induce gentlemen of character and liberal fentiments to engage, and proper care and precaution ufed in the nomination (having more regard to the characters of perfons than the number of men they can enlift), we fhould in a little time have an army able to cope with any that can be oppofed to it, as there are excellent materials to form one out of. But while the only merit an officer poffeffes is his ability to raife men,—while thofe men confider and treat him as an equal, and (in the character of an officer) regard him no more than a broom-ftick, being mixed together as one common herd,—no order nor difcipline can prevail; nor will the officer ever meet with that refpect which is effentially neceffary to due fubordination.

To place any dependence upon militia is affuredly refting upon a broken ftaff,—men juft dragged from the tender fcenes of domeftic life,—unaccuftomed to the din of arms,—totally unacquainted with every kind of military fkill; which being followed by a want of confidence in themfelves, when oppofed to troops regularly trained, difciplined, and
appointed,

appointed, superior in knowledge and superior in arms, makes them timid and ready to fly from their own shadows. Besides, the sudden change in their manner of living (particularly in the lodging) brings on sickness in many, impatience in all, and such an unconquerable desire of returning to their respective homes, that it not only produces shameful and scandalous desertions among themselves, but infuses the like spirit into others.

Again, men accustomed to unbounded freedom and no control, cannot brook the restraint which is indispensably necessary to the good order and government of an army; without which, licentiousness and every kind of disorder triumphantly reign.—To bring men to a proper degree of subordination is not the work of a day, a month, or even a year: and, unhappily for us and the cause we are engaged in, the little discipline I have been laboring to establish in the army under my immediate command is in a manner done away by having such a mixture of troops as have been called together within these few months.

Relaxed and unfit as our rules and regulations of war are for the government of an army, the militia (those properly so called; for of these we have two sorts, the six-months-men, and those sent in as a temporary aid) do not think themselves subject to them, and therefore take liberties which the soldier is punished for. This creates jealousy: jealousy begets dissatisfactions; and these by degrees ripen into mutiny, keeping the whole army in a confused and disordered state,—rendering the time of those who wish to see regularity and good order prevail, more unhappy than words can describe. Besides this, such repeated changes take place, that all arrangement is set at nought, and the constant fluctuation of things deranges every plan as fast as adopted.

These, sir, Congress may be assured, are but a small part of the inconveniences which might be enumerated, and attributed to militia: but there is one that merits particular attention; and that is the expense. Certain I am, that it would be be cheaper to keep fifty or a hundred thousand in constant pay, than to depend upon half the number and supply the other half occasionally by militia. The time the latter are in pay before and after they are in camp, assembling and marching,—the waste of ammunition, the consumption of stores, which, in spite of every resolution or requisition of Congress, they must be furnished with, or sent home,—added to other incidental expenses consequent upon their coming and conduct in camp,—surpasses all idea, and destroys every kind of regularity and economy which you could establish among fixed and settled troops, and will, in my opinion, prove (if the scheme is adhered to) the ruin of our cause.

The jealousies of a standing army, and the evils to be apprehended from one, are remote, and, in my judgment, situated and circumstanced as we are, not at all to be dreaded: but the consequence of wanting one, according to my ideas formed from the present view of things, is certain and inevitable ruin. For, if I was called upon to declare upon oath, whether the militia have been most serviceable or hurtful upon the whole, I should subscribe to the latter. I do not mean by this, however, to arraign the conduct of Congress: in so doing I should equally condemn my own measures, if I did not my judgment: but experience, which is the best criterion to work by, so fully, clearly and decisively reprobates the practice of trusting to militia, that no man who regards order, regularity and economy, or who has any regard for his own honor, character, or peace of mind, will risk them upon this issue. * * *

An army formed of good officers moves like clock-work: but there is no situation upon earth less enviable nor more distressing than that person's who is at the head of troops who are regardless of order and discipline, and who are unprovided with almost every necessary. In a word, the difficulties which have for ever surrounded me since I have been in the service, and kept my mind constantly upon the stretch,—the wounds which my feelings (as an officer) have received

by

by a thoufand things which have happened contrary to my expectation and wifhes, * * *—added to a confcioufnefs of my inability to govern an army compofed of fuch difcordant parts, and under fuch a variety of intricate and perplexing circumftances,—induce not only a belief, but a thorough conviction in my mind, that it will be impoffible (unlefs there is a thorough change in our military fyftem) for me to conduct matters in fuch a manner as to give fatisfaction to the public, which is all the recompenfe I aim at, or ever wifhed for.

Before I conclude, I muft apologife for the liberties taken in this letter, and for the blots and fcratchings therein, not having time to give it more correctly.—With truth I can add, that, with every fentiment of refpect and efteem, I am yours and the Congrefs's moft obedient, &c. G. W.

Head-Quarters, Haerlem Heights, September 25, 1776.
SIR,

HAVING wrote you fully on fundry important fubjects this morning as you will perceive by the letter which accompanies this, I mean principally now to inclofe a copy of a letter received from general Howe on funday morning, with the lifts of the prifoners in his hands,—of thofe in our poffeffion belonging to the army immediately under his command,— and of my anfwer, which were omitted to be put in the other. His letter will difcover to Congrefs his refufal to exchange lord Stirling for Mr. M'Donald, confidering the latter only as a major. They will be pleafed to determine how he is to be ranked in future.

The number of prifoners according to thefe returns is greater than what we expected. However, I am inclined to believe, that, among thofe in the lift from Long-Ifland, are feveral militia of general Woodhull's party, who were never arranged in this army.—As to thofe taken on the fifteenth, they greatly exceed the number that I fuppofed fell into their hands in the retreat from the city. At the time that I transmitted an account of that affair, I had not obtained returns, and took the matter upon the officers' reports. They are difficult to get with certainty at any time.—In the skirmish of monday se'nnight, they could have taken but very few.

Before I conclude, I shall take occasion to mention that those returns made with such precision, and the difficulty that will attend the proposed exchange on account of the dispersed and scattered state of the prisoners in our hands, will clearly evince the necessity of appointing commissaries and proper persons to superintend and conduct in such instances. This I took the liberty of urging more than once, as well on account of the propriety of the measure and the saving that would have resulted from it, as that the prisoners might be treated with humanity, and have their wants particularly attended to.

I would also observe (as I esteem it my duty) that this army is in want of almost every necessary,—tents, camp kettles, blankets, and clothes of all kinds. But what is to be done with respect to the two last articles, I know not, as the term of enlistment will be nearly expired by the time they can be provided. This may be exhibited as a further proof of the disadvantages attending the levying of an army upon such a footing as never to know how to keep them without injuring the public or incommoding the men.—I have directed the colonel or commanding officer of each corps to use his endeavors to procure such clothing as is absolutely necessary: but at the same time I confess, that I do not know how they are to be got.—I have the honor to be, &c.   G. W.

Head-Quarters, Heights of Haerlem, September 27, 1776.

SIR,

I HAVE nothing in particular to communicate to Congress by this day's post, as our situation is the same as when I last wrote.

We

We are now sitting on the business the committee came upon, which, it is probable, will be finished this evening. The result they will duly report upon their return.

I received yesterday the inclosed declaration by a gentleman from Elizabethtown who told me many copies were found in the possession of the soldiers from Canada, that were landed there a day or two ago by general Howe's permission. I shall not comment upon it. It seems to be founded on the plan that has been artfully pursued for some time past.—I have the honor to be, &c. G. W.

P. S. The account of the troops, &c, in Canada, comes from a person who is among the prisoners sent from Canada. It was anonymous, nor do I know the intelligencer. According to him, the enemy in that quarter are stronger than we supposed, and their naval force much greater on the lakes than we had any idea of. I trust he has taken the matter up on the enemy's report.

Head-Quarters, Heights of Haerlem, September 28, 1776.
SIR,

BEING about to cross the North-river this morning in order to view the post opposite, and the grounds between that and Paulus-Hook, I shall not add much more than that I have been honored with your favor of the twenty-fourth and its several inclosures; and that, since my letter of yesterday, no important event has taken place.

As colonel Hugh Stephenson, of the rifle regiment ordered lately to be raised, is dead according to the information I have received, I would beg leave to recommend to the particular notice of Congress captain Daniel Morgan just returned among the prisoners from Canada, as a fit and proper person to succeed to the vacancy occasioned by his death. The present field-officers of the regiment cannot claim any right in preference to him, because he ranked above them, and as a captain, when he first entered the service. His conduct as an officer, on the expedition with general Arnold laſt fall,—his intrepid behavior in the aſſault upon Quebec, when the brave Montgomery fell,—the inflexible attachment he profeſſed to our cauſe during his impriſonment, and which he perſeveres in,—added to theſe, his reſidence in the place colonel Stephenſon came from, and his intereſt and influence in the ſame circle, and with ſuch men as are to compoſe ſuch a regiment,—all, in my opinion, entitle him to the favor of Congreſs, and lead me to believe that in his promotion the ſtates will gain a good and valuable officer for the ſort of troops he is particularly recommended to command. * * *—I have the honor to be, &c. G. W.

Head-Quarters, Heights of Haerlem, September 30, 1776.

SIR,

SINCE I had the honor of addreſſing you laſt, nothing of importance has tranſpired; though, from ſome movements yeſterday on the part of the enemy, it would ſeem as if ſomething was intended.

The incloſed memorial, from lieutenant-colonel Shephard of the fourth regiment, I beg leave to ſubmit to the conſideration of Congreſs, and ſhall only add that I could wiſh they would promote him to the command of the regiment and ſend him a commiſſion, being a good and valuable officer, and eſpecially as the vacancy is of a pretty long ſtanding, and I have not had (nor has he) any intelligence from colonel Learned himſelf (who had the command, and who obtained a diſcharge on account of his indiſpoſition), of his deſign to return.—I have alſo incloſed a letter from captain Ballard, which Congreſs will pleaſe to determine on, the ſubject being new and not within my authority.

I have the honor to be, &c. G. W.

P. S. A commiſſion was ſent for colonel Learned, which is now in my hands, having received no application, or heard from him ſince it came.

OFFICIAL LETTERS.

Sir, *Head-Quarters, Haerlem Heights, Oct.* 2, 1776.

I DO myself the honor of transmitting to you the inclosed letter from lieutenant-colonel Livingston, with sundry copies of general Delancey's orders, which discover the measures the enemy are pursuing on Long-Island for raising recruits and obtaining supplies of provisions. In consequence of the intelligence they contain, and authentic advices through other channels respecting these matters, I have sent brigadier-general George Clinton to meet general Lincoln who has got as far as Fairfield with part of the troops lately ordered by the Massachusetts assembly, to concert with him and others an expedition across the Sound with those troops, three companies under colonel Livingston, and such further aid as governor Trumbull can afford, in order to prevent if possible their effecting those important objects, and to assist the inhabitants in the removal of their stock, grain, &c, or in destroying them, that the enemy may not derive any advantage or benefit from them.

The recruiting scheme they are prosecuting with uncommon industry; nor is it confined to Long-Island alone. Having just now received a letter from the committee of West-Chester-county, advising that there are several companies of men in that and Duchess-county preparing to go off and join the king's army, I have given directions to our guard-boats and the centries at our works at Mount-Washington to keep a strict look-out in case they attempt to come down the North-river; also to general Heath at Kingsbridge, that the utmost vigilance may be observed by the regiments and troops stationed above there and down towards the East-river, that they may intercept them, should they take that route with a view of crossing to Long-Island.—I will use every precaution in my power to prevent those parricides from accomplishing their designs: but I have but little hopes of success, as it will be no difficult matter for them to procure a passage over some part or other of the Sound.

I have

I have been applied to lately by colonel Weedon of Virginia, for permission to recruit the deficiency of men in his regiment out of the troops composing the flying camp,—informing me at the same time that some of those from Maryland had offered to engage. Colonel Hand of the rifle batallion made a similar application to-day. If the enlistments could be made, they would have this good consequence,—the securing of so many in the service. However, as the measure might occasion some uneasiness in their own corps, and be considered as a hardship by the states to which they belong, and the means of their furnishing more than the quota exacted from them in the general arrangement, and would make it more difficult for them to complete their own levies, I did not conceive myself at liberty to authorise it without submitting the propriety of it to the consideration of Congress, and obtaining their opinion whether it should be allowed or not.

I have inclosed a list of warrants granted from the second to the thirtieth ultimo inclusive, the only return of the sort that I have been able to make since the resolution for that purpose,—owing to the unsettled state of our affairs, and my having sent my papers away.—You will also receive sundry letters, &c, from general Schuyler, which came under cover to me, and which I have the honor of forwarding.

By a letter just received from the committee of safety of the state of New-Hampshire, I find a thousand of their militia were about to march on the twenty-fourth ultimo to reinforce this army in consequence of the requisition of Congress. Previous to their march, general Ward writes me he was obliged to furnish them with five hundred pounds of powder and a thousand pounds of musket-ball; and I have little reason to expect that they are better provided with other articles than they were with ammunition. In such case they will only add to our present distress which is already far too great, and become disgusted with the service, though

the

the time they are engaged for is only till the first of December.—This will injure their enlisting for a longer term, if not wholly prevent it.

By three deserters who came from the Galatea man-of-war about five days ago, we are informed that several transports had sailed, before they left her, for England, as it was generally reported, in order to return with a supply of provisions, of which they say there is a want.—General Mercer, in a letter, informed me that general Thompson said he had heard they were going to dismiss about a hundred of the ships from the service.—I am also advised by a letter from Mr. Derby at Boston, of the twenty-fixth ultimo, that, the day before, a transport snow had been taken and sent into Piscatawa by a privateer, in her passage from New-York to the West-Indies. She sailed with five more under the convoy of a man-of-war, in order to bring from thence the troops that are there, to join general Howe.—They were all victualled for four months.—From this intelligence it would seem as if they did not apprehend any thing to be meditating against them by the court of France.

October 3.———I have nothing in particular to communicate respecting our situation, it being much the same as when I wrote last.—We had an alarm this morning a little before four o'clock, from some of our out-centries, who reported that a large body of the enemy was advancing towards our lines. This put us in motion: however it turned out entirely premature; or at least we saw nothing of them.

I have the honor to be, &c, G. W.

SIR, *Haerlem, October* 4, 1776.

BEFORE I knew of the late resolutions of Congress which you did me the honor to inclose in your letter of the twenty-fourth, and before I was favored with the visit of your committee, I took the liberty of giving you my sentiments on several points which seemed to be of importance.—

I have no doubt but that the committee will make such report of the state and condition of the army, as will induce Congress to believe that nothing but the most vigorous exertions can put matters upon such a footing as to give this continent a fair prospect of success. Give me leave to say, sir,—I say it with due deference and respect (and my knowledge of the facts, added to the importance of the cause, and the stake I hold in it, must justify the freedom),—that your affairs are in a more unpromising way than you seem to apprehend.

Your army, as I mentioned in my last, is on the eve of its political dissolution. True it is, you have voted a larger one in lieu of it: but the season is late; and there is a material difference between voting of batallions and raising of men. In the latter there are more difficulties than Congress are aware of; which makes it my duty (as I have been informed of the prevailing sentiments of this army) to inform them, that, unless the pay of the officers, especially that of the field-officers, is raised, the chief part of those that are worth retaining will leave the service at the expiration of the present term, as the soldiers will also, if some greater encouragement is not offered them than twenty dollars and a hundred acres of land.

Nothing less, in my opinion, than a suit of clothes annually given to each non-commissioned officer and soldier, in addition to the pay and bounty, will avail; and I question whether that will do, as the enemy (from the information of one John Mash, who, with six others, was taken by our guards) are giving ten pounds bounty for recruits, and have got a batallion under major Rogers nearly completed upon Long-Island.

Nor will less pay, according to my judgment, than I have taken the liberty of mentioning in the inclosed estimate, retain such officers as we could wish to have continued. The difference per month in each batallion will amount to better than a hundred pounds. To this may be added the pay of

the

the staff-officers; for it is presumable they will also require an augmentation: but, being few in number, the sum will not be greatly increased by them, and consequently is a matter of no great moment: but it is a matter of no small importance to make the several offices desirable. When the pay and establishment of an officer once become objects of interested attention, the sloth, negligence, and even disobedience of orders, which at this time but too generally prevail, will be purged off. But while the service is viewed with indifference,—while the officer conceives that he is rather conferring than receiving an obligation,—there will be a total relaxation of all order and discipline, and every thing will move heavily on, to the great detriment of the service, and inexpressible trouble and vexation of the general.

The critical situation of our affairs at this time will justify my saying that no time is to be lost in making of fruitless experiments. An unavailing trial of a month to get an army upon the terms proposed may render it impracticable to do it at all, and prove fatal to our cause; as I am not sure whether any rubs in the way of our enlistments, or unfavorable turn in our affairs, may not prove the means of the enemy recruiting men faster than we do. To this may be added the inextricable difficulty of forming one corps out of another, and arranging matters with any degree of order, in the face of an enemy who are watching for advantages.

At Cambridge, last year, where the officers (and more than a sufficiency of them) were all upon the spot, we found it a work of such extreme difficulty to know their sentiments (each having some terms to propose), that I despaired once of getting the arrangements completed: and I do suppose, that at least a hundred alterations took place before matters were finally adjusted. What must it be then under the present regulation, where the officer is to negotiate this matter with the state he comes from, distant perhaps two or three hundred miles?—some of whom, without leave or licence from me, set out to make personal application, the

moment

moment the refolve got to their hands. What kind of officers thefe are, I leave Congrefs to judge.

If an officer of reputation (for none other fhould be applied to) is afked to ftay, what anfwer can he give, but in the firft place, that he does not know whether it is at his option to do fo, no provifion being made in the refolution of Congrefs, even recommendatory of this meafure; confequently, that it refts with the ftate he comes from (furrounded perhaps with a variety of applications, and influenced probably by local attachments) to determine whether he can be provided for or not ? In the next place, if he is an officer of merit, and knows that the ftate he comes from is to furnifh more batallions than it at prefent has in the fervice, he will fcarcely, after two years' faithful fervices, think of continuing in the rank he now bears, when new creations are to be made, and men appointed to offices (nowife fuperior in merit, and ignorant perhaps of fervice) over his head. A committee, fent to the army from each ftate, may upon the fpot fix things with a degree of propriety and certainty, and is the only method I can fee of bringing matters to a decifion with refpect to the officers of the army. But what can be done in the mean while towards the arrangement in the country, I know not. In the one cafe you run the hazard of lofing your officers; in the other, of encountering delay, unlefs fome method could be devifed of forwarding both at the fame inftant.

Upon the prefent plan, I plainly forefee an intervention of time between the old and new army, which muft be filled up with militia (if to be had), with whom no man who has any regard for his own reputation can undertake to be anfwerable for confequences. I fhall alfo be miftaken in my conjectures, if we do not lofe the moft valuable officers in this army, under the prefent mode of appointing them : confequently, if we have an army at all, it will be compofed of materials not only entirely raw, but (if uncommon pains are not taken) entirely unfit; and I fee fuch a diftruft and jealoufy lousy of military power, that the commander-in-chief has not an opportunity, even by recommendation, to give the least assurances of reward for the most essential services. In a word, such a cloud of perplexing circumstances appear before me, without one flattering hope, that I am thoroughly convinced, unless the most vigorous and decisive exertions are immediately adopted to remedy these evils, that the certain and absolute loss of our liberties will be the inevitable consequence; as one unhappy stroke will throw a powerful weight into the scale against us, enabling general Howe to recruit his army as fast as we shall ours,—numbers being disposed [*to join him*], and many actually doing so already. Some of the most probable remedies, and such as experience has brought to my more intimate knowledge, I have taken the liberty to point out: the rest I beg leave to submit to the consideration of Congress.

I ask pardon for taking up so much of their time with my opinions. But I should betray that trust which they and my country have reposed in me, were I to be silent upon a matter so extremely interesting.—With the most perfect esteem, I have the honor to be, &c. G. W.

Sir, *Head-Quarters, Haerlem Heights, Oct. 5, 1776.*

I WAS last night honored with your favor of the second with sundry resolutions of Congress. * * *

In respect to the exchange of prisoners, I fear it will be a work of great difficulty, owing to their dispersed and scattered situation throughout the states. In order to effect it, I have wrote to the eastern governments to have them collected, and to transmit me an account of their number, distinguishing the names and ranks of the field and commissioned officers, and the corps they belong to. I have also wrote to governor Livingston of the Jerseys upon the subject, and must take the liberty of requesting Congress to give directions that a similar return may be made of those in Pennsylvania

vania and Maryland, and for their being brought to Brunſwic, that they may be ready to be exchanged for an equal number of thoſe of the ſame rank.

I obſerve, by the reſolve of the twenty-ſixth ultimo, that the exchange is particularly directed to be made of the officers and ſoldiers taken on Long-Iſland. But ſhould not that follow the exchange of thoſe officers and men who have lately returned from Quebec, whoſe impriſonment has been much longer, and whoſe ſervice has not been leſs ſevere, and, in many inſtances, conducted with great intrepidity? I have had many applications ſince their arrival, by which they claim a kind of preference as far as their number and the circumſtances of their rank will allow, and which I thought it my duty to mention, that I may obtain ſome direction upon the ſubject.

You will obſerve by a paragraph of a letter received yeſterday from general Howe, a copy of which you have at length, that the non-performance of the agreement between captain Forſter and general Arnold, by which the latter ſtipulated for the return of an equal number of officers and priſoners in our hands for thoſe delivered him, is conſidered in an unfavorable light, and entirely imputed to me, as having the chief command of the armies of the ſtates, and a controlling power over general Arnold.—The pointed manner in which Mr. Howe is pleaſed to expreſs himſelf could not perſonally affect me, ſuppoſing there had been no good grounds for the treaty not being ratified, having been nothing more than an inſtrument of conveying to him the reſolutions formed upon the ſubject. * * *

However, I would beg leave to obſerve, from the letters from the hoſtages,—from what has been reported by others reſpecting captain Forſter's having uſed his endeavors to reſtrain the ſavages from exerciſing their wonted barbarities, though in ſome inſtances they did,—his purchaſing ſome of the priſoners for a pretty conſiderable premium,—but, above all, from the delicate nature of ſuch treaties, and becauſe

the

the non-obfervance of them muſt damp the ſpirits of the officers who make them, and add affliction to the misfortunes of thoſe whom neceſſity and the nature of the caſe force into captivity to give them a ſanction by a long and irkſome confinement,—for theſe reaſons and many more that will readily occur, I could wiſh Congreſs to reconſider the matter, and to carry it into execution.

I am ſenſible the wrong was originally in their employing ſavages, and that whatever cruelties were committed by them ſhould be eſteemed their own acts: yet perhaps, in point of policy, it may not be improper to overlook theſe infractions on their part, and to purſue that mode which will be the moſt likely to render the hardſhips incident to war moſt tolerable, and the greateſt benefits to the ſtate.

I have ventured to ſay thus much upon the ſubject from a regard to the ſervice, and becauſe ſuch gentlemen of the army as I have heard mention it ſeem to wiſh the treaty had been ratified rather than diſallowed.

Incloſed is a liſt of vacancies in the third regiment of Virginia troops, in part occaſioned by the death of major Leitch who died of his wounds on tueſday morning,—and of the gentlemen who ſtand next in regimental order, and who are recommended to ſucceed to them.—You will obſerve that captain John Fitzgerald is ſaid to be appointed to the duty of major. This I have done in order, being the oldeſt captain in the regiment, and, I believe, an officer of unexceptionable merit, and as it was highly neceſſary at this time to have the corps as well and fully officered as poſſible.—There is alſo a vacancy in the firſt continental batallion by the promotion of lieutenant Clarke to a majority in the flying camp, to which colonel Hand has recommended William Patten to ſucceed, as you will perceive by his letter incloſed.

I have taken the liberty to tranſmit a plan for eſtabliſhing a corps of engineers, artificers, &c, ſketched out by colonel Putnam, and which is propoſed for the conſideration

of

of Congress. How far they may incline to adopt it, or whether they may chuse to proceed upon such an extensive scale, they will be pleased to determine. However, I conceive it a matter well worthy of their consideration, being convinced from experience, and from the reasons suggested by colonel Putnam who has acted with great diligence and reputation in the business, that some establishment of the fort is highly necessary, and will be productive of the most beneficial consequences.

If the proposition is approved by Congress, I am informed by good authority that there is a gentleman in Virginia, in the colony service, John Stadler, esquire, a native of Germany, whose abilities in this way are by no means inconsiderable. I am told he was an engineer in the army under general Stanwix, and is reputed to be of skill and ingenuity in the profession. In this capacity I do not know him myself, but am intimately acquainted with him in his private character, as a man of understanding and of good behavior. I would submit his merit to the inquiry of Congress; and if he should answer the report I have had of him, I make no doubt but he will be suitably provided for.

The convention of this state have lately seized and had appraised two new ships, valued at six thousand two hundred and twenty-nine pounds York currency, which they have sent down for the purpose of sinking, and obstructing the channel opposite Mount-Washington. The price being high, and the opinions various as to the necessity of the measure, some conceiving the obstruction nearly sufficient already, and others that they would render it secure, I would wish to have the direction of Congress upon the subject by the earliest opportunity, thinking myself, that, if the enemy should attempt to come up, they should be used, sooner than to hazard their passing.—I must be governed by circumstances, yet hope for their sentiments before any thing is necessary to be done.

Sundry disputes having arisen of late between officers of
different

different regiments and of the same rank, respecting the right of succession to such vacancies as happen from death or other causes,—some suggesting that it should be in a colonial line and governed by the priority of their commissions,—others, that it should be regimentally,—and there being an instance now before me, between the officers of the Virginia regiments, occasioned by the death of major Leitch,— it has become absolutely necessary that Congress should determine the mode by which promotions are to be regulated, —whether colonially and by priority of commissions, or regimentally, reserving a right out of the general rule they adopt, to reward for particular merit, or of with-holding from office such as may not be worthy to succeed.

I have only proposed two modes for their consideration, being satisfied that promotions through the line (as they are called) can never take place without producing discord, jealousy, distrust, and the most fatal consequences. In some of my letters upon the subject of promotions, and one which I had the honor of addressing to the board of war on the thirtieth ultimo, I advised that the mode should be rather practised than resolved on : but I am fully convinced now of the necessity there is of settling it in one of the two ways I have taken the liberty to point out, and under the restrictions I have mentioned ; or the disputes and applications will be endless, and attended with great inconveniences.

I have the honor to be, &c.   G. W.

SIR,   *Head-Quarters, Heights of Haerlem, Oct. 7, 1776.*

I DO myself the honor of transmitting to you a copy of a letter from the comte D'Emery, governor-general of the French part of Saint-Domingo, which I received yesterday, and also my answer, which I have inclosed and left open for the consideration of Congress, wishing that it may be sealed if they approve of the sieur De Chambeau's releasement, which I think may be attended with many valuable consequences.

quences. If Congress concur in sentiment with me, they will be pleased to give direction for his passage by the first opportunity to the French islands: if they do not, I shall be obliged by your returning my letter.

I have also the pleasure of inclosing a copy of a letter from monsieur P. Pennel, which came to hand last night, and which contains intelligence of an agreeable and interesting nature, for which I beg leave to refer you to the copy. The polite manner in which monsieur Pennel has requested to be one of my aides-de-camp demands my acknowledgments. As the appointment will not be attended with any expense, and will shew a proper regard for his complaisance and the attachment he is pleased to express for the service of the American states, I shall take the liberty of complying with his requisition, and transmit him a brevet commission, provided the same shall be agreeable to Congress.—Their sentiments upon this subject you will be kind enough to favor me with by the first opportunity.—The inclosed letter for the sieur De Chambeau you will please to forward to him (if he is to be enlarged) after closing it.

Before I conclude, I must take the liberty to observe that I am under no small difficulties on account of the French gentlemen that are here in consequence of the commissions they have received,—having no means to employ them, or to afford them an opportunity of rendering that service they themselves wish to give, or which perhaps is expected by the public. Their want of our language is an objection to their being joined to any of the regiments here at this time, were there vacancies, and not other obstacles. These considerations induce me to wish that Congress would adopt and point out some particular mode to be observed respecting them. What it should be, they will be best able to determine. But to me it appears that their being here now can be attended with no valuable consequences, and that, as the power of appointing officers for the new army is vested in the conventions, &c, of the several states, it will be necessary

for

for Congress to direct them to be provided for in the regiments to be raised, according to the ranks they would wish them to bear—(or I am convinced they will never be taken in, let their merit be what it may);—or to form them into a distinct corps which may be increased in time. They seem to be genteel, sensible men; and I have no doubt of their making good officers as soon as they can learn as much of our language as to make themselves well understood: but, unless Congress interfere by their particular direction to the states, they will never be incorporated in any of the regiments to be raised: and, without they are, they will be entirely at a loss, and in the most irksome situation, for something to do, as they now are.—I have the honor to be, &c.　　G. W.

Sir,　　*Head-Quarters, Haerlem Heights, Oct.* 8, 1776.

SINCE I had the honor of writing you yesterday, I have been favored with a letter from the honorable council of Massachusetts-Bay, covering one from Richard Derby, esquire, a copy of which is herewith transmitted, as it contains intelligence of an important and interesting nature.

As an exchange of prisoners is about to take place, I am induced, from a question stated in a letter I received from governor Trumbull this morning, to ask the opinion of Congress, in what manner the states that have had the care of them are to be reimbursed the expenses incurred on their account. My want of information in this instance, or whether any account is to be sent in with the prisoners, would not allow me to give him an answer, as nothing that I recollect has ever been said upon the subject.—He also mentions another matter, viz. whether such privates as are mechanics, and others who may desire to remain with us, should be obliged to return.—In respect to the latter, I conceive there can be no doubt of our being under a necessity of returning the whole, a proposition having been made on our part for a general exchange, and that agreed to: besides,

sides, the balance of prisoners is greatly against us; and I am informed it was particularly stipulated by general Montgomery, that all those that were taken in Canada should be exchanged whenever a cartel was settled for the purpose.

Under these circumstances, I should suppose the several committees having the care of them should be instructed to make the most exact returns of the whole, however willing a part should be to continue with us. At the same time I should think it not improper to inform them of the reasons leading to the measure, and that they should be invited to escape afterwards, which, in all probability, they may effect without much difficulty if they are attached to us, extending their influence to many more, and bringing them away also.

The situation of our affairs and the present establishment of the army requiring our most vigorous exertions to engage a new one, I presume it will be necessary to furnish the paymaster-general as early as possible with money to pay the bounty, lately resolved on, to such men as will enlist. Prompt pay perhaps may have a happy effect, and induce the continuance of some who are here: but, without it, I am certain that nothing can be done; nor have we time to lose in making the experiment. But then it may be asked, who is to recruit? or who can consider themselves as officers for that purpose, till the conventions of the different states have made the appointments?

Yesterday afternoon the exchange between lord Stirling and governor Browne was carried into execution; and his lordship is now here. He confirms the intelligence mentioned by captain Souther, about the transports he met, by the arrival of the Daphne man-of-war (a twenty-gun ship) a few days ago, with twelve ships under her convoy, having light-horse on board. They sailed with about twenty in each, and lost about eighty in their passage, besides those in the vessel taken by captain Souther.—He further adds that he had heard it acknowledged more than once, that, in the action of the sixteenth ultimo, the enemy had a hundred men killed,

—about

—about sixty Highlanders of the forty-second regiment, and forty of the light infantry. This confession coming from themselves, we may reasonably conclude, did not exaggerate the number. * * *

October 9.——About eight o'clock this morning, two ships, of forty-four guns each (supposed to be the Roebuck and Phœnix), and a frigate of twenty guns, with three or four tenders, got under way from about Bloomingdale where they had been lying some time, and stood with an easy southerly breeze towards our chevaux-de-frise, which we hoped would have intercepted their passage while our batteries played upon them: but, to our surprise and mortification, they ran through without the least difficulty, and without receiving any apparent damage from our forts, though they kept up a heavy fire from both sides of the river. Their destination or views cannot be known with certainty: but most probably they are sent to stop the navigation, and cut off the supplies of boards, &c, which we should have received, and of which we are in great need. They are standing up, and I have dispatched an express to the convention of this state, that notice may be immediately communicated to general Clinton at the Highland fortifications, to put him on his guard in case they should have any designs against them, and that precautions may be taken to prevent the craft belonging to the river falling into their hands.

I have the honor to be, &c. G. W.

SIR, *Head-Quarters, Haerlem Heights, Oct.* 11, 1776.

I BEG leave to inform you, that, since my letter of the eighth and ninth instant which I had the honor of addressing you, nothing of importance has occurred, except that the ships of war which I then mentioned, in their passage up the river, took a sloop that was at anchor off the mouth of Spitendevil, and two of our row-gallies which they out-sailed. The crews, finding that they could not prevent them falling into the enemy's hands, ran them near the shore, and effected their own escape. From the intelligence I have received, the ships are now lying at Tarrytown, without having landed any men (which seemed to be apprehended by some), or attempted any thing else. Their principal views, in all probability, are, to interrupt our navigation, and to receive such disaffected persons as incline to take part against us. The former they will effect beyond all question; and I fear that their expectations respecting the latter will be but too fully answered.

October 12.——The inclosed copy of a letter received last night from the convention of this state will shew you the apprehensions they are under on account of the disaffected among them.—I have ordered up a part of the militia from the Massachusetts under general Lincoln, to prevent, if possible, the consequences which they suggest may happen, and which there is reason to believe the conspirators have in contemplation. I am persuaded that they are upon the eve of breaking out, and that they will leave nothing un-essayed that will distress us and favor the designs of the enemy, as soon as their schemes are ripe for it.

October 13.——Yesterday the enemy landed at Frog's-Point, about nine miles from hence, further up the Sound. Their number we cannot ascertain, as they have not advanced from the point,—which is a kind of island,—but the water that surrounds it is fordable at low tide. I have ordered works to be thrown up at the passes from the point to the main. From the great number of sloops, schooners, and nine ships, that went up the Sound in the evening, full of men, and from the information of two deserters who came over last night, I have reason to believe that the greatest part of their army has moved upwards or is about to do it, pursuing their original plan of getting in our rear, and cutting off our communication with the country.

The grounds from Frog's-Point are strong and defensible, being full of stone fences, both along the road and across

the

the adjacent fields, which will render it difficult for artillery, or indeed a large body of foot, to advance in any regular order, except through the main road.—Our men who are posted on the passes seemed to be in great spirits when I left them last night.—I have the honor to be, &c. G. W.

Sir, *Head-Quarters, Haerlem Heights, Oct. 14, 1776.*

HIS excellency having gone this morning to visit our posts beyond Kingsbridge and the several passes leading from Frog's-Point and the necks adjacent, I have the honor to inform you by his command, that no interesting event has taken place since his letter by yesterday's post.

Every day's intelligence from the convention of this state holds forth discoveries of new plots and of new conspiracies. Some of the members seem to apprehend that insurrections are upon the eve of breaking out, and have suggested the necessity of seizing and securing the passes through the Highlands, lest the disaffected should do it. Their preservation being a matter of the greatest importance, his excellency, notwithstanding the situation we are in with respect to troops, has detached colonel Tash with his regiment, lately from New-Hampshire, in addition to the militia mentioned in his last, with directions to receive orders from the convention, as to the station and posts he is to occupy.

There are now in our possession several persons, inhabitants of this state, who had engaged to join the enemy, and were intercepted in going to them. There are also two who confess they have been with them, and that they had actually engaged in their service; but, finding the terms (the bounty, pay, &c,) not so advantageous as they expected from the information they had received, they were induced to return.—As the affairs of this government are in a precarious situation, and such as, the convention themselves seem to think, forbid their interposition farther than taking measures to apprehend them, his excellency would wish to obtain the sentiments of Congress,

Congress, and their direction upon a subject so extremely critical and delicate, and which, in the consideration of it, involves many important consequences.

Your favor of the ninth, with its several inclosures, his excellency received yesterday morning by the express, who proceeded immediately on his journey.

October 17.——I am directed by his excellency to acquaint you that we are again obliged to change our disposition, to counteract the operations of the enemy. Declining an attack upon our front, they have drawn the main body of their army to Frog's-Point, with a design of hemming us in, and drawing a line in our rear. To prevent the consequences which would but too probably follow the execution of their scheme, the general officers determined yesterday that our forces must be taken from hence, and extended towards East and West Chester, so as to out-flank them. General Lee, who arrived on monday, has strongly urged the absolute necessity of the measure. It is proposed to leave a garrison at Fort-Washington, and to maintain it if possible, in order to preserve the communication with the Jerseys.— They are landing their artillery and waggons upon the point; and there are now several boats passing up the Sound, full of men.

I have the honor to be, &c. R. H. Harrison.

P. S. The post having not come in since sunday, till to-day, has been the occasion of not writing to you since that time. He was expected as usual; which prevented an express being sent.

Sir, *Haerlem Heights, October* 18, 1776.

I WAS yesterday morning honored with your favor of the fifteenth, with the resolutions of the eleventh and fourteenth. The latter, by which Congress have authorised me to appoint monsieur Pennel a brevet aide-de-camp, claims a return of my acknowledgments.

Last

Last night I received a letter from Mr. Varick, secretary to general Schuyler, inclosing a copy of one from general Arnold to general Gates. The intelligence transmitted by general Arnold being of an extremely interesting and important nature, I thought it advisable to forward the same immediately by express. You have a copy herewith, which contains the particulars, and to which I beg leave to refer you.

The accounts transmitted yesterday by post will inform you of the movements of the enemy, and of the measures judged necessary to be pursued by us, to counteract their designs. I have nothing to add on this head, except that ten or eleven ships, which have been prevented passing Hell-gate for two or three days for want of wind, are now under way, and proceeding up the Sound. Amongst them there appear to be two frigates: the rest probably have in stores, &c.

Inclosed is a copy of the last general return I have been able to obtain. It only comes down to the fifth instant: the situation of our affairs, and the almost constant necessity of sending detachments from one place to another to watch the enemy's motions, have prevented the officers from making them with regularity.

I have the honor to be, &c.   G. W.

Kingsbridge, October 20, 1776, half after one o'clock, P. M.
SIR,

I HAVE it in command from his excellency to transmit you the inclosed copies of dispatches which just now came to hand, and which contain intelligence of the most interesting and important nature respecting our affairs in the northern department. His excellency would have wrote himself, but was going to our several posts, when the express arrived.

The enemy are pursuing with great industry their plan of penetrating the country from the Sound, and of fo-line in our rear. They are now extended from Frog's-Point to New-Rochelle, from whence it is generally conjectured they mean to take their route by way of the White-Plains, and from thence to draw a line to the North-river. We on our part have drawn our whole force, except the regiments intended to garrison Fort-Washington, from the island of New-York, and have possessed ourselves of the heights, passes, and advantageous grounds, between New-Rochelle where the van of their army now lies, and the North-river. —They will in all probability attempt to effect their purpose by moving higher up. If they do, our forces will move accordingly, it being a principal object to prevent their outflanking us.

On friday, one of their advanced parties, near East Chester, fell in with part of colonel Glover's brigade, and a smart and close skirmish ensued, in which, I have the pleasure to inform you, our men behaved with great coolness and intrepidity, and drove the enemy back to their main body.

I have the honor to be, &c.   R. H. HARRISON.

SIR,   *Head-Quarters, Valentine's Hill, Oct. 21, 1776.*

HIS excellency being absent on a visit to the several posts on the left of our lines and at the White-Plains, I have the honor to inform you, by the favor of colonel Whipple, that, since my letter of yesterday, no event of importance has occurred.

I have the honor to be, &c.   R. H. HARRISON.

To the Board of War.

GENTLEMEN,   *Camp on Valentine's Hill, Oct. 22, 1776.*

I AM directed by his excellency whose business has called him from hence, to acknowledge his receipt of your favors of the twelfth and fifteenth instant, and to inform you in answer to the first, that he will mention the case of the

French

French gentlemen to general Lee, and obtain his opinion as to the beſt mode of providing for them in a uſeful way. The horſes belonging to the light dragoons who were taken, he thinks, will be very ſerviceable; and he will write to general Ward or one of the agents to purchaſe them.

In reſpect to your requiſition for an immediate return of ordnance ſtores, his excellency ſays it cannot poſſibly be complied with in the preſent unſettled ſtate of the army. In order to effect the good purpoſes you have in view, he would take the liberty to recommend the eſtabliſhing of magazines of ammunition and other ordnance ſtores in proper places of ſecurity, from whence ſupplies could be occaſionally drawn. As large quantities are conſtantly in demand in time of war, he does not conceive your proviſion in theſe inſtances can be too great.

He will direct the regimental returns in future to include arms and accoutrements, and the commiſſary-general to tranſmit monthly liſts of rations. He thinks the regulation extremely proper, though he apprehends the information to be premature reſpecting the over-quantity ſuggeſted to have been drawn, having heard no ſuſpicion of the ſort in this army of late.

I have the honor to be, &c.   R. H. HARRISON.

SIR,   *Head-Quarters, White-Plains, Oct.* 25, 1776.

THE whole of our army is now here and on the neighboring heights, except the troops left at Mount-Waſhington and Kingſbridge (about fourteen hundred at the former, and ſix hundred at the latter), and general Lee's diviſion which now forms the rear, and which is on their march. Our removal, and that of the ſtores, have been attended with a great deal of trouble, owing to the ſcarcity and difficulty of procuring waggons. However, they are nearly effected, and without any loſs.—The general officers are
now

now reconnoitring the several passes leading from the enemy, that the most important may be immediately secured.—The situation of their army remains nearly the same as when I had the honor of addressing you on the twenty-first instant. It differs in nothing unless it is that their main body is more collected about New-Rochelle. A few of their troops are extended as far as Momarioneck.

On monday night a detachment of our men, under the command of colonel Hazlet, was sent out to surprise and cut off major Rogers, if possible, with his regiment which was posted there. By some accident or other the expedition did not succeed so well as I could have wished. However our advanced party, led on by major Greene of the first Virginia regiment, fell in with their out-guard, and brought off thirty-six prisoners, sixty muskets, and some blankets. The number killed is not certainly known: but it is reported by an officer who was there, that he counted about twenty-five. —Our loss, two killed, and ten or twelve wounded; among the latter, major Greene, whose recovery is very doubtful.

On wednesday there was also a smart skirmish between a party of colonel Hand's riflemen,—about two hundred and forty,—and nearly the same number of Hessian chasseurs, in which the latter were put to the rout. Our men buried ten of them on the field, and took two prisoners, one badly wounded. We sustained no other loss than having one lad wounded, supposed mortally.

The ships of war that are in the North-river fell down, yesterday morning or the evening before, to Dobbs's ferry, to prevent our bringing stores from below by water, and the removal of those that are landed there. As soon as the waggons, employed in bringing the baggage and stores of general Lee's division, are disengaged, they will be immediately sent to assist those already there to remove them.

On saturday night we had the misfortune to lose one of the new ships intended to be sunk for obstructing the channel. She parted her cables in a severe squall, when properly ballasted,

ballasted, and bilged as soon as she struck the shore. The other ship was sunk well; and yesterday morning two brigs, both ready, were sent down for the same purpose.

About two o'clock this afternoon, intelligence was brought to head-quarters that three or four detachments of the enemy were on their march, and had advanced within about four miles of this place. It has been fully confirmed since by a variety of persons who have been out to reconnoitre.— Their number cannot be ascertained: but it is generally conjectured that the detachments are or will be succeeded by as many columns composing their main body.—Our drums have beat to arms, and the men are ordered to their several posts.—Most probably some important event is upon the eve of taking place: I hope it will be victory in favor of our arms. —General Lee, with his division, has not got up; but I hear he is on his march.

Experiment having proved it difficult, if not impossible, to prevent the enemy from possessing the navigation of the North-river, and rendering the communication and intercourse between the states divided by it extremely hazardous and precarious by means of their ships of war, it has become a matter of important consideration how to remedy the evil, and to guard against the consequences which may result from it. I am charged by his excellency to mention it to Congress as a matter that has employed much of his thought, and that seems worthy of their most serious attention. He has communicated it to several of the general and other officers, and to many gentlemen of sense and discernment, who all agree with him, not only upon the propriety but the absolute necessity that two distinct armies should be formed,—one to act particularly in the states which lie on the east, the other in those that are on the south of the river;— the whole however to be raised on a general plan, and not to be confined to any particular place by the terms of enlistment. These matters,—the apparent difficulty and perhaps impracticability of succours being thrown across the river
while

while the enemy can command it,—have induced his excellency to submit the measure to their consideration, not knowing how their operations may be directed, and foreseeing that innumerable evils may arise if a respectable force is not appointed to oppose their arms wheresoever they are carried.—I have the honor to be, in great haste, &c.

R. H. HARRISON.

SIR,   *White-Plains, October* 29, 1776.

THE situation of our affairs not permitting his excellency to write himself, I have it in charge to inform you, that, on yesterday morning about ten o'clock, the enemy appeared in several large columns in our front, and, from their first movements, seemed as if they meant an attack there. However, halting for a little time, their main body filed off to our left, and presently began a most severe and incessant cannonade at a part of our troops who had taken post on a hill, with a view of throwing up some lines. At the same time they advanced in two divisions, and, after a smart engagement for about a quarter of an hour, obliged our men to give way.

Our loss is not certainly known; but, from conjecture, is between four and five hundred in killed, wounded, and missing.—What theirs was, we have not heard.

After gaining the hill (upon which they are intrenching), and leaving a sufficient number of men and artillery to prevent our repossessing it, they proceeded to advance by our left; and, as far as I can discover, their posts or encampments now form nearly a semicircle. It is evident their design is to get in our rear according to their original plan.— Every measure is taking to prevent them: but the removal of our baggage, &c, is attended with infinite difficulty and delays.

Our post, from its situation, is not so advantageous as could be wished, and was only intended as temporary and occasional, till the stores belonging to the army, which had
been

been deposited here, could be removed. The enemy coming on so suddenly has distressed us much. They are now close at hand, and most probably will in a little time commence their second attack: we expect it every hour:—perhaps it is beginning: I have just heard the report of some cannon.—I have the honor to be, &c. R. H. HARRISON.

SIR, *White-Plains, October* 31, 1776.

SINCE I had the honor of addressing you on the twenty-ninth instant, no event of importance has occurred. The enemy are throwing up some lines and redoubts in our front, with a view of cannonading as soon as they are ready; and at the same time are extending their wings farther by our right and left. It is supposed that one of their objects is to advance a part of their troops, and seize on the bridge over Croton river, that the communication may be cut off with the upper country. To prevent this, a part of our force is detached, with orders to proceed with the utmost expedition, and to secure the pass if possible.

We are trying to remove, to guard against their designs, but are greatly impeded by reason of the scarcity of waggons in proportion to our baggage and stores. Every exertion has been employed to obtain a sufficiency; but they cannot be had in this part of the country. The quarter-master has sent to Connecticut to get a supply if possible.

Our army is decreasing fast. Several gentlemen, who have come to camp within a few days, have observed large numbers of militia returning home on the different roads: nor are any measures taken as yet to raise the new army, no commissions having come from the states to appoint or signify the nomination of their officers. If this was done, perhaps many who are now here might be induced to engage: but at present there are none authorised to recruit.

His excellency would have wrote himself by the person who carries this (to the care of general Greene); but his attention

tention is totally engaged in ordering the affairs of the army, and the beft mode for its removal.

I have the honor to be, &c.   R. H. HARRISON.

SIR,   *White-Plains, November* 1, 1776.

I AM directed by his excellency to acknowledge his receipt of your favor of the twenty-eighth ultimo which came to hand yefterday evening, and to tranfmit you a copy of the letter I had the honor of writing you by the Bofton exprefs by his command. Had the exprefs been charged with no other letter, the lofs would not have been attended with any material injury to us, or advantage to the enemy, provided it fhould come to their hands: but there were others from his excellency, of a very interefting nature, the mifcarriage of which gives him much concern. As the bundle was taken away in fo fudden and fecret a manner, I fear there is but little hope of recovering it,—being done moft probably for the exprefs purpofe of furnifhing the enemy with intelligence, and a ftate of our army. Befides his excellency's letters, the moft material of which was to Mr. Rutledge, there were five or fix more from the gentlemen of his family.

My letters of the twenty-ninth and of yefterday, which I had the honor of addreffing you, will give a pretty full account of our fituation, and of every matter refpecting this army antecedent to this date. I only omitted to mention that we have taken thirteen of the Waldeckers, and that, for feveral days paft, our fcouting parties have brought in one, two, or three prifoners. In addition to thefe, we have every day a deferter or two.

About fix o'clock this morning, a meffenger arrived from lord Stirling (who is with his brigade between two and three miles from White-Plains, on our right, and rather nearer the North-river) with intelligence that the enemy were advancing towards him in two columns. This information has carried his excellency and aides out. The refult of their movement

movement I have not heard: but most likely they are pursuing their original design of getting by our flanks and seizing the heights above us. Every precaution is taking to prevent them, and to hurry away our stores to a more interior part of the country.

I have the honor to be, &c.   R. H. HARRISON.

P. S. His excellency has just returned, and says the alarm was premature. It arose from some of lord Stirling's advanced guards seeing a body of our men who had been ordered to reinforce him, who were supposed to be the enemy. His excellency is very apprehensive that the army will be greatly distressed for want of provision, particularly in the article of flour, owing to the water-conveyance, both in the North and East river, being in the enemy's possession. He has wrote to the convention of this state, and directed Mr. Trumbull, that their utmost exertions in this instance may be used. There is a good deal of flour on the Jersey side: but there is no other way to get it, but by carting and ferrying it over to Peekskill. This I have wrote to general Greene to have done, by his excellency's direction.

SIR,   *White-Plains, November 3, 1776.*

BY command of his excellency, I have the honor to inform you that our situation is nearly the same as when I had the pleasure of writing you last. It is altered in no instance, unless in the number of our troops, which is every day decreasing by their most scandalous desertion and return home. The inclosed letter from general Parsons, who is stationed near the Saw-pits, and which his excellency directed me to transmit, will inform you of the prevalency of this disgraceful practice.

I have the honor to be, &c.   R. H. HARRISON.

To the Board of War.

Gentlemen, *White-Plains, November* 4, 1776.

BY command of his excellency, I have the honor to acknowledge his receipt of your favor of the twenty-fourth ultimo, and to inform you that he esteems the plan you propose to lay before Congress, for preventing more rations being drawn than may be due, well calculated to answer the end. That respecting the sick seems to him not entirely perfect. The captains or commanders of companies are prohibited from drawing pay for such sick as may be discharged from the hospitals as unfit for service. If, during their stay, and before it can be known whether their case will or will not admit of their return, it should become necessary to make up a regimental pay-abstract, in what manner are the officers to make up their rolls? are they to include the sick, or not?

As this is a case which may and must of necessity frequently happen, it appears to his excellency that the intended regulations should be more general, and restrain the officers from including in their pay-abstracts or rolls all the sick they send to the hospitals, and the pay due 'em previous to their going. In such case, those who are discharged as unfit for service may receive their pay as intended; and those who return to duty can obtain what was due to them when the regiment was paid, by applying to the paymaster with the officer and surgeon's certificates, or be included in a subsequent abstract. The inconveniences and abuses which are designed to be remedied by these regulations, his excellency does not apprehend to arise so much from necessity (as incident to the nature of armies), as from the imperfect institution of the present, and the great mixture and diversity of troops composing it, and also from the inattention of the officers. * * *

The defenceless state of Pennsylvania, as communicated by

by the committee of safety to your honorable body, is a matter of much concern to his excellency, which is not a little aggravated by the part too many seem ready to take in favor of the enemy. He trusts, however, the defection will be too inconsiderable to threaten any alarming consequences.

Before the receipt of your letter, his excellency had wrote to the commanding officer of the Virginia regiments at Trenton, directing him to march them forward towards general Greene's post, and there remain under his command till further orders, unless special instructions had been or should be given to the contrary by Congress, or for their particular destination.

Agreeable to your request, his excellency has consulted with general Lee upon the best mode for employing the French gentlemen, and making them serviceable. The result is that they should be appointed to regiments by Congress according to the ranks they have been pleased to give them, and with the same pay as is allowed other officers in such cases. Their want of our language is rather an objection: but it is hoped they will attain a sufficient knowledge of it, ere it be long, to be of great service; and that, in the interim, their advice and assistance in directing of works may be of use where they may be stationed.

With great respect, I have the honor to be, &c.

R. H. HARRISON.

SIR, *White-Plains, November 6, 1776.*

I HAVE the honor to inform you that on yesterday morning the enemy made a sudden and unexpected movement from the several posts they had taken in our front. They broke up their whole encampments the preceding night, and have advanced towards Kingsbridge and the North-river. The design of this manœuvre is a matter of much conjecture and speculation, and cannot be accounted for with any degree of certainty. The grounds we had taken possession of were strong and advantageous, and such as they could not have gained without much loss of blood in case an attempt had been made. I had taken every possible precaution to prevent their outflanking us;—which may have led to the present measure. They may still have in view their original plan, and, by a sudden wheel, try to accomplish it. Detachments are constantly out to observe their motions, and to harrass them as much as possible.

In consequence of this movement I called a council of general officers to-day, to consult of such measures as should be adopted in case they pursued their retreat to New-York; the result of which is herewith transmitted. In respect to myself, I cannot indulge an idea that general Howe, supposing he is going to New-York, means to close the campaign, and to sit down without attempting something more. I think it highly probable, and almost certain, that he will make a descent with a part of his troops into Jersey: and, as soon as I am satisfied that the present manœuvre is real and not a feint, I shall use every means in my power to forward a part of our force to counteract his designs: nor shall I be disappointed if he sends a detachment to the southward for the purpose of making a winter campaign.

From the information I have received, there is now a number of transports at Red-Hook, with about three thousand troops on board. Their destination, as given out, is to Rhode-Island: but this seems altogether improbable for various reasons; among others, the season is much against it. In the southern states they will find it milder, and much more favorable for their purposes. I shall take the liberty of mentioning that it may not be improper to suggest the probability of such a measure to the assemblies and conventions in those states, that they may be on their guard,—and the propriety of their establishing and laying up magazines of provisions and other necessaries in suitable places. This is a matter of exceeding importance, and what cannot be too much attended to.

From

From the approaching dissolution of the army, and the departure of the new levies which is on the eve of taking place, and the little prospect of levying a new one in time, I have wrote to the eastern states by the unanimous advice of the general officers, to forward supplies of militia in the room of those that are now here, and who, it is feared, will not be prevailed on to stay any longer than the time they are engaged for. The propriety of this application, I trust, will appear, when it is known that not a single officer is yet commissioned to recruit, and when it is considered how essential it is to keep up some shew of force and shadow of an army.

I expect the enemy will bend their force against Fort-Washington, and invest it immediately. From some advices, it is an object that will attract their earliest attention.

I am happy to inform you, that, in the engagement on monday se'nnight, I have reason to believe our loss was by no means so considerable as was conjectured at first. By some deserters and prisoners we are told, that of the enemy was tolerably great: some accounts make it about four hundred in killed and wounded: all agree that among the former there was a colonel Carr of the thirty-fifth regiment.

The force that will be sent to Jersey after I am satisfied of Mr. Howe's retreat, in addition to those now there; according to my present opinion, will make it necessary for me to go with them, to put things in a proper channel, and such a way of defence as shall seem most probable to check the progress of the enemy, in case they should attempt a descent there, or a move toward Philadelphia.

I have the honor to be, &c.   G. W.

To the Board of War.

GENTLEMEN,   *White-Plains, November 8, 1776.*

I HAVE been favored with yours of the thirty-first ultimo, by monsieur Laytaniac, and must take the liberty of referring you to my former letters upon the subject of providing for the French gentlemen who shall incline to enter the service of the states. To me it appears that one of two modes must be adopted: they must either be appointed to places in some of the regiments, or formed into a distinct corps. The former was advised as the most eligible in respect to the gentlemen who were here before. It requires time to form an accurate opinion of the merits of an officer; and the present situation of the army will not allow me to pay a particular attention to monsieur Laytaniac, or such notice as he may wish to receive, or I to give: nor is there any way of making his stay here agreeable.

I have the honor to be, &c. G. W.

Sir, *White-Plains, November* 9, 1776.

I HAVE the honor to transmit you a copy of a letter from general Gates to general Schuyler, and of another paper containing intelligence respecting the northern army and the situation of the enemy in that department. They this minute came to hand; and to them I beg leave to refer you for particulars.

By every information I can obtain, and the accounts I had last night by two deserters who were very intelligent and particular, general Howe still has in view an expedition to the Jerseys, and is preparing for it with the greatest industry. I have detached the first division of our troops which was thought necessary to be sent, and which I hope will cross the river at Peekskill to-day. The second, I expect, will all march this evening; and to-morrow morning I propose to follow myself, in order to put things in the best train I can, and to give him every possible opposition.—I hope (when the two divisions arrive, and are joined to such other force as I expect to collect) to check his progress and prevent him from penetrating any distance from the river, if

not

not to oblige him to return immediately with some loss. Whatever is in my power to effect, shall be done.

I have the honor to be, &c. G. W.

———

Sir, *Peekskill, November* 11, 1776.

I HAVE only time to acknowledge the honor of your letter of the fifth instant, and its several inclosures, and to inform you, that, agreeable to the resolves of Congress, I shall use every measure in my power that the moving and present confused state of the army will admit of, to appoint officers for recruiting.

You will have been advised, before this, of the arrival of commissioners from the Massachusetts. Others have come from Connecticut: but, from the present appearance of things, we seem but little if any nearer to levying an army. I had anticipated the resolve respecting the militia, by writing to the eastern states and to the Jersey, by the advice of my general officers, and from a consciousness of the necessity of getting in a number of men if possible, to keep up the appearance of an army. How my applications will succeed, the event must determine. I have little or no reason to expect that the militia now here will remain a day longer than the time they first engaged for. I have recommended their stay, and requested it in general orders. General Lincoln and the Massachusetts commissioners are using their interest with those from that state: but, as far as I can judge, we cannot rely on their staying.

I left White-Plains about eleven o'clock yesterday;—all peace then. The enemy appeared to be preparing for their expedition to Jersey according to every information. What their designs are, or whether their present conduct is not a feint, I cannot determine.

The Maryland and Virginia troops under lord Stirling have crossed the river, as have part of those from the Jersey: the remainder are now embarking. The troops, judged necessary to secure the several posts through the Highlands, have also got up. I am going to examine the passes, and direct such works as may appear necessary; after which, and making the best disposition I can of things in this quarter, I intend to proceed to Jersey, which I expect to do to-morrow.

The assemblies of Massachusetts and Connecticut, to induce their men more readily to engage in the service, have voted an advance pay of twenty shillings per month, in addition to that allowed by the Congress to privates. It may perhaps be the means of their levying the quotas exacted from them sooner than they could otherwise have been raised: but I am of opinion, a more fatal and mistaken policy could not have entered their councils, or one more detrimental to the general cause. The influence of the vote will become continental, and materially affect the other states in making up their levies. If they could do it, I am certain, when the troops come to act together, that jealousy, impatience and mutiny, would necessarily arise. A different pay cannot exist in the same army. The reasons are obvious, and experience has proved their force in the case of the eastern and southern troops last spring. Sensible of this, and of the pernicious consequences that would inevitably result from the advance, I have prevented the commissioners from proceeding or publishing their terms till they could obtain the sense of Congress upon the subject, and remonstrated against it in a letter to governor Trumbull. I am not singular in opinion: I have the concurrence of all the general officers, of its fatal tendency.

I congratulate you and Congress upon the news from Ticonderoga, and that general Carleton and his army have been obliged to return to Canada without attempting any thing.

I have the honor to be, &c.   G. W.

SIR, *General Greene's Quarters, Nov.* 14, 1776.

I HAVE the honor to inform you of my arrival here yesterday, and that the whole of the troops belonging to the states, which lay south of Hudson's-river, and which were in New-York government, have passed over to this side, except the regiment, lately colonel Smallwood's, which I expect is now on their march.

That they may be ready to check any incursions the enemy may attempt in this neighborhood, I intend to quarter them at Brunswic, Amboy, Elizabethtown, Newark, and about this place, unless Congress should conceive it necessary for any of them to be stationed at or more contiguous to Philadelphia. In such case they will be pleased to signify their pleasure. There will be very few of them after the departure of those who were engaged for the flying camp, which is fast approaching. The disposition I have mentioned seems to me well calculated for the end proposed, and also for their accommodation.

The movements and designs of the enemy are not yet understood. Various are the opinions and reports on this head. From every information, the whole have removed from Dobbs's ferry towards Kingsbridge; and it seems to be generally believed on all hands, that the investing of Fort-Washington is one object they have in view: but that can employ but a small part of their force. Whether they intend a southern expedition, must be determined by time: to me there appears a probability of it, which seems to be favored by the advices we have that many transports are wooding and watering. General Greene's letter would give you the substance of the intelligence brought by Mr. Mersereau from Staten-Island in this instance, which he received before it came to me.

Inclosed you have copies of two letters from general Howe, and of my answer to the first of them. The letter alluded to, and returned in his last, was one from myself to Mrs.

Mrs. Washington, of the twenty-fifth ultimo, from whence I conclude that all the letters which went by the Boston exprefs have come to his poffeffion. You will alfo perceive that general Howe has requefted the return of Peter Jack, a fervant to major Stewart, to which I have confented, as he was not in the military line, and the requifition agreeable to the cuftom of war. This fervant having been fent to Philadelphia with the Waldeckers and other prifoners, I muft requeft the favor of you to have him conveyed to general Greene by the earlieft opportunity, in order that he may be returned to his mafter.

Before I conclude, I beg leave not only to fuggeft but to urge the neceffity of increafing our field artillery very confiderably. Experience has convinced me, as it has every gentleman of difcernment in this army, that, while we remain fo much inferior to the enemy in this inftance, we muft carry on the war under infinite difadvantages, and without the fmalleft probability of fuccefs. It has been peculiarly owing to the fituation of the country where their operations have been conducted, and to the rough and ftrong grounds we poffeffed ourfelves of, and over which they had to pafs, that they have not carried their arms, by means of their artillery, to a much greater extent. When thefe difficulties ceafe by changing the fcene of action to a level champaign country, the worft of confequences are to be apprehended. I would therefore, with the concurrence of all the officers whom I have fpoken to upon the fubject, fubmit to the confideration of Congrefs whether immediate meafures ought not to be taken for procuring a refpectable train.

It is agreed on all hands that each batallion fhould be furnifhed at leaft with two pieces, and that a fmaller number than a hundred of three pounds, fifty of fix pounds, and fifty of twelve pounds, fhould not be provided, in addition to thofe we now have. Befides thefe, if fome eighteen and twenty-four-pounders are ordered, the train will be more ferviceable and complete. The whole fhould be of brafs,

for

for the moſt obvious reaſons: they will be much more portable, not half ſo liable to burſt; and, when they do, no damage is occaſioned by it, and they may be caſt over again. The ſizes before deſcribed ſhould be particularly attended to: if they are not, there will be great reaſon to expect miſtakes and confuſion in the charges in time of action, as it has frequently happened in the beſt-regulated armies. The diſparity between thoſe I have mentioned and ſuch as are of an intermediate ſize is difficult to diſcern.

It is alſo agreed that a regiment of artilleriſts, with approved and experienced officers, ſhould be obtained if poſſible, and ſome engineers of known reputation and abilities. I am ſorry to ſay, too ready an indulgence has been had to ſeveral appointments in the latter inſtance, and that men have been promoted, who ſeem to me to know but little if any thing of the buſineſs.

Perhaps this train, &c, may be looked upon by ſome as large and expenſive. True, it will be ſo: but when it is conſidered that the enemy, having effected but little in the courſe of the preſent campaign, will uſe their utmoſt efforts to ſubjugate us in the next, every conſideration of that ſort ſhould be diſregarded, and every poſſible preparation made to fruſtrate their * * * attempts. How they are to be procured, is to be inquired into.—That we cannot provide them among ourſelves, or more than a very ſmall proportion, ſo trifling as not to deſerve our notice, is evident. Therefore I would adviſe, with all imaginable deference, that, without any abatement of our own internal exertions, application ſhould be immediately made to ſuch powers as can and may be willing to ſupply them. They cannot be obtained too early, if ſoon enough: and I am told they may be eaſily had from France and Holland.

Mr. Trumbull the commiſſary-general has frequently mentioned to me of late the inadequacy of his pay to his trouble and the great riſk he is ſubject to on account of the large ſums of money which paſs through his hands. He has

ſtated

stated his case with a view of laying it before Congress and obtaining a more adequate compensation. My sentiments upon the subject are already known: but yet I shall take the liberty to add that I think his complaint to be well founded, and his pay, considering the important duties and risks of his office, by no means sufficient, and that the footing he seems to think it should be upon, himself, appears just and reasonable.

A proposition having been made long since to general Howe and agreed to by him, for an exchange of prisoners in consequence of the resolutions of Congress to that effect, I shall be extremely happy if you will give directions to the committees and those having the charge of prisoners in the several states south of Jersey, to transmit me proper lists of the names of all the commissioned officers, and of their ranks and the corps they belong to; also the number of non-commissioned and privates, and their respective regiments. You will perceive by his letter, he supposes me to have affected some delay, or to have been unmindful of the proposition I had made.

I propose to stay in this neighborhood a few days, in which time I expect the designs of the enemy will be more disclosed, and their incursions be made in this quarter, or their investiture of Fort-Washington, if they are intended.

I have the honor to be, &c.   G. W.

To the Board of War.

General Greene's Quarters, November 15, 1776.

GENTLEMEN,

ON wednesday evening I received the favor of your letter of the eighth instant, in consequence of which I stopped the flag that was going in with the ladies you mention, pointing out to them the necessity of the measure, and recommending them to write to their husbands and connexions

nexions to obtain general Howe's assurances for the release of Mrs. Lewis, and Mrs. Robinson and her children, with their baggage, as the condition on which they will be permitted to go in themselves. These terms I can only extend to Mrs. Barrow and Mrs. Kemp who had never obtained my leave; Mrs. Watts had, and my promise that she should go in. The whole however were prepared to go, when the letter reached Newark.—The mode I have adopted seems most likely, and the only proper one, to procure the enlargement of our ladies, which I wish for much.

I am, gentlemen, with great respect, &c.   G. W.

To the Board of War.

Gentlemen,   *Hackinsac, November* 15, 1776.

HAVING given my promise to general Howe, on his application, that Peter Jack, a servant of major Stewart, who was sent to Philadelphia with the Waldeckers and other prisoners and who has nothing to do in the military line, should be returned to his master agreeable to the usage of war in such cases,—I must take the liberty to request the favor of you to have him conveyed to general Greene by the earliest opportunity, that he may be forwarded to his master in compliance with my promise.

I also wish that you would have all the British prisoners collected that you conveniently can, and sent to me as soon as possible with the Hessian prisoners, that I may exchange them. The return of the latter I think will be attended with many salutary consequences: but, should it be made without that of a large proportion of other troops, it will carry the marks of design, and occasion precautions to be taken to prevent the ends we have in view.

I have the honor to be, &c.   G. W.

Sir, General Greene's Quarters, Nov. 16, 1776.

SINCE I had the honor of addreſſing you laſt, an important event has taken place, of which I wiſh to give you the earlieſt intelligence.

The preſervation of the paſſage of the North-river was an object of ſo much conſequence that I thought no pains or expenſe too great for that purpoſe: and therefore, after ſending off all the valuable ſtores except ſuch as were neceſſary for its defence, I determined, agreeable to the advice of moſt of the general officers, to riſk ſomething to defend the poſt on the eaſt ſide, called Mount-Waſhington.

When the army moved up in conſequence of general Howe's landing at Frog-point, colonel Magaw was left on that command, with about twelve hundred men, and orders given to defend it to the laſt. Afterwards, reflecting upon the ſmallneſs of the garriſon, and the difficulty of their holding it if general Howe ſhould fall down upon it with his whole force, I wrote to general Greene who had the command on the Jerſey ſhore, directing him to govern himſelf by circumſtances, and to retain or evacuate the poſt as he ſhould think beſt, and revoking the abſolute order to colonel Magaw to defend the poſt to the laſt extremity.—General Greene, ſtruck with the importance of the poſt, and the diſcouragement which our evacuation of poſts muſt neceſſarily have given, reinforced colonel Magaw with detachments from ſeveral regiments of the flying camp, but chiefly of Pennſylvania, ſo as to make up the number about two thouſand.

In this ſituation things were yeſterday, when general Howe demanded the ſurrendry of the garriſon, to which colonel Magaw returned a ſpirited refuſal. Immediately upon receiving an account of this tranſaction, I came from Hackinſac to this place, and had partly croſſed the North-river when I met general Putnam and general Greene, who were juſt returning from thence, and informed me that the

troops

troops were in high spirits, and would make a good defence: and it being late at night, I returned.

Early this morning colonel Magaw posted his troops partly in the lines thrown up by our army on our first coming thither from New-York, and partly on a commanding hill lying north of Mount-Washington,—the lines being all to the southward. In this position the attack began about ten o'clock, which our troops stood, and returned the fire in such a manner as gave me great hopes the enemy was entirely repulsed. But at this time a body of troops crossed Haerlem-river in boats, and landed inside of the second lines, our troops being then engaged in the first.

Colonel Cadwallader, who commanded in the lines, sent off a detachment to oppose them: but they, being overpowered by numbers, gave way; upon which, colonel Cadwallader ordered his troops to retreat in order to gain the fort. It was done with much confusion; and the enemy crossing over came in upon them in such a manner, that a number of them surrendered.

At this time the Hessians advanced on the north side of the fort in very large bodies. They were received by the troops posted there, with proper spirit, and kept back a considerable time: but at length they were also obliged to submit to a superiority of numbers, and retire under the cannon of the fort.

The enemy, having advanced thus far, halted; and immediately a flag went in, with a repetition of the demand of the fortress, as I suppose. At this time I sent a billet to colonel Magaw, directing him to hold out, and I would endeavor this evening to bring off the garrison, if the fortress could not be maintained, as I did not expect it could, the enemy being possessed of the adjacent ground. But, before this reached him, he had entered too far into a treaty, to retract: after which, colonel Cadwallader told another messenger who went over, that they had been able to obtain no other terms than to surrender as prisoners of war. In this situation

tion matters now stand. I have stopped general Beall's and general Heard's brigades, to preserve the post and stores here; which, with the other troops, I hope we shall be able to effect.

I do not yet know the numbers killed or wounded on either side: but, from the heaviness and continuance of the fire in some places, I imagine there must have been considerable execution.

The loss of such a number of officers and men, many of whom have been trained with more than common attention, will, I fear, be severely felt; but, when that of the arms and accoutrements is added, much more so; and must be a further incentive to procure as considerable a supply as possible for the new troops, as soon as it can be done.

I have the honor to be, &c. G. W.

Sir, *Hackinsac, November* 19, 1776.

I HAVE not been yet able to obtain a particular account of the unhappy affair of the sixteenth, nor of the terms on which the garrison surrendered. The intelligence that has come to hand is not so full and accurate as I could wish. One of the artillery, whose information is most direct, and who escaped on sunday night, says the enemy's loss was very considerable, especially in the attack made above the fort by the division of Hessians that marched from Kingsbridge, and where lieutenant-colonel Rawlins, of the late colonel Stephenson's regiment, was posted.

They burned yesterday one or two houses on the heights, and contiguous to the fort, and appeared, by advices from general Greene, to be moving in the evening their main body down towards the city. Whether they will close the campaign without attempting something more, or make an incursion into Jersey, must be determined by the events themselves.

As Fort-Lee was always considered as only necessary in conjunction

conjunction with that on the east side of the river, to preserve the communication across, and to prevent the enemy from a free navigation, it has become of no importance by the loss of the other, or not so material as to employ a force for its defence. Being viewed in this light, and apprehending that the stores there would be precariously situated, their removal has been determined on to Boundbrook above Brunswic, Princeton, Springfield, and Acquackenunk bridge, as places that will not be subject to sudden danger in case the enemy should pass the river, and which have been thought proper as repositories for some of our stores of provision and forage.

The troops belonging to the flying camp under generals Heard and Beall, with what remains of general Ewing's brigade, are now at Fort-Lee, where they will continue till the stores are got away. By the time that is effected, their term of enlistment will be near expiring; and, if the enemy should make a push in this quarter, the only troops that there will be to oppose them, will be Hand's, Hazlett's, the regiments from Virginia, and that, lately Smallwood's, —the latter greatly reduced by the losses it sustained on Long-Island, &c, and sickness: nor are the rest by any means complete. In addition to these, I am told there are a few of the militia of this state, who have been called in by governor Livingston. I shall make such a disposition of the whole at Brunswic and at the intermediate posts, as shall seem most likely to guard against the designs of the enemy, and to prevent them making an irruption or foraging with detached parties.

The inclosed letter from colonels Miles and Atlee will shew Congress the distressed situation of our prisoners in New-York; and their distress will become greater every day by the cold inclement season that is approaching. It will be happy if some expedient can be adopted, by which they may be furnished with necessary blankets and clothing.
Humanity

Humanity and the good of the service require it.—I think the mode suggested by these gentlemen, for establishing a credit, appears as likely to succeed, and as eligible, as any that occurs to me. It is probable many articles that may be wanted can be obtained there, and upon better terms than elsewhere. In respect to provision, their allowance perhaps is as good as the situation of general Howe's stores will admit of: it has been said of late by deserters and others that they were rather scant.

By a letter from the paymaster-general, of the seventeenth, he says there will be a necessity that large and early remittances should be made him. The demands, when the troops now in service are dismissed, will be extremely great. Besides, the bounty to recruits will require a large supply; and he adds that the commissary-general has informed him, that, between this and the last of December, he shall have occasion for a million of dollars.

November 21.——The unhappy affair of the sixteenth has been succeeded by further misfortunes. Yesterday morning a large body of the enemy landed between Dobbs's ferry and Fort-Lee. Their object was, evidently, to inclose the whole of our troops and stores that lay between the North and Hackinsac rivers, which form a very narrow neck of land. For this purpose, they formed and marched as soon as they had ascended the high grounds towards the fort. Upon the first information of their having landed, and of their movements, our men were ordered to meet them: but finding their numbers greatly superior, and that they were extending themselves to seize on the passes over the river, it was thought prudent to withdraw our men; which was effected, and their retreat secured. We lost the whole of the cannon that was at the fort (except two twelve-pounders) and a great deal of baggage, between two and three hundred tents, about a thousand barrels of flour, and other stores in the quartermaster's department. This loss was inevitable.

As many of the stores had been removed as circumstances and time would admit of. The ammunition had been happily got away.

Our present situation between Hackinsac and Passaic rivers being exactly similar to our late one, and our force here by no means adequate to an opposition that will promise the smallest probability of success, we are taking measures to retire over the waters of the latter, when the best disposition will be formed that circumstances will admit of.

By colonel Cadwallader, who has been permitted by general Howe to return to his friends, I am informed the surrender of the garrison on the sixteenth was on the common terms as prisoners of war; the loss of the Hessians, about three hundred privates and twenty-seven officers killed and wounded; about forty of the British troops, and two or three officers; the loss on our side but inconsiderable. I beg leave to refer you to him for a more particular account, and also for his relation of the distresses of our prisoners.— Colonels Miles and Atlee's letter, mentioned above, upon this subject, was through mistake sent from hence yesterday morning. The mode of relief proposed by them was a credit or supply of cash through the means of Mr. Franks. This seems to be doubtful, as he is said to be in confinement by colonel Cadwallader,—provided it would have been otherwise practicable.

I have the honor to be, &c. G. W.

P. S. Your favor of the sixteenth was duly received.—My letter to the board of war, on the subject of the return of the Waldeckers, I presume you will have seen.

Sir, *Newark, November 23, 1776.*

I HAVE not yet heard that any provision is making to supply the place of the troops composing the flying camp, whose departure is now at hand. The situation of our affairs is truly critical, and such as requires uncommon exertions

tions on our part. From the movements of the enemy, and the information we have received, they certainly will make a push to possess themselves of this part of the Jersey.—In order that you may be fully apprised of our weakness, and of the necessity there is of our obtaining early succours, I have, by the advice of the general officers here, directed general Mifflin to wait on you. He is intimately acquainted with our circumstances, and will represent them better than my hurried state will allow.

I have wrote to general Lee to come over with the continental regiments immediately under his command: those with general Heath I have ordered to secure the passes through the Highlands. I have also wrote to governor Livingston requesting of him such aid as may be in his power; and would submit it to the consideration of Congress whether application should not be made for part of the Pennsylvania militia to step forth at this pressing time.

Before I conclude, I would mention, if an early and immediate supply of money could be sent to Mr. Dalham to pay the flying-camp troops, it might have a happy effect. They would subsist themselves comfortably on their return, provide many necessaries of which they are in great want; and moreover it might be the means of inducing many, after seeing their friends, to engage again.

I expected, on coming here, to have met with many of the militia, but find from inquiry that there are not more than from four to five hundred at the different posts.

I have the honor to be, &c.   G. W.

Sir,   *Newark, November* 27, 1776.

I DO myself the honor to acknowledge the receipt of your favors of the twenty-first and twenty-fourth, with their several inclosures. The execution of the resolves has been and will be attended to as far as in my power.

I have wrote to general Schuyler to send down as early

as possible the troops in the northern department from this and the state of Pennsylvania. The proposition for exchanging Mr. Franklin for general Thompson I shall submit to general Howe, as soon as circumstances will allow me.

I have nothing in particular to advise you of, respecting the enemy, more than that they are advancing this way. Part of them have passed the Passaic; and I suppose the main body that they have on this side the North-river would have done the same before now (as they are coming on), had their progress not been retarded by the weather which has been rainy for several days past. I have scouts and detachments constantly out to harrass them and watch their motions, and to gain, if possible, intelligence of their designs.

Colonel Miles, who has been permitted to go to Philadelphia for a few days by general Howe, will deliver you this, and inform you of the distresses of our prisoners, and the necessity of effecting their exchange as far as we have prisoners to give in return.

By a letter from the board of war on the subject of an exchange, they mention that several of the prisoners in our hands have enlisted. It is a measure, I think, that cannot be justified, though the precedent is furnished on the side of the enemy: nor do I conceive it good in point of policy. But, as it has been done, I shall leave it with Congress to order them to be returned or not, as they shall judge fit.

I have the honor to be, &c. G. W.

Sir, *Brunswic, November* 30, 1776.

I HAVE been honored with your favor of the twenty-sixth, and with its inclosures, by which I perceive the measures that have been adopted for forwarding a reinforcement of militia. Their arrival is much to be wished, the situation of our affairs being truly alarming, and such as demands the earliest aids. As general Mifflin's presence may have a happy influence on the disposition and temper of many of the affociators, I fhall not direct his return fo long as he can be done without; and till it becomes indifpenfably neceffary.

On thurfday morning I left Newark, and arrived here yefterday with the troops that were there. It was the opinion of all the generals who were with me, that a retreat to this place was requifite, and founded in neceffity, as our force was by no means fufficient to make a ftand, with the leaft probability of fuccefs, againft an enemy much fuperior in number, and whofe advanced guards were entering the town by the time our rear got out. It was the wifh of all to have remained there longer, and to have halted before we came thus far: but, upon due confideration of our ftrength, the circumftances attending the enliftment of a great part of our little force, and the frequent advices that the enemy were embarking or about to embark another detachment for Staten-Ifland with a view of landing at Amboy to co-operate with this, which feemed to be confirmed by the information of fome perfons who came from the ifland, that they were collecting and impreffing all the waggons they could find,—it was judged neceffary to proceed till we came here, not only to prevent their bringing a force to act upon our front and rear, but alfo that we might be more convenient to oppofe any troops they might land at South-Amboy, which many conjectured to be an object they had in view. This conjecture too had probability and fome advices to fupport it.

I hoped we fhould have met with large and early fuccours by this time: but as yet no great number of the militia of this ftate has come in; nor have I much reafon to expect that any confiderable aid will be derived from the counties which lie beyond this river, and in which the enemy are. Their fituation will prevent it in a great meafure from thofe parts where they are, provided the inclinations of the people were good. Added to this, I have no affurances that more than a very few of the troops compofing the flying camp will remain

remain after the time of their engagement is out: so far from it, I am told that some of general Ewing's brigade, who stand engaged to the first of January, are now going away. If those go whose service expires this day, our force will be reduced to a mere handful.

From intelligence received this morning, one division of the enemy was advanced last night as far as Elizabethtown, and some of their quarter-masters had proceeded about four or five miles on this side, to provide barns, &c, for their accommodation. Other accounts say another division, composed of Hessians, are on the road through Springfield, and are reported to have reached that place last night. I do not know how far their views extend: but I doubt not, they mean to push every advantage resulting from the small number and state of our troops.

I early began to forward part of the stores from this place towards Philadelphia. Many are gone: the rest we are removing, and hope to secure.

I am, sir, very respectfully, &c. G. W.

P. S. I have wrote to governor Livingston, who is exerting himself to throw in every assistance, and to have guards placed at the ferries to prevent the return of the soldiers who are not discharged.

To the Board of War.

Head-Quarters, Brunswic, November 30, 1776.

GENTLEMEN,

I AM to acknowledge the receipt of your favors of the eighteenth, nineteenth, and twenty-third instant, which, from the unsettled situation of our affairs, I have not been able to answer before. That of the eighteenth incloses a list of stores [*imported*] in the Hancock-and-Adams continental ship, and carried into Dartmouth in New-England,—with a resolve of Congress to deliver the muskets, powder, lead, and flints,

flints, to my order. As the other articles of the cargo will be full as useful to the army as those included in the resolve, I would advise that directions be given to have the whole cargo removed from Dartmouth to some secure place in the neighborhood of Philadelphia, and there deposited till called for. It is by no means proper that so great a quantity of military stores should be lodged with the army, especially at present, as we know not to-day where we shall be obliged to remove to-morrow: and that will in all probability be the case while the enemy continue with a light army on this side the North-river.

In answer to that part of yours of the nineteenth in which you ask my advice as to the propriety of enlisting prisoners of war, I would just observe, that, in my opinion, it is neither consistent with the rules of war, nor politic: nor can I think, that, because our enemies have committed an unjustifiable action, by enticing, and, in some instances, intimidating our men into their service, we ought to follow their example. Before I had the honor of yours on this subject, I had determined to remonstrate to general Howe on this head. As to those few who have already enlisted, I would not have them again withdrawn and sent in, because they might be subjected to punishment: but I would have the practice discontinued in future. If you will revert to the capitulation of St. John's and Chamblee, you will find an express stipulation against the enlisting the prisoners taken there.

I remarked that the enlistment of prisoners was not a politic step:—my reason is this, that in time of danger I have always observed such persons most backward, for fear (I suppose) of falling into the hands of their former masters, from whom they expect no mercy: and this fear they are apt to communicate to their fellow-soldiers. They are also most ready to desert when any action is expected, hoping, by carrying intelligence, to secure their peace.

I met captain Hesketh on the road; and, as the situation of

of his family did not admit of delay, I permitted him to go immediately to New-York, not having the least doubt but general Howe will make a return of any officer of equal rank who shall be required.

I have the honor to be, &c.   G. W.

SIR,   *Brunſwic, December* 1, 1776.

I YESTERDAY had the honor of writing you, and to advise you of our arrival here. I am now to inform you that the enemy are still advancing, and that their van-guard had proceeded as far as Bonem, a small town about four miles this side of Woodbridge, according to my last intelligence. As to their number, reports are various. Some say they were joined yesterday by a considerable reinforcement from Staten-Island. How far this fact may be true, I cannot determine: but, from every information, before, they were between six and seven thousand strong.

I have for some time past supposed Philadelphia to be the object of their movement, and have every reason to believe my opinion well founded,—the advices of sundry persons, who have had an opportunity of mixing and conversing with them on the march, agreeing that such is the report. I have wrote to governor Livingston upon the subject, requesting his utmost exertions to forward on every succour in his power. The same, I trust, will be attended to in Pennsylvania. Without a sufficient number of men and arms, their progress cannot be checked:—at present our force is totally inadequate to any attempt.

Several officers belonging to the enemy, who were prisoners, have obtained permission to return. I have not yet sent in the names of those belonging to us, that are to be exchanged for them. By a Virginia paper, I perceive that captain Morgan and lieutenant Heath, who were taken prisoners at Quebec, and now on parole, are promoted in the late arrangement of officers in that state,—the former to a regiment,

regiment, the latter to a majority. It would be well if they were releaſed: but, being Virginians, and not knowing that any gentlemen who were taken at the ſame time are ſo circumſtanced, I have declined claiming their return without the opinion of Congreſs, leſt I ſhould incur the charge of partiality.

I have ſent forward colonel Humpton to collect proper boats and craft at the ferry for tranſporting our troops: and it will be of infinite importance to have every other craft, beſides what he takes for the above purpoſe, ſecured on the weſt ſide of Delaware: otherwiſe they may fall into the enemy's hands and facilitate their views.

I have the honor to be, &c.   G. W.

P. S. *Half after one o'clock, P. M.*—The enemy are faſt advancing: ſome of them are now in ſight. All the men of the Jerſey flying camp under general Heard, being applied to, have refuſed to continue longer in ſervice.

Sir,   *December* 1, 1776, *half after ſeven, P. M.*

IN a little time after I wrote you this evening, the enemy appeared in ſeveral parties on the heights oppoſite Brunſwic, and were advancing in a large body towards the croſſing-place. We had a ſmart cannonade whilſt we were parading our men, but without any or but little loſs on either ſide. It being impoſſible to oppoſe them with our preſent force with the leaſt proſpect of ſucceſs, we ſhall retreat to the weſt ſide of Delaware (and have advanced about eight miles) where it is hoped we ſhall meet a reinforcement ſufficient to check their progreſs. I have ſent colonel Humpton forward to collect the neceſſary boats for our tranſportation, and conceive it proper that the militia from Pennſylvania ſhould be ordered towards Trenton, that they may be ready to join us, and act as occaſion may require.

I am, ſir, your moſt obedient ſervant,   G. W.

P. S. I wiſh my letters of yeſterday may arrive ſafe, being informed

informed that the return expreſs who had them was idling his time, and ſhewing them on the road.

Sir, Princeton, December 2, 1776.

I ARRIVED here this morning with our troops between eight and nine o'clock, when I received the honor of your letter of the firſt with its incloſure.

When the enemy firſt landed on this ſide the North-river, I apprehended that they meant to make a puſh this way; and knowing that the force which I had was not ſufficient to oppoſe them, I wrote to general Lee to croſs with the ſeveral continental regiments in his diviſion, and hoped he would have arrived before now.—By ſome means or other he has been delayed.—I ſuppoſe he has paſſed the river, as his letter of the twenty-ſixth ultimo mentioned that he had marched a brigade the day before, and ſhould follow the next himſelf. The remainder of the troops I conceived neceſſary to guard the ſeveral paſſes through the Highlands; nor do I think they can be called from thence. Their number is very ſmall, being reduced to very few by the departure of the troops who ſtood engaged till the thirtieth ultimo.

I underſtand there are now at Briſtol ſeveral priſoners. As their exchange at this time cannot be effected with propriety, I think it will be neceſſary, under the preſent ſituation of affairs, to have them removed immediately to ſome more interior place, upon their paroles. If they remain, they may be of infinite diſadvantage.

I have the honor to be, &c. G. W.

[*On the outſide of the foregoing letter, which is, as uſual, addreſſed to the preſident of Congreſs, appears the following line, to Mr. Peters, ſecretary to the board of war.*]

Sir, diſpatch an expreſs immediately, to have the priſoners at Briſtol removed. R. H. HARRISON.

SIR, *Head-Quarters, Trenton, Dec. 3, 1776.*

I ARRIVED here myself yesterday morning with the main body of the army, having left lord Stirling with two brigades at Princeton and that neighborhood, to watch the motions of the enemy, and give notice of their approach. I am informed that they had not entered Brunswic yesterday morning at nine o'clock, but were on the opposite side of the Rariton.

Immediately on my arrival here, I ordered the removal of all the military and other stores and baggage over the Delaware: a great quantity are already got over; and as soon as the boats come up from Philadelphia, we shall load them; by which means I hope to have every thing secured this night and to-morrow, if we are not disturbed. After being disencumbered of my baggage and stores, my future situation will depend entirely upon circumstances.

I have not heard a word from general Lee since the twenty-sixth of last month; which surprises me not a little, as I have dispatched daily expresses to him, desiring to know when I might look for him. This makes me fearful that my letters have not reached him. I am informed by report that general St. Clair has joined him with three or four regiments from the northward. To know the truth of this, and also when I may expect him, and with what numbers, I have this minute dispatched colonel Steward (general Gates's aide-de-camp) to meet general Lee and bring me an account.

I look out earnestly for the reinforcement from Philadelphia. I am in hopes, that, if we can draw a good head of men together, it will give spirits to the militia of this state, who have as yet afforded me little or no assistance; nor can I find they are likely to do much.

General Heard just informs me that a person, on whose veracity he can depend, has reported to him that on sunday last he counted a hundred and seventeen sail of ships going out

out of the Hook.—You may depend upon being advised instantly of any further movement in the enemy's army or mine,—I have the honor to be, &c.   G. W.

SIR,   *Trenton, December* 4, 1776.

SINCE I had the honor of addressing you yesterday, I received a letter from general Lee. On the thirtieth ultimo he was at Peekskill, and expected to pass the river with his division two days after. From this intelligence you will readily conclude that he will not be able to afford us any aid for several days. The report of general St. Clair's having joined him with three or four regiments, I believe to be altogether premature, as he mentions nothing of it. It has arisen, as I am informed, from the return of some of the Jersey and Pennsylvania troops from Ticonderoga, whose time of service is expired. They have reached Pluckemin where I have wrote to have them halted and kept together, if they can be prevailed on, till further orders.

The inclosed is a copy of a letter which came to hand last night from major Clark, to which I beg leave to refer you for the intelligence it contains.—The number of the enemy said to be embarked is supposed to be rather exaggerated. That there has been an embarkation, is not to be doubted, it being confirmed through various channels. By colonel Griffin, who went from Brunswic on sunday morning with a captain Sims, to pass him by our guards, and who was detained by lord Cornwallis till monday evening on account of his situation, the amount of general Clinton's force, from what he could collect from the officers, was about six thousand: as to their destination, he could not obtain the least information. By him I also learn the enemy were in Brunswic, and that some of their advanced parties had proceeded two miles on this side. The heavy rain that has fallen has probably checked their progress, and may prevent their further movement for some time.

  I have the honor to be, &c.   G. W.

To Richard Peters, Esquire, Secretary to the Board of War.

SIR, Head-Quarters, Trenton, Dec. 4, 1776.

YOURS of the twentieth of last month was delivered to me by the brigadier La Roche de Fermoy, who is now here, but unable to render me that service, which, I dare say, from his character, he would, were he better acquainted with our language.

I yesterday received a letter from you without a date, mentioning that the prisoners from York-town were directed to halt at Newtown for my orders. On hearing they were there, I sent colonel Moylan to conduct them, and the prisoners from Reading who arrived nearly at the same time, over towards Brunswic, and deliver them in.

I hope you have not sent captain Price, lieutenant Peacock, and major Campbell, on to this place, as it is highly improper they should see and know the situation of our army here and at Princeton. They had better be sent up, under the care of some person, to Newtown or that neighborhood, and there wait the arrival of some larger party, who, I imagine, will be soon forwarded from Lancaster, and go in with them.

Lieutenant Symes came over to me at Brunswic from Bethlehem without the least guard or escort; and a lieutenant of the seventh regiment went through our whole army, and was at last discovered by a mere accident. He had a pass from the council of safety, and that was all. Such an irregular mode of suffering prisoners to go in alone must be put a stop to, or the enemy will be as well acquainted with our situation as we are ourselves. If they are left at liberty to chuse their own route, they will always take that through our army, for reasons too obvious to mention.

I am, sir, your most obedient servant, G. W.

I have been obliged to send down a number of our sick to Philadelphia, to make room for the troops, and to remove them

them out of the way. Be pleafed to have fome care taken to have them properly accommodated. I fhould think part of the Houfe-of-employment might be procured for that purpofe: I have ordered down an officer from each regiment, and a furgeon's mate, if they can be fpared: but I hope they will not want the affiftance of the vifiting phyficians of the hofpital.

Sir, *Trenton, December* 5, 1776.

AS nothing but neceffity obliged me to retire before the enemy and leave fo much of the Jerfeys unprotected, I conceive it my duty, and it correfponds with my inclination, to make head againft them fo foon as there fhall be the leaft probability of doing it with propriety. That the country might in fome meafure be covered, I left two brigades confifting of the five Virginia regiments and that of Delaware, containing in the whole about twelve hundred men fit for duty, under the command of lord Stirling and general Stephen, at Princeton, till the baggage and ftores could crofs the Delaware, or the troops under their refpective commands fhould be forced from thence. I fhall now, having removed the greateft part of the above articles, face about with fuch troops as are here fit for fervice, and march back to Princeton, and there govern myfelf by circumftances and the movements of general Lee. At any event, the enemy's progrefs may be retarded by this means if they intend to come on, and the people's fears in fome meafure quieted, if they do not. Sorry I am to obferve, however, that the frequent calls upon the militia of this ftate, the want of exertion in the principal gentlemen of the country, or a fatal fupinenefs and infenfibility of danger till it is too late to prevent an evil that was not only forefeen but foretold, have been the caufes of our late difgraces.

If the militia of this ftate had ftepped forth in feafon (and timely notice they had), we might have prevented the enemy's
crofling

crossing the Hackinsac, although without some previous notice of the time and place it was impossible to have done this at the North-river. We might with equal probability of success have made a stand at Brunswic on the Rariton. But as both these rivers were fordable in a variety of places (knee-deep only), it required many men to defend the passes; and these we had not. At Hackinsac our force was insufficient, because a part was at Elizabethtown, Amboy, and Brunswic, guarding a coast which I thought most exposed to danger; and at Brunswic, because I was disappointed in my expectation of militia, and because on the day of the enemy's approach (and probably the occasion of it) the term of the Jersey and Maryland brigades' service expired; neither of which would consent to stay an hour longer.

These, among ten thousand other instances, might be adduced to shew the disadvantages of short enlistments, and the little dependence upon militia in times of real danger. But, as yesterday cannot be recalled, I will not dwell upon a subject which, no doubt, has given much uneasiness to Congress, as well as extreme pain and anxiety to myself. My first wish is that Congress may be convinced of the impropriety of relying upon the militia, and of the necessity of raising a larger standing army than what they have voted. The saving in the article of stores, provisions, and in a thousand other things, by having nothing to do with militia unless in cases of extraordinary exigency, and such as could not be expected in the common course of events, would amply support a large army, which, well officered, would be daily improving, instead of continuing a destructive, expensive, and disorderly mob.

I am clear in opinion, that, if forty thousand men had been kept in constant pay since the first commencement of hostilities, and the militia had been excused doing duty during that period, the continent would have saved money. When I reflect on the losses we have sustained for want of good troops, the certainty of this is placed beyond a doubt in my mind. In such case, the militia, who have been harrassed

and

and tired by repeated calls upon them (and farming and manufactures in a manner suspended), would, upon any pressing emergency, have run with alacrity to arms; whereas the cry now is, "they may be as well ruined in one way as another;" and with difficulty they are obtained.

I mention these things, to shew, that, in my opinion, if any dependence is placed in the militia another year, Congress will be deceived. When danger is a little removed from them, they will not turn out at all. When it comes home to them, the well-affected, instead of flying to arms to defend themselves, are busily employed in removing their families and effects,—whilst the disaffected are concerting measures to make their submission, and spread terror and dismay all around, to induce others to follow the example.—Daily experience and abundant proofs warrant this information.

I shall this day reinforce lord Stirling with about twelve hundred men, which will make his number about two thousand four hundred. To-morrow I mean to repair to Princeton myself, and shall order the Pennsylvania troops (who are not yet arrived, except part of the German batallion and a company of light infantry) to the same place.

By my last advices, the enemy are still at Brunswic; and the account adds that general Howe was expected at Elizabethtown with a reinforcement, to erect the king's standard, and demand a submission of this state. I can only give this as a report brought from the enemy's camp by some of the country people.—I have the honor to be, &c.   G. W.

Sir,   *Trenton, December* 6, 1776.

I HAVE not received any intelligence of the enemy's movements since my letter of yesterday. From every information, they still remain at Brunswic, except some of their parties who are advanced a small distance on this side. To-day

day I shall set out for Princeton myself, unless something should occur to prevent me, which I do not expect.

By a letter of the fourteenth ultimo from a Mr. Caldwell, a clergyman, and a staunch friend to the cause, who has fled from Elizabethtown, and taken refuge in the mountains about ten miles from hence, I am informed that general or lord Howe was expected in that town to publish pardon and peace. His words are, " I have not seen his proclamation, but can only say he gives sixty days of grace, and pardons from the Congress down to the committee. No one man in the continent is to be denied his mercy."—In the language of this good man, the lord deliver us from his mercy !

Your letter of the third, by major Livingston, was duly received. Before it came to hand, I had wrote to general Howe about governor Franklin's exchange, but am not certain whether the letter could not be recovered. I dispatched a messenger instantly for that purpose.

I have the honor to be, &c. G. W.

Sir, *Mr. Berkley's Summer Seat, Dec. 8. 1776.*

COLONEL Reed would inform you of the intelligence which I first met with on the road from Trenton to Princeton yesterday. Before I got to the latter, I received a second express informing me, that, as the enemy were advancing by different routes, and attempting by one to get in the rear of our troops which were there (and whose numbers were small, and the place by no means defensible), they had judged it prudent to retreat to Trenton. The retreat was accordingly made, and since to this side of the river.

This information I thought it my duty to communicate as soon as possible, as there is not a moment's time to be lost in assembling such force as can be collected; and as the object of the enemy cannot now be doubted in the

smallest

smallest degree. Indeed I shall be out in my conjecture (for it is only conjecture) if the late embarkation at New-York is not for Delaware river, to co-operate with the army under the immediate command of general Howe, who, I am informed from good authority, is with the British troops and his whole force upon this route.

I have no certain intelligence of general Lee, although I have sent frequent expresses to him, and lately a colonel Humpton to bring me some accurate accounts of his situation. I last night dispatched another gentleman to him (major Hoops) desiring he would hasten his march to the Delaware, in which I would provide boats near a place called Alexandria, for the transportation of his troops.—I cannot account for the slowness of his march.

In the disordered and moving state of the army, I cannot get returns: but, from the best accounts, we had between three thousand and three thousand five hundred men, before the Philadelphia militia and German batallion arrived:—they amount to about two thousand.

I have the honor to be, &c.   G. W.

Sir,   *Head-Quarters, Trenton Falls, Dec. 9, 1776.*

I DID myself the honor of writing to you yesterday, and informing you that I had removed the troops to this side of the Delaware. Soon after, the enemy made their appearance, and their van entered just as our rear guard quitted. We had removed all our stores, except a few boards.—From the best information, they are in two bodies, one at and near Trenton, the other some miles higher up, and inclining towards Delaware; but whether with intent to cross there, or throw themselves between general Lee and me, is yet uncertain.

I have this morning detached lord Stirling with his brigade, to take post at the different landing-places, and prevent them from stealing a march upon us from above; for I am informed,

informed, if they cross at Coryel's ferry or thereabouts, they are as near to Philadelphia, as we are here. From several accounts I am led to think that the enemy are bringing boats with them: if so, it will be impossible for our small force to give them any considerable opposition in the passage of the river, [*as they may*] make a feint at one place, and, by a sudden removal, carry their boats higher or lower before we can bring our cannon to play upon them.

Under these circumstances, the security of Philadelphia should be our next object.—From my own remembrance, but more from information (for I never viewed the ground), I should think that a communication of lines and redoubts might soon be formed from the Delaware to Schuylkill on the north entrance of the city, the lines to begin on the Schuylkill side, about the heights of Springatebury, and run eastward to Delaware, upon the most advantageous and commanding grounds. If something of this kind is not done, the enemy might, in case any misfortune should befall us, march directly in, and take possession. We have ever found that lines, however slight, are very formidable to them: they would at least give a check till people could recover of the fright and consternation that naturally attends the first appearance of an enemy.

In the mean time every step should be taken to collect force, not only from Pennsylvania, but from the most neighborly states. If we can keep the enemy from entering Philadelphia, and keep the communication by water open for supplies, we may yet make a stand, if the country will come to our assistance till our new levies can be collected.

If the measure of fortifying the city should be adopted, some skilful person should immediately view the grounds, and begin to trace out the lines and works. I am informed there is a French engineer of eminence in Philadelphia at this time: if so, he will be the most proper.

I have the honor to be, &c. G. W.

P. S. I have just received the inclosed from general Heath.
—General

—General Mifflin is this moment come up, and tells me that all the military stores yet remain in Philadelphia. This makes the immediate fortifying of the city so necessary, that I have desired general Mifflin to return to take charge of the stores; and have ordered major-general Putnam immediately down to superintend the works and give the necessary directions.

Sir, *Head-Quarters, Falls of Delaware, Dec.* 10, 1776.

SINCE I had the honor of addressing you yesterday, nothing of importance has occurred.—In respect to the enemy's movements, I have obtained no other information than that they have a number of parties patroling up and down the river, particularly above. As yet they have not attempted to pass; nor do any of their patroles, though some are exceedingly small, meet with the least interruption from the inhabitants of Jersey.

By a letter received last night from general Lee, of the eighth instant, he was then at Morristown, where he entertained thoughts of establishing a post: but, on receiving my dispatches by major Hoops, I should suppose he would be convinced of the necessity of his proceeding this way with all the force he can bring.

I have the honor to be, &c. G. W.

P. S. *Nine o'clock, A. M.*—I this minute received information that the enemy were repairing the bridges three or four miles below Trenton; which seems to indicate an intention of their passing lower down, and suggests to me the necessity that some attention should be had to the fort at Billingsport, lest they should possess themselves of it; the consideration of which I beg leave to submit to Congress.— I have wrote to the council of safety on the subject.

Sir, *Head-Quarters, Falls of Delaware, Dec. 11, 1776.*

AFTER I had wrote you yesterday, I received certain information that the enemy, after repairing Crofwix's bridge, had advanced a party of about five hundred to Bordentown. By their taking this route, it confirms me in my opinion, that they have an intention to land between this and Philadelphia, as well as above, if they can procure boats for that purpose.

I last night directed commodore Seymour to station all his gallies between Bordentown and Philadelphia, to give the earliest intelligence of any appearance of the enemy on the Jersey shore.

I yesterday rode up the river about eleven miles, to lord Stirling's post, where I found a prisoner of the forty-second regiment who had been just brought in. He informed me that lord Cornwallis was at Pennytown with two batallions of grenadiers, and three of light infantry, all British, the Hessian grenadiers, the forty-second Highland regiment, and two other batallions, the names of which he did not remember. He knew nothing of the reasons of their being assembled there, nor what were their future intentions. But I last night received information from my lord Stirling, which had been brought in by his scouts, which in some measure accounted for their being there. They had made a forced march from Trenton on sunday night, to Coryel's ferry, in hopes of surprising a sufficient number of boats to transport them; but, finding themselves disappointed, had marched back to Pennytown, where they remained yesterday. From their several attempts to seize boats, it does not look as if they had brought any with them, as I was at one time informed. I last night sent a person over to Trenton, to learn whether there was any appearance of building any: but he could not perceive any preparations for a work of that kind; so that I am in hopes, if proper care is taken to keep all the craft out

of

of their way, they will find the crossing Delaware a matter of considerable difficulty.

I received another letter from general Lee last evening: it was dated at Chatham (which I take to be near Morristown) the eighth of this month. He had then received my letter sent by major Hoops, but seemed still inclined to hang upon the enemy's rear, to which I should have no objection, had I a sufficient force to oppose them in front: but, as I have not at present, nor do I see much probability of further reinforcement, I have wrote to him in the most pressing terms, to join me with all expedition.

Major Sheldon, who commands the volunteer horse from Connecticut, waits upon Congress to establish some mode of pay. I can only say that the service of himself and his troop has been such as merits the warmest thanks of the public, and deserves a handsome compensation for their trouble. Whatever is settled now, will serve for a precedent in future.—From the experience I have had, this campaign, of the utility of horse, I am convinced there is no carrying on the war without them; and I would therefore recommend the establishment of one or more corps (in proportion to the number of foot) in addition to those already raised in Virginia. If major Sheldon would undertake the command of a regiment of horse on the continental establishment, I believe he could very soon raise them; and I can recommend him as a man of activity and spirit, from what I have seen of him.—I have the honor to be, &c.   G. W.

Sir,   *Trenton Falls, December* 12, 1776.

I LAST night received the favor of Mr. Thompson's letter inclosing the proceedings of Congress, of the eleventh instant.—As the publication of their resolve, in my opinion, will not lead to any good end, but, on the contrary, may be attended with some bad consequences, I shall take the liberty to decline inserting it in this day's orders. I am persuaded, if the subject is taken up and reconsidered, that Congress will concur with me in sentiment. I doubt not but there are some who have propagated the report: but what if they have? Their remaining in or leaving Philadelphia must be governed by circumstances and events. If their departure should become necessary, it will be right: on the other hand, if there should not be a necessity for it, they will remain, and their continuance will shew the report to be the production of calumny and falsehood. In a word, sir, I conceive it a matter that may be as well disregarded; and that the removal or staying of Congress, depending entirely upon events, should not have been the subject of a resolve.

The intelligence we obtain respecting the movements and situation of the enemy is far from being so certain and satisfactory as I could wish, though every probable means in my power, and that I can devise, are adopted for that purpose. The latest I have received was from lord Stirling last night. He says that two grenadiers of the Inniskillen regiment, who were taken and brought in by some countrymen, inform that generals Howe, Cornwallis, Vaughan, &c, with about six thousand of the flying army, were at Pennytown, waiting for pontoons to come up, with which they mean to pass the river near the Blue Mounts, or at Coryel's ferry;— they believe, the latter;—that the two batallions of guards were at Brunswic, and the Hessian grenadiers, chasseurs, and a regiment or two of British troops, are at Trenton.

Captain Miller of colonel Hand's regiment also informs me, that a body of the enemy were marching to Burlington yesterday morning. He had been sent over with a strong scouting party, and, at day-break, fell in with their advanced guards consisting of about four hundred Hessian troops, who fired upon him before they were discovered, but without any loss; and obliged him to retreat with his party and to take boat. The number of the whole he could not ascertain: but it appeared to be considerable. Captain Miller's account is partly confirmed by commodore Seymour who reports

ports that four or five hundred of the enemy had entered the town. Upon the whole, there can be no doubt but that Philadelphia is their object, and that they will pass the Delaware as soon as possible. Happy should I be if I could see the means of preventing them: at present, I confess, I do not. All military writers agree that it is a work of great difficulty, nay impracticable, where there is any extent of coast to guard. This is the case with us; and we have to do it with a force, small and inconsiderable, and much inferior to that of the enemy. Perhaps Congress have some hope and prospect of reinforcements: I have no intelligence of the sort, and wish to be informed on the subject. Our little handful is daily decreasing by sickness and other causes: and, without aid, without considerable succours and exertions on the part of the people, what can we reasonably look for or expect, but an event that will be severely felt by the common cause, and that will wound the heart of every virtuous American,—the loss of Philadelphia? The subject is disagreeable: but yet it is true. I will leave it, wishing that our situation may become such as to do away the apprehensions which at this time seem to fill the minds of too many, and with too much justice.

By a letter from general Heath, dated at Peekskill, the eighth, I am advised that lieutenant-colonel Vose was then there with Greaton's, Bond's, and Porter's regiments, amounting in the whole to between five and six hundred men, who were coming this way. He adds that generals Gates and Arnold would be at Goshen that night, with Stark's, Poor's, and Read's regiments; but for what purpose, he does not mention.

The inclosed extract of a letter which I received last night contains intelligence of an agreeable nature. I wish to hear its confirmation by the arrival of the several prizes; that with clothing and arms will be an invaluable acquisition.

I shall be glad to be advised of the mode I am to observe

in paying the officers; whether they are to be allowed to draw the pay lately established, and from what time, or how long they are to be paid under the old establishment. A pay-roll which was presented yesterday, being made up for the new, has given rise to these propositions. Upon my objecting to it, I was told that Congress or the board of war had established the precedent, by paying the sixth regiment of Virginia troops commanded by colonel Buckner, agreeable to the latter, as they came through Philadelphia.

I have the honor to be, &c.   G. W.

Sir,   *Head-Quarters, Trenton Falls, Dec.* 13, 1776.

THE apparent designs of the enemy being to avoid this ferry, and land their troops above and below us, have induced me remove from this place the greater part of the troops, and throw them into a different disposition on the river, whereby I hope not only to be more able to impede their passage, but also to avoid the danger of being inclosed in this angle of the river. And notwithstanding the extended appearances of the enemy on the other side, made, at least in part, to divert our attention from any particular point as well as to harrass us by fatigue, I cannot divest myself of the opinion that their principal design is to ford the river somewhere above Trenton; to which design I have had particular respect in the new arrangement, wherein I am so far happy as to have the concurrence of the general officers at this place.

Four brigades of the army, under generals lord Stirling, Mercer, Stephen and De Fermoy, extend from Yardley's up to Coryel's ferry, posted in such a manner as to guard every suspicious part of the river, and to afford assistance to each other in case of attack. General Ewing, with the flying camp of Pennsylvania, and a few Jersey troops under general Dickinson, are posted from Yardley's ferry down to the ferry opposite Bordentown. Colonel Cadwallader, with the Pennsylvania militia, occupies the ground above and below

the

the mouth of Neshaminy river as far down as Dunk's ferry; at which place colonel Nixon is posted with the third batallion of [*Pennsylvania*]. A proper quantity of artillery is appointed to each brigade; and I have ordered small redoubts to be thrown up opposite every place where there is a possibility of fording.—I shall remove further up the river to be near the main body of my small army, with which every possible opposition shall be given to any further approach of the enemy towards Philadelphia.

As general Armstrong has a good deal of influence in this state, and our present force is small and inconsiderable, I think he cannot be better employed than to repair to the counties where his interest lies, to animate the people, promote the recruiting service, and encourage the militia to come in. He will also be able to form a proper judgment of the places suitable for magazines of provision to be collected. I have requested him to wait upon Congress on this subject: and if general Smallwood should go to Maryland on the same business, I think it would have a happy effect: he is popular and of great influence, and, I am persuaded, would contribute greatly to that state's furnishing her quota of men in a little time. He is now in Philadelphia.

I have the honor to be, &c, G. W.

SIR, *Head-Quarters, at Keith's, Dec.* 15, 1776,

ABOUT one o'clock to-day I received a letter from general Sullivan, a copy of which you have inclosed. I will not comment on the melancholy intelligence which it contains, only adding that I sincerely regret general Lee's unhappy fate, and feel much for the loss of my country in his captivity.

In respect to the enemy, they have been industrious in their attempts to procure boats and small craft: but as yet their efforts have not succeeded. From the latest advices that I have of their movements by some prisoners and others,
they

they appear to be leaving Trenton, and to be filing off towards Princeton and Allentown. What their designs are, whether they mean to retreat, or only a feint, cannot be determined. I have parties out to watch their motions, and to form, if possible, an accurate opinion of their plans.

Our force, since my last, has received no augmentation,— of course, by sickness and other causes, has diminished: but I am advised by a letter from the council of safety, which just came to hand, that colonels Burd and Gilbreath are marching with their batallions of militia, and also that some small parties are assembling in Cumberland county. * * *

I have the honor to be, &c. G. W.

SIR, *Head-Quarters, at Keith's, Dec.* 16, 1776.

IN a late letter which I had the honor of addressing you, I took the liberty to recommend that more batallions should be raised for the new army than what had been voted. Having fully considered the matter, I am more and more convinced not only of the propriety but of the necessity of the measure. That the enemy will leave nothing un-essayed in the course of the next campaign to reduce these states to the rule of a most * * *, must be obvious to every one; and that the militia is not to be depended on, or aid expected from them but in cases of the most pressing emergency, is not to be doubted. The first of these propositions is unquestionable, and fatal experience has given her sanction to the truth of the latter: indeed their lethargy of late, and backwardness to turn out at this alarming crisis, seem to justify an apprehension that nothing can bring them from their homes. For want of their assistance, a large part of Jersey has been exposed to ravage and to plunder; nor do I know that Pennsylvania would share a better fate, could general Howe effect a passage across the Delaware with a respectable force. These considerations have induced me to wish that no reliance, except such as may arise from necessity,

should

should ever be had in them again; and to make further mention to Congress of the expediency of increasing their army.—I trust the measure will meet their earliest attention.

Had I leisure and were it necessary, I could say much upon this head: but, as I have not, and the matter is well understood, I will not add much. By augmenting the number of your batallions, you will augment your force: the officers of each will have their interest and influence; and, upon the whole, their numbers will be much greater, though they should not be complete. Added to this, from the present confused state of Jersey, and the improper appointment of officers in many instances, I have little or no expectation that she will be able to raise all the troops exacted from her, though I think it might be done, were suitable spirited gentlemen commissioned, who would exert themselves, and encourage the people, many of whom (for a failure in this instance, and who are well disposed) are making their submissions.—In a word, the next will be a trying campaign: and as all that is dear and valuable may depend upon the issue of it, I would advise that nothing should be omitted, that shall seem necessary to our success. Let us have a respectable army, and such as will be competent to every exigency.

I will also add that the critical situation of our affairs, and the dissolution of our present force (now at hand), require that every nerve and exertion be employed for recruiting the new batallions. One part of general Howe's movements at this time, I believe, is with a design to distract us and prevent this business. If the inclemency of the weather should force him into winter-quarters, he will not remain there longer than necessity shall oblige him: he will commence his operations in a short space of time; and in that time our levies must be made up, to oppose him, or I fear the most melancholy of all events must take place.

The inclosed extract of a letter from the commissary-general will shew his demands for money, and his plans for

procuring

procuring salted provisions and a quantity of flour from the southward. The whole is submitted to the consideration of Congress; and I wish the result of their opinion to be transmitted him, with such supplies of money as may be necessary for himself and the departments he mentions.

The clothing of the troops is a matter of infinite importance, and, if it could be accomplished, would have a happy effect. Their distresses are extremely great, many of them being entirely naked, and most so thinly clad as to be unfit for service. I must entreat Congress to write to the agents and contractors upon this subject, that every possible supply may be procured and forwarded with the utmost expedition. I cannot attend to the business myself, having more than I can possibly do besides.

I have the honor to be, &c. G. W.

SIR, *Camp, above Trenton Falls, Dec.* 20, 1776.

I HAVE waited with much impatience to know the determinations of Congress on the propositions made some time in October last for augmenting our corps of artillery and establishing a corps of engineers. The time is now come when the first cannot be delayed without the greatest injury to the safety of these states; and therefore, under the resolution of Congress bearing date the twelfth instant, at the repeated instances of colonel Knox, and by the pressing advice of all the general officers now here, I have ventured to order three batalions of artillery to be immediately recruited. These are two less than colonel Knox recommends, as you will see by his plan inclosed; but then this scheme comprehends all the United States, whereas some of the states have corps already established, and these three batalions are indispensably necessary for the operations in this quarter, including the northern department.

The pay of our artillerists bearing no proportion with that in the English or French service,—the murmuring and dissatisfaction

dissatisfaction thereby occasioned, and the absolute impossibility (as I am told) of getting them upon the old terms,—and the unavoidable necessity of obtaining them at all events,—have induced me (also by advice) to promise officers and men that their pay should be augmented twenty-five per cent, or that their engagements shall become null and void. This may appear to Congress premature and unwarrantable. But, sir, if they view our situation in the light it strikes their officers, they will be convinced of the utility of the measure, and that the execution could not be delayed till after their meeting at Baltimore. In short, the present exigency of our affairs will not admit of delay either in council or the field: for well convinced I am, that, if the enemy go into quarters at all, it will be for a short season. But I rather think the design of general Howe is to possess himself of Philadelphia this winter, if possible; and in truth I do not see what is to prevent him, as ten days more will put an end to the existence of our army. That one great point is to keep us as much harrassed as possible, with a view to injure the recruiting service and hinder a collection of stores and other necessaries for the next campaign, I am as clear in, as I am of my existence. If therefore,--[when] we have to provide in this short interval, and make these great and arduous preparations,—every matter that in its nature is self evident is to be referred to Congress at the distance of a hundred and thirty or forty miles, so much time must necessarily elapse, as to defeat the end in view.

It may be said that this is an application for powers that are too dangerous to be entrusted. I can only add that desperate diseases require desperate remedies; and with truth declare that I have no lust after power, but wish with as much fervency as any man upon this wide-extended continent for an opportunity of turning the sword into a ploughshare. But my feelings, as an officer and a man, have been such as to force me to say that no person ever had a greater choice of difficulties to contend with than I have:—It is

needless

needless to add that short enlistments, and a mistaken dependence upon militia, have been the origin of all our misfortunes and the great accumulation of our debt.

We find, sir, that the enemy are daily gathering strength from the disaffected. This strength, like a snow-ball, by rolling, will increase, unless some means can be devised to check effectually the progress of the enemy's arms. Militia may possibly do it for a little while: but in a little while also, the militia of those states which have been frequently called upon will not turn out at all; or, if they do, it will be with so much reluctance and sloth, as to amount to the same thing:—instance, New-Jersey!—witness, Pennsylvania!—Could any thing but the river Delaware have saved Philadephia?—Can any thing (the exigency of the case indeed may justify it) be more destructive to the recruiting service, than giving ten dollars bounty for six weeks' service of the militia, who come in, you cannot tell how,—go, you cannot tell when,—and act, you cannot tell where,—consume your provisions, exhaust your stores, and leave you at last at a critical moment?

These, sir, are the men I am to depend upon, ten days hence: this is the basis on which your cause will and must forever depend, till you get a large standing army sufficient of itself to oppose the enemy. I therefore beg leave to give it as my humble opinion, that eighty-eight batallions are by no means equal to the opposition you are to make, and that a moment's time is not to be lost in raising a greater number,—not less, in my opinion and the opinion of my officers, than a hundred and ten. It may be urged that it will be found difficult enough to complete the first number. This may be true, and yet the officers of a hundred and ten batallions will recruit many more men, than those of eighty-eight. In my judgment this is not a time to stand upon expense: our funds are the only object of consideration. The state of New-York have added one batallion (I wish they had made it two) to their quota.—If any good officers offer

offer to raise men upon continental pay and establishment in this quarter, I shall encourage them to do so, and regiment them when they have done it. If Congress disapprove of this proceeding, they will please to signify it, as I mean it for the best.

It may be thought that I am going a good deal out of the line of my duty, to adopt these measures, or to advise thus freely. A character to lose,—an estate to forfeit,—the inestimable blessings of liberty at stake,—and a life devoted,—must be my excuse.

I have heard nothing of the light-horse from Virginia, nor the regiment from the Eastern-Shore. I wish to know what troops are to act in the different departments, and to have those from the southward (designed for this place) ordered on as fast as they shall be raised. The route should be pointed out by which they are to march; assistant-commissaries and quarter-masters upon the communication, to supply their wants; the first or second officer of each batallion to forward them, and the other to come on, receive and form them at their place of destination. Unless this is immediately set about, the campaign, if it should be closed, will be opened in the spring before we have any men in the field.

Every exertion should be used to procure tents: a clothier-general should be appointed without loss of time for supplying the army with every article in that way:—he should be a man of business and abilities. A commissary of prisoners must be appointed to attend the army:—for want of an officer of this kind, the exchange of prisoners has been conducted in a most shameful and injurious manner. We have had them from all quarters pushed into our camps at the most critical junctures, and without the least previous notice. We have had them travelling through the different states in all directions by certificates from committees, without any kind of control; and have had instances of some going into the enemy's camp without my privity or knowledge,

ledge, after paſſing in the manner before mentioned.—There may be other officers neceſſary which I do not recollect at this time, and which, when thought of, muſt be provided for; this, ſir, you may rely on, that the commanding officer, under the preſent eſtabliſhment, is obliged to attend to the buſineſs of ſo many different departments, as to render it impoſſible to conduct that of his own with the attention neceſſary;—than which, nothing can be more injurious.

In a former letter, I intimated my opinion of the neceſſity of having a brigadier for every three regiments, and a major-general to every three brigades, at moſt. I think no time is to be loſt in making the appointments, that the arrangements may be conſequent. This will not only aid the recruiting ſervice, but will be the readieſt means of forming and diſciplining the army afterwards, which, in the ſhort time we have to do it, is of amazing conſequence. I have labored, ever ſince I have been in the ſervice, to diſcourage all kinds of local attachments and diſtinctions of country, denominating the whole by he greateſt name of '*American*:' but I found it impoſſible to over come prejudices; and, under the new eſtabliſhment, I conceive it beſt to ſtir up an emulation; in order to do which, would it not be better for each ſtate to furniſh (though not to appoint) their own brigadiers?—This, if known to be part of the eſtabliſhment, might prevent a good deal of contention and jealouſy; and would, I believe, be the means of promotions going forward with more ſatisfaction, and quiet the higher officers.

Whilſt I am ſpeaking of promotions, I cannot help giving it as my opinion, that, if Congreſs think proper to confirm what I have done with reſpect to the corps of artillery, colonel Knox (at preſent at the head of that department, but who, without promotion, will reſign) ought to be appointed to the command of it, with the rank and pay of brigadier. I have alſo to mention, that, for want of ſome eſtabliſhment in the department of engineers agreeable to the plan laid before Congreſs in October laſt, colonel Putnam, who was at the head of it, has quitted, and taken a regiment in the state of Massachusetts. I know of no other man tolerably well qualified for the conducting of that business. None of the French gentlemen whom I have seen with appointments in that way appear to me to know any thing of the matter. There is one in Philadelphia, who, I am told, is clever: but him I have never seen.

I must also once more beg leave to mention to Congress the expediency of letting promotions be in a regimental line. The want of this has already driven some of the best officers that were in your army, out of the service. From repeated and strict inquiry I am convinced you can adopt no mode of promotion that will be better received, or that will give more general satisfaction. I wish therefore to have it announced.

The casting of cannon is a matter that ought not to be one moment delayed: and therefore I shall send colonel Knox to put this in a train, as also to have travelling carriages and shot provided,—elaboratories to be established, one in Hartford, and another in York. Magazines of provisions should also be laid in. These I shall fix with the commissary. As our great loss last year proceeded from a want of teams, I shall direct the quarter-master-general to furnish a certain number to each regiment to answer the common purposes thereof, that the army may be enabled to remove from place to place differently from what we have done, or could do, this campaign. Ammunition carts, and proper carts for intrenching tools, should also be provided, and I shall direct about them accordingly. Above all, a store of small arms should be provided, or men will be of little use. The consumption and waste of these, this year, has been great:—militia, flying-camp men, &c, coming in without, were obliged to be furnished, or become useless. Many of these threw their arms away: some lost them, whilst others deserted, and took them away. In a word, although I used every precaution to preserve them, the loss has been great; and this will forever be the case in such a mixed and irregular army as ours has been.

If no part of the troops already embarked at New-York has appeared in Virginia, their destination doubtless must be to some other quarter; and that state must, I should think, be freed from any invasion, if general Howe can be effectually opposed in this. I therefore inclose a memorandum given me by brigadier Stephen of Virginia, which Congress will please to adopt in the whole,—in part,—or reject,—as may be consistent with their plans and intelligence.

The division of the army, late under the command of general Lee, now general Sullivan, is just upon the point of joining us. A strange kind of fatality has attended it. They had orders on the seventeenth of November to join, now more than a month. General Gates, with four eastern regiments, is also near at hand: three others from those states were coming on, by his order, by the way of Peekskill, and had joined general Heath whom I had ordered on with Parsons's brigade, to join me, leaving Clinton's brigade and some militia (that were at Forts Montgomery and Constitution) to guard those important passes of the Highlands. But the convention of the state of New-York seeming to be much alarmed at Heath's coming away,—a fleet appearing off New-London,—and some part of the enemy's troops retiring towards Brunswic,—induced me to countermand the order for the march of Parsons's brigade, and to direct the three regiments from Ticonderoga to halt at Morristown in Jersey (where I understand about eight hundred militia had collected), in order to inspirit the inhabitants, and, as far as possible, cover that part of the country. I shall send general Maxwell this day to take the command of them, and, if to be done, to harrass and annoy the enemy in their quarters, and cut off their convoys.

The care and vigilance, which were used in securing the boats

boats on this river, have hitherto baffled every attempt of the enemy to crofs: but, from concurring reports and appearances, they are waiting for ice to afford them a paffage.

Since writing the foregoing I have received a letter from governor Cooke of Rhode-Ifland, of which the inclofed is a copy. Previous to this, and immediately upon the firft intelligence obtained of a fleet's going through the Sound, I difpatched orders to generals Spencer and Arnold to proceed without the leaft delay to the eaftward. The firft, I prefume, is gone: the latter, not getting my letter till he came to a place called Eafton, was, by advice of general Gates who alfo met my letter at the fame place, induced to come on hither before he proceeded to the eaftward.—Moft of our brigadiers are laid up: not one has come on with the divifion under general Sullivan, but they are left fick at different places on the road.

By accounts from the eaftward, a large body of men had affembled in Rhode-Ifland from the ftates of Maffachufetts and Connecticut. I prefume (but I have no advice of it) that the militia ordered from the firft, to rendez-vous at Danbury (fix thoufand in number) under the command of major-general Lincoln, for fupplying the place of the difbanded men of that ftate in the continental army, will now be ordered to Rhode-Ifland.

In fpeaking of general Lincoln, I fhould not do him juftice, were I not to add that he is a gentleman well worthy of notice in the military line. He commanded the militia from Maffachufetts laft fummer, or fall rather, and much to my fatisfaction,—having proved himfelf on all occafions an active, fpirited, fenfible man. I do not know whether it is his wifh to remain in the military line, or whether, if he fhould, any thing under the rank he now holds in the ftate he comes from would fatisfy him. How far an appointment of this kind might offend the continental brigadiers, I cannot undertake to fay:—many there are, over whom he ought not to be placed; but I know of no way to difcriminate.—Brigadier Reed of New-Hampfhire does not, I presume,

presume, mean to continue in service: he ought not,—as I am told, by the severity of the small-pox, he is become both blind and deaf.—I have the honor to be, &c. G. W.

P. S. Generals Gates and Sullivan have this instant come in. By them I learn that few or no men are recruited out of the regiments coming on with them, and that there is very little reason to expect that these regiments will be prevailed upon to continue after their term of service expires. If militia then do not come in, the consequences are but too evident.

Sir,   *Camp above Trenton Falls, Decem.* 24, 1776.

THAT I should dwell upon the subject of our distresses, cannot be more disagreeable to Congress than it is painful to myself. The alarming situation to which our affairs are reduced impels me to the measure. Inquiry and investigation,—which in most cases serve to develop and point out a remedy,—in ours, present more and greater difficulties. Till of late, I was led to hope from report that no inconsiderable part of the troops composing the regiments that were with general Lee, and those from Ticonderoga under general Gates, had enlisted again. This intelligence, I confess, gave me reason to expect that I should have, at the expiration of the present year, a force somewhat more respectable than what I find will be the case.

Having examined into the state of those regiments, I am authorised to say from the information of their officers, that but very few of the men have enlisted. Those who have are of the troops from Ticonderoga, and were permitted to visit their friends and homes, as part of the terms on which they would re-engage. In respect to those who marched with general Lee, I cannot learn that any have. Their refusal, I am told, has not proceeded more from an aversion to the service, or any fixed determination not to engage again, than from their wishes to return home,—the non-appointment of officers in some instances,—the turning out of good, and appointing of bad,—in others, and the incomplete or rather no arrangement of them,—a work unhappily committed to the management of their states: nor have I the most distant prospect of retaining them a moment longer than the last of this instant, notwithstanding the most pressing solicitations and the obvious necessity for it.

By the departure of these regiments I shall be left with five from Virginia, Smallwood's from Maryland, a small part of Rawlins's, Hand's from Pennsylvania, a part of Ward's from Connecticut, and the German batallion, amounting in the whole at this time from fourteen to fifteen hundred effective men. This handful, and such militia as may chuse to join me, will then compose our army.

When I reflect upon these things they fill me with much concern, knowing that general Howe has a number of troops cantoned in the towns bordering on and near the Delaware, —his intentions to pass, as soon as the ice is sufficiently formed, to invade Pennsylvania and to possess himself of Philadelphia if possible. To guard against his designs and the execution of them, shall employ my every exertion: but how is this to be done? As yet but few militia have gone to Philadelphia, and they are to be our support at this alarming crisis. Had I entertained a doubt of general Howe's intentions to pass the Delaware on the dissolution of our army, and as soon as the ice is made, it would now be done away. An intercepted letter from a gentleman of Philadelphia (who has joined the enemy), to his friend and partner in the city declares that to be their design,—that the army would be there in ten or twenty days from the sixteenth instant, the time of his writing, if the ice should be made;—advises him by no means to remove their stores,—that they would be safe.

The obstacles which have arisen to the raising of the new army, from the mode of appointing the officers, induce me to hope, if Congress resolve on an additional number of batallions

batallions to those already voted, that they will devise some other rule by which the officers, especially the field-officers, should be appointed. In case an augmentation should be made to the eastern regiments, a deviation from the former mode will operate more strongly as to them than to other batallions, because there have been many more officers in service from those states, than the regiments voted to be raised would admit of; by which means several deserving men could not have been provided for, had the utmost pains been used for the purpose; and many others of merit have been neglected in the late appointments, and those of little worth and less experience put in their places or promoted over their heads. This has been the case with many of the best officers.

The inclosed letter from the paymaster-general will shew the state of the military chest, and the necessity of a large and immediate supply of cash. The advances to the officers, for bounty and the recruiting service, are great: besides, the regiments, at the expiration of this month, will require pay of their claims. * * *

I have the honor to be, &c. G. W.

P. S. If the public papers have been removed from Philadelphia, I hope those which I sent by lieutenant-colonel Reed before we left New-York have not been forgot. If they have not, I beg the favor of you to break open the chest, and send me the several letter-books sealed up, having frequent occasion to refer to them.

To Robert Morris *Esquire.*

Dear Sir, *Head-Quarters, December* 25, 1776.

I HAVE your obliging favors of the twenty-first and twenty-third. The blankets are come to hand; but I would not have any of the other goods sent on till you hear again from me.

I agree with you that it is in vain to ruminate upon, or even

even reflect upon the authors or causes of, our present misfortunes: we should rather exert ourselves, and look forward with hopes that some lucky chance may yet turn up in our favor. Bad as our prospects are, I should not have the least doubt of success in the end, did not the late treachery and defection of those, who stood foremost in the opposition while fortune smiled upon us, make me fearful that many more will follow their example, who, by using their influence with some and working upon the fears of others, may extend the circle so as to take in whole towns, counties, nay provinces. Of this we have a recent instance in Jersey; and I wish many parts of Pennsylvania may not be ready to receive the yoke.

The security of the continental ships of war in Delaware is certainly a capital object; and yet to draught the many hands, necessary to fit them out, from the militia, might be dangerous just now: perhaps in a little time hence their places may be supplied with country militia; and then, if the exigency of affairs requires it, they certainly ought to be spared. —I will just hint to you a proposition that was made, or rather talked of, a few days ago by the officers of two New-England regiments whose time of service will expire on the first of January. They are most of them water men: and they said their men would willingly go on board the frigates, and navigate them round to any of the ports in New-England, if it was thought they would be safer there than in Delaware. You may think of this, and let me hear from you on the subject, if the proposition pleases you.

Lieutenant Boger of the navy is already gone in, and I have made a demand of lieutenant Josiah in exchange; but I have not heard whether lord Howe accedes to it. I will procure the release of doctor Hodge as soon as it can be done without injuring others by giving him the preference, as I have always made it a rule to demand those first who have been longest in captivity. I will take the same steps in regard to Mr. Jones, commander of the sloop taken by the Andrew Doria.

I shall

I shall take the earliest opportunity of sending in your letter to general Lee, with the bill drawn upon major Small.

From an intercepted letter from a person in the secrets of the enemy, I find their intentions are to cross Delaware as soon as the ice is sufficiently strong. I mention this, that you may take the necessary steps for the security of such public and private property as ought not to fall into their hands should they make themselves masters of Philadelphia, of which they do not seem to entertain the least doubt.

I hope the next christmas will prove happier than the present, to you, and to, dear sir, your sincere friend and humble servant, G. W.

P. S. I would just ask whether you think Christiana a safe place for our stores. Do not you think they would be safer at Lancaster, or somewhere more inland?

Sir, *Head-Quarters, Morristown, Dec.* 27, 1776.

I HAVE the pleasure of congratulating you upon the success of an enterprise which I had formed against a detachment of the enemy lying in Trenton, and which was executed yesterday morning.

The evening of the twenty-fifth I ordered the troops intended for this service to parade back of M‘Konkey's ferry, that they might begin to pass as soon as it grew dark, imagining we should be able to throw them all over, with the necessary artillery, by twelve o'clock, and that we might easily arrive at Trenton by five in the morning, the distance being about nine miles. But the quantity of ice, made that night, impeded the passage of the boats so much, that it was three o'clock before the artillery could all be got over; and near four, before the troops took up their line of march.

This made me despair of surprising the town, as I well knew we could not reach it before the day was fairly broke. But as I was certain there was no making a retreat without being discovered, and harrassed on repassing the river, I determined

termined to push on at all events. I formed my detachment into two divisions, one to march by the lower or river road, the other by the upper or Pennington road. As the divisions had nearly the same distance to march, I ordered each of them, immediately upon forcing the out guards, to push directly into the town, that they might charge the enemy before they had time to form.

The upper division arrived at the enemy's advanced post exactly at eight o'clock; and in three minutes after, I found, from the fire on the lower road, that that division had also got up. The out-guards made but small opposition, though, for their numbers, they behaved very well, keeping up a constant retreating fire from behind houses. We presently saw their main body formed: but, from their motions, they seemed undetermined how to act.

Being hard pressed by our troops who had already got possession of their artillery, they attempted to file off by a road on their right, leading to Princeton. But, perceiving their intention, I threw a body of troops in their way; which immediately checked them. Finding from our disposition, that they were surrounded, and that they must inevitably be cut to pieces if they made any further resistance, they agreed to lay down their arms. The number that submitted in this manner was twenty-three officers and eight hundred and eighty-six men. Colonel Rahl the commanding officer, and seven others, were found wounded in the town. I do not exactly know how many they had killed; but I fancy, not above twenty or thirty, as they never made any regular stand. Our loss is very trifling indeed,—only two officers and one or two privates wounded.

I find that the detachment of the enemy consisted of the three Hessian regiments of Lanspach, Kniphausen, and Rahl, amounting to about fifteen hundred men, and a troop of British light-horse: but, immediately upon the beginning of the attack, all those who were not killed or taken pushed directly down the road towards Bordentown. These would

would likewife have fallen into our hands, could my plan have been completely carried into execution. General Ewing was to have croffed before day at Trenton ferry, and taken poffeffion of the bridge leading out of town: but the quantity of ice was fo great, that, though he did every thing in his power to effect it, he could not get over. This difficulty alfo hindered general Cadwallader from croffing with the Pennfylvania militia from Briftol. He got part of his foot over: but finding it impoffible to embark his artillery, he was obliged to defift.

I am fully confident, that, could the troops under generals Ewing and Cadwallader have paffed the river, I fhould have been able with their affiftance to have driven the enemy from all their pofts below Trenton. But the numbers I had with me being inferior to theirs below me, and a ftrong batallion of light infantry being at Princeton above me, I thought it moft prudent to return the fame evening with the prifoners and the artillery we had taken. We found no ftores of any confequence in the town.

In juftice to the officers and men, I muft add that their behavior upon this occafion reflects the higheft honor upon them. The difficulty of paffing the river in a very fevere night, and their march through a violent ftorm of fnow and hail, did not in the leaft abate their ardor: but, when they came to the charge, each feemed to vie with the other in preffing forward: and were I to give a preference to any particular corps, I fhould do great injuftice to the others.

Colonel Baylor, my firft aide-de-camp, will have the honor of delivering this to you; and from him you may be made acquainted with many other particulars. His fpirited behavior upon every occafion requires me to recommend him to your particular notice.

I have the honor to be, &c. G. W.

Inclofed you have a particular lift of the prifoners, artillery and other ftores.

Sir,   *Newtown, December* 29, 1776.

I AM juft fetting out to attempt a fecond paffage over the Delaware with the troops that were with me on the morning of the twenty-fixth. I am determined to effect it if poffible; but know that it will be attended with much fatigue and difficulty on account of the ice, which will neither allow us to crofs on foot, nor give us an eafy paffage with boats. General Cadwallader croffed from Briftol on the twenty-feventh, and, by his letter of yefterday, was at Bordentown with about eighteen hundred men. In addition to thefe, general Mifflin fent over five hundred from Philadelphia on friday, three hundred yefterday evening from Burlington, and will follow to-day with feven or eight hundred more. I have taken every precaution in my power for fubfifting the troops, and fhall, without lofs of time, and as foon as circumftances will admit of it, purfue the enemy in their retreat,—try to beat up more of their quarters,—and, in a word, in every inftance, adopt fuch meafures as the exigency of our affairs requires, and our fituation will juftify.

Had it not been for the unhappy failure of generals Ewing and Cadwallader in their attempts to pafs on the night of the twenty-fifth,—and if the feveral concerted attacks could have been made;—I have no doubt but that our views would have fucceeded to our warmeft expectations. What was done occafioned the enemy to leave their feveral pofts on the Delaware with great precipitation. The peculiar diftreffes to which the troops who were with me were reduced by the feverities of cold, rain, fnow, and ftorm,—the charge of the prifoners they had taken,—and another reafon that might be mentioned,—and the little profpect of receiving fuccours on account of the feafon and fituation of the river,—would not authorife a further purfuit at that time.

Since tranfmitting the lift of prifoners, a few more have been difcovered and taken in Trenton,—among them a

lieutenant-

lieutenant-colonel, and a deputy-adjutant-general,—the whole amounting to about a thousand.

I have been honored with your letter of the twenty-third and its several inclosures, to which I shall pay due attention.—A flag goes in this morning with a letter to general Howe, and another to general Lee. For the latter, Robert Morris esquire has transmitted a bill of exchange, drawn by two British officers, for a hundred and sixteen pounds, nine shillings, and three pence, on major Small, for money furnished them in South-Carolina, which I trust will be paid. This supply is exclusive of the sum you have resolved to be sent him, and which Mr. Morris will procure in time.

I have the honor to be, &c.   G. W.

P. S. I am under great apprehensions about obtaining proper supplies of provision for our troops: I fear it will be extremely difficult, if not impracticable, as the enemy, from every account, have taken and collected every thing they could find.

END OF THE FIRST VOLUME.

www.ingramcontent.com/pod-product-compliance
Lightning Source LLC
Chambersburg PA
CBHW020307240426
43673CB00039B/725